D1234734

Thought and Emotion
Developmental Perspectives

The Jean Piaget Symposium Series
Available from LEA

SIGEL, I. E., BRODZINSKY, D. M., & GOLIN-KOFF, R. M. (Eds.) • New Directions in Piagetian Theory and Practice

OVERTON, W. F. (Ed.) • Relationships Between Social and Cognitive Development

LIBEN, L. S. (Ed.) • Piaget and the Foundations of Knowledge

SCHOLNICK, E. K. (Ed.) • New Trends in Conceptual Representation: Challenges to Piaget's Theory?

NEIMARK, E., DeLISI, R., & NEWMAN, J. (Eds.) • Moderators of Competence

BEARISON, D. J., & ZIMILES, H. (Eds.) • Thought and Emotion: Developmental Perspectives

Thought and Emotion

—————Developmental Perspectives

Edited by

David J. Bearison
The Graduate School and
University Center of the
City University of New York

Herbert Zimiles
Bank Street College of Education

LEA LAWRENCE ERLBAUM ASSOCIATES, PUBLISHERS
1986   Hillsdale, New Jersey   London

155.412
T524

Lawrence Erlbaum Associates, Inc., Publishers
365 Broadway
Hillsdale, New Jersey 07642

Library of Congress Cataloging in Publication Data
Main entry under title:

Thought and emotion.

   Bibliography: p.
   Includes index.
   1. Cognition in children — Addresses, essays, lectures.
2. Emotions in children — Addresses, essays, lectures.
3. Piaget, Jean, 1896-   — Addresses, essays, lectures.
I. Bearison, David J.   II. Zimiles, Herbert.
BF723.C5T48   1986   155.4'12   85-4517
ISBN 0-89859-530-4

Printed in the United States of America
10 9 8 7 6 5 4 3 2 1

To Gilbert Voyat, in memoriam

Contents

Contributors

David J. Bearison, Ph.D. Program in Developmental Psychology, The Graduate School and University Center of the City University of New York, New York, NY

Augusto Blasi, Department of Psychology, University of Massachusetts, Dorchester, MA

Jerome Bruner, Department of Psychology, New School for Social Research, New York, NY

William Damon, Department of Psychology, Clark University, Worcester, MA

Amy P. Demorest, Judge Baker Guidance Center, Boston, MA; and The Laboratory of Human Development, Harvard Graduate School of Education, Cambridge, MA

Carroll Izard, Department of Psychology, University of Delaware, Newark, DE

Jane Loevinger, Social Science Institute, Washington University, St. Louis, MO

Robert J. Oresick, Department of Psychology, University of Massachusetts, Dorchester, MA

Sebastiano Santostefano, McLean Hospital, Belmont, MA; and Harvard Medical School, Boston, MA

Robert Selman, Judge Baker Guidance Center, Boston MA; and The Laboratory of Human Development, Harvard Graduate School of Education, Cambridge, MA

Irving E. Sigel, Institute for Research in Human Development, Educational Testing Service, Princeton, NJ

Robert H. Wozniak, Department of Human Development, Bryn Mawr College, Bryn Mawr, PA

Herbert Zimiles, Bank Street College of Education, New York, NY

1

Developmental Perspectives on Thought and Emotion: An Introduction

David J. Bearison
*The Graduate School and University Center
of the City University of New York*
Herbert Zimiles
Bank Street College of Education

The purpose of this book reflects the 1983 Piaget Society decision to contribute some ideas to a critical problem in psychology: how the structure and function of intelligence and affectivity are developmentally related. Although this is a fundamental question in psychology, it has largely been ignored at different periods in its history. With the maturing of the cognitive sciences in the past quarter of a century, there today is a recrudescence of interest in the ways in which affect influences cognition.

Twenty-five years ago, with the exception of the Geneva School, there was virtually no organized research in the field of cognitive psychology. Today, the field represents the prevailing scientific orientation to the study of human behavior and its development. The rapidity with which psychologists embraced the opportunity to explore new ways of studying the cognitive features of behavior in the early 1960s reflected how confining and artificial many of them had regarded the prevailing behavioristic ethos of American psychology. They cast aside the taboo against mentalism and theoretical speculations that restricted psychology to the study of overt behaviors. The new cognitive psychology was a reaction against the sterility of a behavioral science that was primarily based on principles of associative conditioning.

Until then, the tide of behaviorism seemed too powerful to resist in this country. The exceptions were Tolman (1932) and a small group of his followers, those sympathetic to the theoretical structure of psychoanalysis (e.g., Rapaport, 1951), Gestalt psychologists (e.g., Koehler, 1929: Koffka, 1935), and a small group of neo-gestaltists or organismic psychologists led by Heinz Werner (1948)

1

at Clark University. The field of cognitive psychology encouraged speculations about what was in the forbidden "black box." It dismissed elementaristic and mechanistic models of behavior that belied the texture of the behavioral events and social processes that they had observed.

The growth of cognitive psychology as a reaction against the orthodoxy of behaviorism gradually solidified into a distinctive style that established its own boundaries of scientific inquiry. Greatest progress was had in studying cognition from a developmental viewpoint, an approach that had largely been ignored at midcentury except for Piaget's pioneering studies. As Piaget's work became better known in America, developmental psychologists began to focus on different aspects of children's logico-mathematical reasoning, including the classical Kantian categories of space, time, number, and causality. This wave of research established, in turn, its own paradigmatic approaches to the study of development that, in some respects, were as limiting as the methodological orthodoxy of behaviorism. One critical limitation was the relative neglect of the ways in which affect influences cognition. By considering the guiding framework for virtually all realms of psychological functioning to be the orderly progress of abstract and reflective reasoning, affect was "cognized." Instead of being seen as a primary source of individual differences in our interests, efforts, and interpersonal commitments, affect somehow became epiphenomenal to cognition. The motivating force behind development was the construction of increasingly rational views of reality. Insofar as the goals of development were defined in terms of universal rationality and logical consistency, affect often was perceived as a detour or obstacle to the telos.

Today, there is among cognitive developmental theorists a revival of interest in the affective side of development that is part of, and consistent with, a greater appreciation for the ecological, behavioral, contextual, and narrative components of cognition. To many cognitive developmentalists, issues and problems about the social pragmatics of cognition capture the complexity of the interplay of these components and have led to innovative approaches to understanding the role of affect in cognition. Although it is customary to attribute the neglect of affectivity in the study of cognition to the influence of Piaget's research and his consuming interest in the evolution of logical-mathematical knowledge structures, he was not entirely silent on matters regarding affectivity and how they relate to the core elements of his theory of development.

PIAGET'S PERSPECTIVE ON INTELLIGENCE AND AFFECTIVITY

Although Piaget emphasized the cognitive-structural bases of human development in terms of concepts related to objects and physical relations, his early studies of children's social reasoning point to another, warmer side of cognition.

Its focus is on the thoughts, feelings, and motives of people (including the self) as they are known through the coordination of interpersonal perspectives that are derived within socially mediated value systems. Cognitive development, viewed from this orientation, raises questions concerning the affective, emotional, and volitional components of development—what Vygotsky (1968) claimed to be "the answer to the last 'why' in the analysis of thought" (p. 354).

Consequently, many investigators who have begun to reexamine Piaget's theory critically in regard to its recognition of the social foundations and affective features of knowledge have begun to appreciate that not only is the theory considerably broader in scope than the voluminous research it has thus far generated, but also it can accommodate further modifications and revisions without violating its core assumptions (Beilin, in press). Despite focus on empirical problems having to do with intelligence, perception, semiotics, and memory, for him, social interaction and affectivity remain essential dimensions of human development, beginning with the socialization of verbal intelligence and interpersonal coordinations in the preoperational period. Prior to preoperational development, affectivity is intraindividual and associated with feelings of practical success or failure of one's own sensorimotor actions (Piaget, 1981, Table 1, p. 14).

The 1981 publication in English of Piaget's 1954 Sorbonne lectures on intelligence and affectivity helped to explain how his cognitive structural model of development can account for the expression and development of affectivity (Piaget, 1954a; 1981). Piaget also considered the development of affectivity and intelligence in a series of lectures he delivered at the Menninger Clinic (Piaget, 1962a, 1962b). These two sources constitute his only major statements on this topic, although he had considered it as early as 1932 in his studies of children's moral reasoning (in which he referred to morality as "the conservation of affective values"). When Piaget was questioned about why he gave such relatively scant recognition to the problems of affectivity in development, he replied, "Only because I'm not interested in it. . . . The problem doesn't interest me as a scientific inquiry because it isn't a problem of knowledge, which is my specialty; . . ." Bringuier, 1980, p. 49). Elsewhere, Piaget replied, "Freud focused on emotions, I chose intelligence" (Décarie, 1978, p. 183). Consequently, in all of Piaget's work there are no data-based studies of affect development that either parallel his ingenious studies of the evolution of children's logical reasoning in cognitive domains or inspire others to empirically explore variations on the Piagetian theme. However, Piaget's (1962a) theoretical discussions of affectivity demonstrate that, in spite of his reluctance to admit it, he understood affect as being very much a "problem of knowledge" and, indeed, he recognized that "without affect there would be no interest, no need, no motivation; and consequently . . .there would be no intelligence" (p. 129).

Piaget rejects the dualism that is usually envisioned between intelligence and affectivity as constituting two distinct but analogous modes of behavior, each acting on the other. Instead, intelligence and affectivity are indissociable from one another and are co-constructed by a constant interaction between them. " . . . [T]here is as much construction in the affective domain as there is in the cognitive" (Piaget, 1981, p. 12). In the dialectic between intelligence and affectivity, neither is reducible nor causal of the other ("Understanding is no more the cause of affectivity than affectivity is the cause of understanding" [Piaget, 1981, p. 25]). Thus, for Piaget, the dichotomy between intelligence and affectivity has been artifically created by analytical abstractions to serve as an axiomatic device for the convenience of exposition, whereas in reality, neither can function without the other. Therefore, questions about whether affect is postcognitive or, by contrast, whether affective reactions temporally precede cognitive judgments are dismissed as being irresolvable. Arguments for the primacy of one behavioral mode over the other are mutually contradictory; each recasts in its own terms the guiding principles of the other and, thereby, alters its meaning (cf. Zajonc, 1980).

According to Piaget, the developmental relationship between intelligence and affectivity can be explained only by a theoretical perspective in which both modes are subsumed by a common system of mental structures. Such a position is entirely consistent with the core of theoretical and empirical assumptions of Piaget's model of development in which all mental processes, including language, thought, perception, and memory are organized by a common and universal system of interiorized, coordinated, and reversible set of transformations, correspondences, and morphisms (Piaget, 1979). Therefore, Piaget is able to claim that "the reaction of intelligence . . . to the social environment is exactly parallel to its reaction to the physical environment . . ." (1963, p. 160), that the "coordination of the actions of individuals obeys the same laws as intra-individual coordinations" (1970, p. 729), and that "affective structures are isomorphic with intellectual structures . . ." (1981, p. 9). Consistent with the structural correspondence between affect and intellect, Piaget (1954b) has maintained that "there are not two developments, one cognitive and the other affective, two separate functions, nor are there two kinds of objects; all objects are simultaneously cognitive and affective" (p. 32).

Structure and Energetics   Piaget sees the relationship between intelligence and affectivity as having to do with structural and energetic components of behavior. Affect reflects the energetics of behavior, including subjective interests, efforts, and feelings, whereas intelligence reflects its organization or structure. To illustrate this relationship, Piaget proposes the metaphor of how an automobile functions. Affect is like gasoline that fuels the engine, whereas intelligence is like an engine which provides structure and direction to the movement of the automobile. Like an engine, intelligence is fueled but not modified by affect. In this way, affect regulates subjective intentions to approach or avoid cognitive activities and, in turn, selectively influences rates of cognitive development across domains, accelerating it in some domains and retarding it in others. However, affect neither causes nor modifies the cognitive structures in whose functioning it inheres: "Feelings explain the interest for the object, but the structure of the object is related to space, time and causality" (Piaget, 1962a, p. 134). As one of several examples, Piaget (1981) considers the case of mathematical operations: "Feelings of success or failure may facilitate or inhibit a student's learning math, but the structure of mathematical operations will not be changed. A child may make mistakes because of affective interference; but even so, he will not invent new rules of addition. One child may understand more quickly than another, but the operation will always be the same" (p. 6). This way of distinguishing between structure and energetics demonstrates how affectivity, although not a generative source of new or modified structures of reasoning, is an essential condition for cognition. There is no such thing as a purely cognitive state without affect or a purely affective state without cognition, no matter how elementary it might be[1].

Affect, Will, and the Conflict of Tendencies.   Although dismissing a causal relationship between intelligence and affectivity in which one is somehow primary to the other, Piaget proposes that they are structurally parallel and it is the stage sequential properties of their corresponding evolution that constitute the cynosure of intelligence and affectivity. It is the ontogenesis of internalized operations that become reversible and coordinated with other operations to form cognitive schemes (which themselves are reversible) that define and explain increasingly more mature forms of intelligence, and that also define and explain affect development. In other words, affective operations are developmentally isomorphic to the cognitive operations that explain intelligence. Their only difference, according to Piaget (1962b), is that an "affective operation . . . bears only on the conservation and coordination of values, and on reversibility in the domain of values, while the intellectual operation bears on the coordination and the conservation of verifications, or of relations" (p. 143).

Affective operations intervene in the process by which individuals resolve conflicting intentions, intentions being the expressive components of values and desires. Extending the ideas of James (1890) and Lewin (1951), Piaget considered

---

[1]Although Piaget recognizes that there can be no intelligence without affectivity and no affectivity without intelligence, he acknowledges behavioral variations in the balance between the two. Most notably, Piaget (1981) distinguishes between "behaviors related to objects and behaviors related to people" (p. 74). Although each domain has both cognitive and affective aspects, in the former, logico-mathematical knowledge structures usually are emphasized; in the latter, interpersonal affect. However, affectivity in the object domain is present in the form of interests and effort; and cognitive structures in the people domain, in the form of reflective interpretations and understandings of the self and social relations. Recent advances in social cognitive theory, however, have diminished the distinction between these two behavioral domains by emphasizing interpersonal transactions inherent in knowledge of both objects and people (Bearison, this volume).

the problem of conflicting intentions to be a form of value disequilibration in which an immediately saliant value is assimilated to a reversible and coordinated system of prior values, intentions, and belief systems. Thus, affective decentration and the coordination of values is the prototype of all acts of will, in which an initially weaker intention becomes the stronger of two conflicting intentions. Without this conflict of intentions, there could be no will, only simple desire. Will intervenes when an individual is confronted with a situation in which there are conflicting tendencies. In order to illustrate how the affective operation of will, which bears upon the decentration of values, parallels an intellectual operation, which bears upon the decentration of verifications, Piaget (1962b) considers James' example of the scholar preparing a lecture while outside the weather is beautiful and the scholar suddenly feels overcome by a desire to leave the lecture and take a walk in the countryside. On the one hand, there is a desire to leave the lecture and take a walk, while, on the other hand, there is the felt obligation to complete the task. The intention to walk outside is initially the stronger of the two conflicting tendencies because it is an actual and immediate desire. The intention to continue working, however, is initially weaker because it corresponds not to an actual desire but to a sense of duty or obligation that is valued as being relatively superior to the actual desire only within a cognitively structured system of value schemes. The act of will operates to reconstruct the situation so that the initially weaker intention overcomes the intially stronger desire. "Therefore, the act of will consists here simply in relying upon a decentration, upon something which is exactly analogous to the reversibility of the intellectual operation and which consists in subordinating the actual value, the desire, to a larger scale of (permanent, coordinated, and reversible) values . . ." (p. 143).

Will, then is the affective analogue of the intellectual operation. Just as there are conservations of physical relations (e.g., number, weight, volume, etc.), there are conservations of values. In both domains, salient dimensions of the immediate stimulus field are assimilated to a prior context of equilibrated schemes (i.e., decentration). A radical distinction, however, between affective and intellectual operations is that the conservation of values, in contrast to physical relations, is relative to cultural and contextual constraints instead of being universal. Thus, values are not verifiable by appeals to extensional or mathematical logic or by empirical proof[2]. This explanation of affectivity in terms of coordinating and conserving values should not be confused with the "intellectualization" of affectivity. Affective operations do not yield cognitive representations,

---

[2]This distinction between logical formalism and social contextualism raises important implications regarding the universality of stages of moral reasoning. Insofar as morality constitutes a conservation of values, there could not exist a system of universal moral principles. Although the formal properties of the ontogenesis of stages of moral reasoning, predicated as they are on the reciprocity of mutual intentions, would follow a universal sequence of cognitive operations, the values that are being operated upon and that determine the content of these stages would remain relative (Bearison, 1983).

memories, or ways of understanding values (i.e., forms of knowing) but are phenomenologically felt as values having either positive or negative valences. "To decentrate in the domain of will is not to invoke memories through the intelligence, but to revive permanent values, . . . to feel them, which means that it is an affective operation and not an intellectual one" (Piaget, 1962b, p. 144). In other words, will is not simply the imposition of rational discourse on intuitive desires; it is not a product of knowing. Will recreates in the subject feelings and values that have been forgotten or contested. Therefore, although there exist no purely affective or purely intellectual modes of behaving, the decentration of values (paralleling and co-occuring with cognitive decentration) cannot be reduced to cognitive decentration.

The Development of Normative Affects.   The development of affectivity mirrors intellectual development because each is correlative of the other. They are subsumed by the same underlying cognitive operations. With development, children attain progressively greater competencies in subordinating (decentering) their affective experience to operational systems of permanent, reversible and coordinated values, interpersonal obligations, and moral imperatives. This development has its origins in the sensorimotor strivings toward object permanence in infancy. In the preoperational period, affectivity is dominated by the immediacy of subjective desires in the absence of cognitive decentration. There are no conflicts of intentions (i.e., will) because the concrete operations allowing for the coordination and conservation of values are lacking. Instead, the affective conflicts associated with the preoperational period are conflicts of immediately salient desires. With the advent of concrete operations, affectivity becomes organized into a system of coordinated and reversible values that become evident in the expression of intra- and interpersonal feelings based on the reciprocity of mutual intentions within and between the self and others, respectively. Piaget (1932) describes this period as the beginning of the child's autonomous moral feelings that replace an earlier heteronomous morality of obedience. At the beginning of the formal operational period in early adolescence, affective development is marked by the collective idealization of values, albeit initially fragile and contextually labile, regarding propositional realities and social orders that leads to a stable conception of the self in reciprocal relation to other selves. Thus, this final stage in the development of affectivity culminates in the subordination of the self to a collective ideal within a socio-cultural context.

AUTHORS' CONTRIBUTIONS

The authors were invited to contribute to the Symposia of the Piaget Society not because they hold a singular commitment to Piaget's theory of intelligence and affectivity, but because their thinking represents profound, innovative, and creative approaches to the revivisence of interest in the connection between thought and feeling. Some of the authors expound on Piaget's theory more than others, but they all are sympathetic to Piaget's genetic epistemology and the basic principles regarding the organismic qualities of human development that logically follow from it. In the ensuing chapters, the authors elaborate upon theoretical themes and methodological techniques and strategies regarding the relationship between thought and emotion that advance this organismic perspective of development.

The chapters in this volume deal with a broad range of general and specific issues that promote new directions in our understanding of how intelligence and affectivity are developmentally and reciprocally related. They do not, collectively, provide a singularly cohesive and balanced developmental theory of thought and emotion. Instead, the authors approached the problem in varied ways using different methodologies to advance different, yet complementary and theoretically compatible positions. Indeed, an overriding theme of the volume is that approaches to the problem of thought and emotion require diverse perspectives that approach traditional problems in novel ways.

In spite of their diversity, the authors share a compelling commitment that one cannot study intellectual development without considering affectivity, nor can one study emotional development apart from intelligence. In their efforts to balance these complementary and reciprocal features of behavior, most of them have approached the thought/feeling connection primarily from backgrounds and training in cognitive development. Consequently, there is a greater implicit consensus among them about the nature of thought than emotion. Because, in their research, they operationally define emotion from different yet theoretically consistent vantage points, they collectively are able to contribute broader and conceptually more challenging ideas about the larger, more comprehensive issues of human development than have traditionally been available to us.

Bruner considers the relation between thought and emotion in terms of how we selectively view the stream of experience; how and why we come to adopt multiple stances by which we construct our representations of "realities." He describes the factors and agents associated with stance switching by considering the social pragmatics of language that guide interpersonal relations within the constraints of a given culture and thereby shape the construction of the concept of self.

Izard questions the utility of cognition-primacy approaches to thought and emotion. He discusses a series of cogent findings that support what he describes as "differential emotions theory," which focuses on the biological/genetic components of affect development as they interact with cue-producing and motivational aspects of the social-signal functions of emotional expressions beginning in infancy.

Wozniak critically contrasts several meta-theoretical principles that guide theoretical assumptions regarding the nature of thought and emotion and the quality of our psychological explanations of them. The principles he describes are implicit in all psychological considerations of thought and emotion.

An analysis of some of the methodological problems associated with assessing the integrative functions of thought and emotion is offered in separate chapters by Loevinger and Zimiles. Loevinger outlines the methodological decisions to be made at various choice points in designing a system for measuring ego development. She contrasts her approach with the hypothetico-deductive approach of Kohlberg. Zimiles calls for a revision in current approaches to the assessment of cognition in order to facilitate the study of cognitive-affective interaction. He proceeds to examine some contradictory and paradoxical lines of thought associated with the traditional view of the affective disruption of cognition.

Selman and Demorest provide a cognitive developmental analysis of interpersonal conflicts among groups of emotionally troubled children. Their analysis is derived from a model of children's interpersonal negotiation strategies that considers the cognitive, emotional, motivational, and action-oriented components of social cognition in practice. Bearison discusses these kinds of sociocognitive approaches to understanding thought and emotion in the context of recent efforts to accommodate empirically the transactional features of social cognition as they are construed in psycholinguistic models, script models, sociocognitive conflict models of peer interaction, and socio-historical models of adult-child interaction.

Blasi and Oresick focus on the concept of self as a central paradigm for understanding the relation between thought and emotion. They are particularly interested in the affectively charged experience of self-inconsistency. They discuss the subject's affective experiences as he or she struggles to regain self-consistency. They consider this to be analogous in form to Piaget's model of cognitive disequilibrium. Damon expands on this consideration of the self-concept in terms of advancing principles of moral development that reflect both affective and cognitive orientations.

Santostefano reviews the relationship between thought and emotion as a function of how cognitive control mechanisms function to modulate organismic interactions between the subject and the environment as the interactions vary in response to different affective contextual features. Data-based findings are amplified and corroborated by an interpretation of a longitudinal case study of a child in analysis. In this way, Santostefano illustrates how developmental theories contribute to the practice of child analysis and, conversely, how practice informs theory.

In the concluding chapter, Sigel considers Santostefanos' findings in order to formulate his own meta-theoretical analysis of the issues that need to be addressed in advancing our understanding of the developmental relationship between thought and emotion.

REFERENCES

Bearison, D. J. (1983). Who killed the epistemic subject? In W. Overton (ed.), *The relationship between social and cognitive development* (pp. 143–146). Hillsdale, NJ: Lawrence Earlbaum Associates.

Beilin, H. (in press). Dispensable and core elements in Piaget's research program. *The Genetic Epistemologist*.

Bringuier, J. (1980). Conversations with Jean Piaget. Chicago: University of Chicago Press.

Décarie, T. G. (1978). Affect development and cognition in a Piagetian context. In M. Lewis & L. A. Rosenblum (Eds.), *The development of affect* (pp. 183–204). New York: Plenum.

James, W. (1890). *The principles of psychology*. New York: Henry Holt.

Koehler, W. (1929). *Gestalt psychology*. New York: Liveright.

Koffka, K. (1935). *Principles of Gestalt psychology*. New York: Harcourt, Brace.

Lewin, K. (1951). Intention, will and need. In D. Rapaport (Ed.), *Organization and pathology of thought* (pp. 95–150). New York: Columbia University Press.

Piaget, J. (1932). *The moral judgment of the child*. London: Routledge & Kegan Paul.

Piaget, J. (1954a). *Les relations entre l'affectivité et l'intelligence dans le développment mental de l'enfant*. Paris: Centre de Documentation Univ.

Piaget, J. (1954b). *The construction of reality in the child*. New York: Basic Books.

Piaget, J. (1962a). The relation of affectivity to intelligence in the mental development of the child. *Bullentin of the Menninger Clinic, 26*, 129–137.

Piaget, J. (1962b). Will and action. *Bulletin of the Menninger Clinic, 26*, 138–145.

Piaget, J. (1963). *The psychology of intelligence*. Paterson, NJ: Littlefield, Adams.

Piaget, J. (1970). Piaget's theory. In P. Mussen (Ed.), *Carmichael's manual of child psychology*. (Vol. I, pp. 703–732). New York: Wiley.

Piaget, J. (1979). Correspondences and transformations. In F. B. Murray (Ed.), *The impact of Piagetian theory on education, philosophy, psychiatry and psychology* (pp. 17–28). Baltimore, MD: University Park.

Piaget, J. (1981). Intelligence and affectivity: Their relationships during child development. *Annual Review Monograph*. Palo Alto, CA: Annual Reviews.

Rapaport, D. (1951).*Organization and pathology of thought*. New York: Columbia University Press.

Tolman, E. (1932). *Purposive behavior in animals and men*. Berkeley, CA: University of California.

Vygotsky, L. S. (1968). In A. N. Leontiev and A. L. Luria, The psychological ideas of L. S. Vygotaky. In B. Solman. *Historical roots of contemporary psychology*. New York: Harper & Row.

Werner, H. (1948). *Comparative psychology of mental development* (Rev. ed.). Chicago: Follet.

Zajonc, R. B. (1980). Feeling and thinking: Preferences need no inferences. *American Psychologist, 35*, 151–175.

2 Thought and Emotion: Can Humpty Dumpty Be Put Together Again?

Jerome Bruner
New School for Social Research

Our topic risks being another Humpty Dumpty unless we take care. It could end up as in the celebrated story of the man who, eager to learn about Chinese metaphysics, first looks up "China" in the Encyclopedia Britannica, and then "metaphysics." In fact, it could produce a more serious catagory error than that.

For indeed, the concept of thought is itself a highly refined abstraction in both philosophy and psychology, an abstraction initially undertaken precisely to purify problem solving of all taint of passion, to force it to conform to something approaching the rules of right reasoning or science. It was no accident that the mathematician, George Boole (1854) entitled his famous work on logic, *The Laws of Thought*. Suppose now we attempt to relate an account of right thinking such as Boole's or Whitehead and Russell's, or for that matter, accounts such as Piaget's (1980) or Newell and Simon's (1972) or Bruner, Goodnow and Austin's (1956), and relate them to *emotion*, which is itself an abstraction from the stream of mental activity specifically designed to exclude reasoning. We shall land either in contradiction if we adhere to strict logic or in a muddle if we try to proceed by some blunt version of correlating measures of the two.

We can avoid these troubles, I think, by taking a fresh look at what we intend by such terms as mental activity or knowledge or judgment without performing the classical abstraction that divides them into the famous trinity of cognition, conation, and affection or reason, motive and emotion. That is what I shall try to do.

Let me begin with the principle of constructivism. We know the world in different ways, from different stances, and each of the ways in which we know it produces different structures or representations, or, indeed, "realities." As we grow to adulthood (at least in Western culture), we become increasingly adept at seeing the same set of events from multiple perspectives or stances and of entertaining the results as, so to speak, alternative possible worlds. The child is less adept at achieving such multiple perspectives—although it is highly dubious whether in fact he or she is as cripplingly egocentric as formerly claimed (e.g., Hogan, 1975; Nelson & Gruendel, 1977; Scaife & Bruner, 1975). There is every reason to insist, moreover, that the human capacity for multiple perspectives and for constituting alternative realities is not simply a result of a higher order interpretive activity operating upon some initial sensory apprehension of the "real" world, some form of veridical perception. A generation of research extending from the New Look through contemporary studies in filtering and information processing tells us that the naive realism of sense-data theories of perception and knowledge acquisition is profoundly misleading. The banal and obvious point is that the limits of our processing system forces us into selectivity at every choice point in the system, from the entry port of the senses to the highest reaches of interpretation. And if we are uncomfortable with the psychological evidence on this matter, we still are forced by the neurophysiology of the case to accede to this view. As Woodworth (1938) put it half a century ago, there is no seeing without looking, no hearing without listening, and both looking and listening are shaped by expectancy, stance and intention.

To be sure, we give privileged ontic status for different reasons to various structures created from our selective encounters with the world. It also could be said that we place a canonical value on certain stances that yield certain forms of knowledge, certain possible worlds. One such stance is scientific or rational or logical, and it is distinguished by being able to yield accounts of experience that are replicable, consistent, and/or coherent. Only the most antirational or relativistic theorist would reject the achievement of such scientific accounts as trivial. But, as the philosopher, Austin (1962), remarked two decades ago, the greater part of human discourse is not in the form either of analytic propositions subject to tests of consistency or of synthetic ones subject to tests of correspondence. We seem, instead, to deal mainly with constitutive realities having to do with requests, promises, affiliations, threats, encouragements, and the like. We even create such bricks-and-mortar realities as jails to deal with people who fail to conform to the felicity conditions that are socially imposed by such forms of discourse and the realities they create. We are forever asking about what people really intended, whether they were sincere, whether they were justified. In its own way, the ontic status imposed on aspects of human interaction is just as arbitrary or just as natural, just as real or imaginary, just as rigorous or loose as the world we describe by statements that are consistent or empirically testable. Viewing one as more personal or impersonal, objective or subjective, thought-related or emotion-related than the other may have significance in some metaphysical account concerning the nature of things. But as for their psychological status, all are outcomes of taking particular perspectives on the stream of experience and creating structures or representations in particular ways. All are selective, stance-dependent, and driven by a selective principle.

Each way of experiencing and structuring the world, in consequence, must be regarded in some non-trivial way as the extension of some stance—and some of these stances we call *emotional*. Althought others escape this label, I think that this is where our troubles begin. We would do far better to postpone the pinning of labels and look instead at what is involved in stance adoption, how it is regulated, and by what means it operates in creating conceptions of the world.

The issue is not *whether* emotion (or stance) affects the selectivity of knowledge and its elaboration in thought, but rather *which* stance is taken. One is always taken in facing the world. We require some sort of stance-switching principle, some executive-routine to deal with the *which*. And with no further ado, I want to give the switch a simple, if cantankerous name: Self. It is intended as a place-holder, a blank check to be filled in as we proceed. In order to jettison as much of that four letter word's historical freight as possible, let me approach it in a somewhat novel way—through language, through the idea of a *Pragmatic Agent*. To do so, I must back away a little from the immediate topic at hand, thought and emotion—as the French say, *reculer pour mieux sauter*, draw back to make a better leap.

Until the latter 1960s, the study of language acquisition in children focused upon the miracle of syntax: how the child mastered the rules for putting together grammatical utterances. More recently, the focus of interest in child language has shifted to the related question of how the child "learns to mean"—that is to say, not only how he acquires the skill of putting together well-formed grammatical utterances, but how he learns to use these for referring to the world in the semantic sense. The latter process is somewhat less miraculous than the former, but nonetheless is still fraught with mystery. In the last several years, a new focus has emerged. Children, it seems, do not simply master syntax for its own sake or learn how to mean simply as an intellectual exercise—like little scholars or lexicographers. They acquire these skills in the interest of getting things done in the world: requesting, indicating, affiliating, protesting, asserting, possessing, and the rest.

It is plain that these uses of communication develop before language proper comes on the scene: They are realized by gesture, by vocalization, by "body language," by regulation of gaze. When language proper is acquired, the process of acquisition appears to be dedicated to perfecting, differentiating, and extending these functions or uses of communication. Eventually, the child learns to perform certain acts that can be performed only by the use of language proper. A typical example is promising and there are many others. Philosophers of language have come to refer to the creation of social realities by language as the *performative* function of language (e.g. Austin, 1962; Searle, 1969). Anthropologists speak of these social realities as *constituted* by conventions of language. Today, it is commonplace in the social sciences to refer to culture itself as consisting of the constitutive realities that are formed by the use of a shared and conventional system.

One striking fact about such constitutive reality is that it is basically trans-actional. It involves at least two human beings in interaction. And certainly the acquisition of language and its conventions of use—its pragmatics—depends upon the close interaction of two human beings, one of whom already knows how to do it, or at least knows some part of how to do it. It is obvious, yet still remarkable, that human beings manage to make their intentions clear and accept-able to each other by the use of speech. What Sullivan (1953) long ago called *parataxis*, the sort of misunderstanding of which both parties are unaware, is the exception. Given the opportunities for misunderstanding, its incidence is astonishingly low—the more astonishing because natural language is polysemic even at the lexical level. Words mean different things even in the dictionary sense and may mean even more different things when uttered in the context of discourse. Our utterances rarely mean exactly what they say. We would be in deep trouble if we interpreted the statement, "Would you be kind enough to pass the salt?" as an inquiry into the limits of our compassion.

All of this suggests that our interpretation of what others say, or our framing of what we say ourselves, must be guided by some rather cunning rules—rules even more cunning than the rules of syntax by which we construct grammatically acceptable sentences or the ones by which we refer and mean in the semantic sense. There is an ancient Chinese proverb that says, "Let not the word interfere with the sentence nor the sentence with the intention." Yet this subtle matter of making our intentions clear is not just a matter of our learning rules, like the rules of grammar. Instead, the process of getting things done with words, the task of making good the pragmatics of language, depends on some rather subtle but robust skills for negotiating the intended meanings of our utterances in interaction with others.

Moreover, it is precisely in the negotiation of intended meaning that the self is formed in such a way that we can relate ourselves not only to the others immediately around us—particularly to the family (and its myths about social reality)—but also to the broader culture into which we must eventually move. It is in this process that we create the internal scripts with which we interpret the transactional world in which we move as socialized human beings.

The bulk of the literature on language acquisition is divergent on many points of serious issue. But on one point of pragmatics, there is unanimous agreement: Listeners to language always operate on the assumption that the speaker is intending to communicate something. Macfarlane's (1977) observations on moth-ers' talk to infants brought to them for the first time after delivery underlines this irresistability. His recordings (often highly amusing when listened to in the aseptic atmosphere of a linguistics laboratory) are full of the usual chatter, "What's that frown for? The world a little surprising, you trying to tell me?"— and so on and on. Mothers will tell you that they really don't think it is for real. But they know only half the truth. For their efforts to "assign an interpretation" to the gestures and vocalizations of their infants inevitably will have the effect of shaping first the prelinguistic and then the linguistic utterances of their children toward conformity with the expectations of the family and of the broader speech community—not grammatically at first, but pragmatically in terms of speech acts and broader patterns of discourse. There are two areas in which the mother and child are closely attuned in this endeavor. For there appear to be two major natural functions served by the infants communicative acts (whether intentionally or not is, of course, not the point). The first is that, from nearly the beginning, the infant uses vocalization and gesture to regulate his or her own attention by communicative means. The second is that the child uses vocalization and gesture to regulate his or her own intention-driven actions and the actions of others. Halliday (1975) regards these two functions—he calls them "mathetic" and "pragmatic" respectively—as the roots of language. At first, as I shall relate in a moment, there are certain natural ways in which these functions express themselves and through which they produce uptake in the mother. But, in their very nature, these early communicative efforts are underdetermined with respect to specifying their target. What saves the day, of course, is that the mother has the complementary tendency to offer interpretations until a satisfactory compromise is reached. The infant is satisfied and the mother is relieved that some acceptable outcome has been achieved. Very soon, certain of the successful exchanges of this kind become stabilized into mutually contingent *formats*—formats of reference and request. In a volume, *Child's Talk: Learning to Use Language* (1983), I have described these formats in very close detail. They involve maintenance by the mother of a succession of invariant reactions to the child's efforts as the child gradually moves toward more fully comprehensible communication procedures for directing her attention or directing her actions. She is at once shaping his communicative behavior and being shaped by it. The two of them are constructing a microcosm, a jointly constructed world in which they can assure reference, presupposition and a communicative code—but it is, above all, a microcosm in which the child learns how he or she may effectively act on the world and on others. The concepts that the child forms must be congruent with the requirements imposed by the interaction and the discourse that holds that interaction together. The child, as Vygotsky (1962) has urged, is not learning about the world, not gaining knowledge in solo encounters, but in concert with others who, so to speak, are representative members of both the culture and the linguistic community. The selective elaboration of the child's knowledge structures and the affect that characterizes his or her knowledge structures are not something added to thought. They are as immanent and as intrinsic as the stances the child takes in the first place in the construction of knowledge. Eventually as the child comes to use the language and to participate in the culture, the affective element becomes so locked in with the knowledge that it requires such major institutions as schooling, science, and a written language to create a new set of rational concepts that can be operated upon by those famous (but non-natural) rules of right reasoning.

So, I must say a word about language and culture as conservers of the intertwining of affect and cognition. Two points that must be made about language are both related to the self or pragmatic agent. The first already has been made in passing and relates to the ubiquitousness of speech acts in human communication: that language in use always involves communicating an intention by conventional linquistic means, that a locution reflects an illocutionary force that defines its intended occasion meaning in that interaction rather than some timeless, universal meaning. Concepts, rather than being cleansed of their affect when embodied in language, are caught in the stance that governs the utterance.

Or to put it another way, this time following Fillmore's (1968) terminology, grammar itself serves the function of "imposing perspectives on scenes," forefronting, marking, emphasizing, assigning agency and causation. The act of speaking grammatically commits one to a point of view concerning the referent. But over and above the usual grammatical devices inherent in a language, there also are quasi-autonomous pragmatic markers that serve to emphasize the stance of the speaker, not only toward the referent, but toward the interlocutor. Feldman (1974), for example, has shown how such words as *just*, *even*, and *only*, provide purely pragmatic marking in such ordinary declarative sentences as:

Jack loves Jill   (1)

with variants such as

Even Jack loves Jill.   (2)
Jack even loves Jill.   (3)
Jack loves even Jill.   (4)

In each case, the pragmatic marker virtually creates presuppositions concerning the stance of speaker toward the actors and action in the sentence.

But there is a second, even more powerful point to be made about the manner in which language assures that concepts do not cool too far below the level of their occasion of use. It relates to the narrative or syntagmatic or what Jakobson (1965) called the metonymic or horizontal combinatorical axis of language. It is governed by the loose relation of predication or topic-comment structure— what can be said about what. Topic-comment structures at the trans-sentential level cohere, then, into thematic accounts, language games. We know it in psychology as the syntagmatic response in word assocation: kitchen–table, woman–dress, paper–pencil. It contrasts linguistically with the vertical metaphoric axis of selection in language having to do with substitutability of words through synonymy, hyperonymy and hyponymy, oppositional contrast, and so on. Its function is categorial: based on the rules for forming linguistic equivalence classes and their transformations. Ordinary language requires dual processing by syntagmatic, metonymic and metaphoric, paradigmatic principles. Semantic memory, moreover, depends on the construction of lexical and topical networks that are joined by links of both types. Indeed, most acts of concept formation proceed as readily by joining together elements that fit into syntagmatic clusters as they do by joining elements that fit into paradigmatic tree structures governed by subordination and superordination: household goods, things you can trade with, people I've liked, the subdivisions of a supermarket, important people, things inherited from my Aunt Sarah. As Wittgenstein (1958) assured us, these are categories that derive their coherence from usage, family resemblance, thematic sharing and the like. They virtually guarantee that only by an act of abstraction can elements be disembodied from their syntagmatic connections and treated in that formal way demanded by the principles of right reasoning or formal logic.

It is not surprising then, that studies of children's reasoning (or "pure" cognition) show them to be "paralogical" or lacking in formal operations or, indeed, even incapable of tracking invariance across transformations in appearance. For, if we take seriously the claim that language gradually becomes a major instrument of thought—that is to say, that humans as they develop come increasingly to operate on linguistic representations of their knowledge rather than on images or habits or whatever, and, so to say, by something approximating inner speach— if we take this view seriously, then we must conclude that ordinary mental activity does not have an isolated "objective" cognitive component that then interacts with an affective or emotional component. The two from the start function together and it is only by taking a specialized stance that they can be abstracted from each other. And at that, the capacity of even educated adults to perform easily the necessary acts of abstraction is brought into question by the work of Kahneman and Tversky (1973) and by some recent studies of Zukier and Pepitone (1984) illustrating how readily the Bayesian reasoning of subjects is diverted by giving their reasoning a richly syntagmatic context.

So, now we may ask a final question before returning finally to the concept of Self. If, in fact, mental activities and the language on which they rely are shot through with syntagmatic, stance-marked, perspectival structures or representations, what determines the form that these take? Let me take my argument from contemporary anthropology. My point is that the manner in which stance, perspective, and emotion, affect the elaboration of mental activity (i.e., how we go about our reasoning, our judging, our problem solving) is determined by a negotiatory process that characterizes the culture.

There has been a profound revolution in the last decade in the definition of human culture. It takes the form of a move away from the strict structuralism that held that culture was a set of learned, interconnected rules from which one derived particular behaviors, to the idea of culture as implicit and only semiconnected knowledge of the world from which, through, negotiations with others, we arrive at satisfactory ways of acting in given contexts. The anthropologist, Geertz (1973), likens the process to interpreting an ambiguous text. Rosaldo (1980) puts it exceptionally well:

In anthropology, the key development . . . is a view of culture probably best articulated in the words of Clifford Geertz, wherein meaning is proclaimed a public fact—or better yet, where culture and meaning are described as processes of interpretive apprehension by individuals of symbolic models. These models are both 'of' the world in which we live and 'for' the organization of activities, responses, perceptions and experiences by the conscious self. For the present purposes, what is important here is first of all the claim that meaning is a fact of public life, and secondly, that cultural patterns—social facts—provide the template for all human action, growth and understanding. Culture so construed, is further-more, a matter less of artifacts and propositions, rules, schematic programs, or beliefs, than of associative chains and images that tell what can be reasonably linked up with what; we come to know it through collective stories that suggest the nature of coherence, probability and sense within the actor's world. Culture is, then, always richer than the traits recorded in the ethnographer's accounts because its truth resides not in explicit formulations of the rituals of daily life but in the daily practices of persons who in acting take for granted an account of who they are and how to understand their fellows' moves (p.6).

On this view, the conventional processes of establishing occasion meanings and of making known our intentions and stances are cultural and subject to linguistic practices. *How* we decide to enter into transaction with others lingu-istically and by other exchanges, how *much* we wish to speak up and out (in contrast to remaining detached and silent and otherwise private) will shape the sense of Self that we form. As Rosaldo (1980) reminds us (using her Ilongot people as contrast), our Western concern with individuals and with their inner hidden selves may well be features of *our* world of action and belief—itself to be explained and not assumed as the foundation of cross-cultural study. Indeed, the image that we provide for guidance to speakers with respect to when they may speak and what they may say in what situations may be a first constraining definition of what constitutes public and private "Self". We even specify cul-turally how one shall evaluate the private non-negotiating Self in contrast to the public, communicating one.

On this view, moreover, the degree to which, the manner in which, and the occasions on which decontextualized and decathected reasoning will occur (if at all) also is culturally specified. In our culture, for example, we are enjoined to temper the universalism of justice with the particularism of mercy—and Par-sons and Shils (1951) make the interplay of the two a general principle of sociological theory. Among Rosaldo's Ilongot, for example, anger held in too long destroys one's relations. Each culture has a way of patterning the cathected and decathected, the contextualized and decontextualized, and each individual as well. And that is where Self or Pragmatic Agent comes into play.

For one of the crucial "executive" decisions involved in carrying out any mental activity is precisely whether to attend to context and stance marking and go the syntagmatic, metonymic way, or whether to strip down to the paradig-matic, the ritual zero stance mark, the rational. In many instances, it is obvious how to proceed: Your arithmetic class is clearly one extreme, thinking about your best friend is clearly the other. But in most instances, it is a balance of the two that is crucial, and that creates difficulties. Perhaps it is why moral judgment (depending as it does on a balance of the two) is so slow, so gradual, and so uncertain in development (Colby, Kohlberg, Gibbs, & Lieberman, 1983) in contrast to the development, say, of conservation of quantity—although even the conservation of quantity can be made uncertain by highlighting or submerging contextual cues.

Whenever a balance is required, then, negotiation with others becomes crucial, and it is here that the skills and subtleties stored in the implicit knowledge of the culture becomes critical—how to make the implicit explicitly relevant to particular situations in a manner to suit the requirements of the particular actors involved. I conceive of the detachment of Self as requiring mastery of the possibilities of getting things done in a manner congruent with constraints of the culture and with one's own perceived requirements—getting things done both with words and with acts. But getting things done with words is the essence of negotiation, of going from the culturally implicit to the situationally explicit. That is why I place such emphasis on the mastery of the pragmatics of language as a key feature of Self: on mastery of the felicity conditions on speech acts, on indicating and being able to decode stance marking, on being able deictically to unpack contextual presupposition. And that too is why Self is so heavily dependent on interaction with the culure.

One final word about development. If what I have said is even minimally true, it should be plain that we have been remiss in our research emphasis on the mastery of decontextualized cognition alone. It has been important, to be sure, to get a deeper sense of how children move through stages in the understanding of the constancies and invariances. But we will deceive ourselves about mental development if we stop at that. We must be as mindful of how children develop the skills of spotting relevant context, mastering uptake of stances and speech acts, knowing when to be particular rather than universal. And, above all, we must study how children learn to regulate the balance between the two main modes of using mind: the metonymic, syntagmatic, stance-marked context sensitive and the metaphoric, paradigmatic, ritual zero, context free. If we fail to do this, we shall think of emotion as somehow interfering with or being antithetical to thought. In fact, they are features of a common stream of mental activity. Iago, Hamlet and Lear are as much products of thought as Mendelev's Table or Einstein's equations.

REFERENCES

Austin, J. (1962). *How to do things with words*. Oxford: Oxford University Press.
Boole, G. (1854). *The laws of thought*. New York: Dover Publications.
Bruner, J. (1983). *Child's talk: Learning to use language*. New York: Norton.

Bruner, J., Goodnow, J., & Austin, G. (1956). *A study of thinking*. New York: Wiley.

Colby, A., Kohlberg, L. Gibbs, J., & Lieberman, M. (1983). A longitudinal study of moral judgment. *Monographs of the Society for Research in Child Development, 48* (1-2), Serial No. 200.

Feldman, C. (1974). Pragmatic features of natural language. In M.W. LaGally, R. A. Fox, & A. Bruck (Eds.). *Papers from the tenth Regional Meeting, Chicago Linguistic Society* (pp. 151–160). Chicago: Chicago Lingistic Society, 1974.

Fillmore, C. (1968). The case for case reopened. In P. Cole & J.M. Seadock (Eds.). *Syntax & semantics, Vol 3: Speech acts*. New York: Academic Press.

Geertz, C. (1973). *The interpretation of cultures: Selected essays* New York: Basic Books.

Halliday, M. (1975). *Learning how to mean*. London: Edward Arnold.

Hogan, R. (1975, May). Theoretical egocentrism and the problem of compliance. *American Psychologist*, 533—540.

Jakobson, R. (1965). The functions of language. In T.A. Sebeok (Ed.), *Poetics*. The Hague: Mouton.

Kahneman, O., & Tversky, A. (1973). On the psychology of prediction. *Psychological Review, 80*, 237–251.

Macfarlane, A. (1977). *The psychology of childbirth*. Cambridge, MA: Harvard University Press.

Nelson, K. & Gruendel, J. (1977). *At morning it's lunch time: A scriptal view of children's dialogue*. Paper presented at the Conference on Dialogue. University of Michigan, Ann Arbor.

Newell, A. & Simon, H.A. (1972). *Human problem solving*. Englewood Cliffs, NJ: Prentice-Hall.

Parsons, T. & Shils, E. (1951). *Toward a general theory of action*. Cambridge, MA: Harvard University Press.

Piaget, J. (1980). *Adaptation and intelligence*. Chicago: University of Chicago Press.

Rosaldo, M. (1980). *Knowledge and passion*. Stanford, CA: Stanford University Press.

Scaife, M. & Bruner, J. (1975). The capacity for joint visual attention in the infant. *Nature, 253*, 263–266.

Searle, J. (1909). *Speech acts: An essay in the philosophy of language*. New York: Cambridge University Press.

Sullivan, H.S. (1953). *Interpersonal theory of psychiatry*. New York: Norton.

Vygotsky, L. (1962). *Thought and language*. Cambridge: MIT Press.

Whitehead, A. & Russell, B. (1984). *Principia mathematica*. Cambridge: Cambridge University Press. (Original work published 1938)

Wittgenstein, L. (1958). *Philosophical investigations*. Oxford: Basil Blackwell.

Woodworth, R. (1938). *Experimental psychology*. New York: Henry Holt.

Zukler, H. & Pepitone, A. (1984). Social roles and strategies in prediction: Some determinants of the use of base rate information. *Journal of Personality and Social Psychology, 47*, 349–360.

3 Approaches to Developmental Research on Emotion-Cognition Relationships

Carroll E. Izard
University of Delaware

INTRODUCTION

Two types of theories guide most of the research on the study of relationships between emotion and cognition. I shall refer to the first class as *cognitive theory* because these theories conceive of cognition as the primary mental process and as the cause of emotion. The other type shall be referred to as *dynamic theory* because theories of this type view emotion as the primary mental process and as the primary cause or motivation for cognition. Although these synoptic descriptions suggest that these positions are in total disagreement on all issues, they are not. I suggest some of the important ways in which they do differ.

In recent years a number of investigators have made distinct contributions to cognitive theory of emotional development. In this brief review I omit some major contributions to general cognitive theory of emotion because they have not addressed developmental issues.

EMOTIONAL DEVELOPMENT AS A FUNCTION OF COGNITIVE DEVELOPMENT

Emotion is seen by Mandler (1982), and by Kagan (1984) as a function of cognition. Mandler has not written much about emotional development, but he is in agreement with Piaget on the issue of the inseparability of affect and cognition. He sees emotion as a cognitive construction, its intensity determined by perceived level of autonomic arousal and its quality by evaluative processes.

Thus, for Mandler, the study of emotional development is the study of two apparently parallel processes—autonomic-visceral development and cognitive-evaluative development—whose interaction produces emotion. The development of evaluative perception is seen as proceeding in the same fashion as the object concept and spatio/temporal perception. Mandler thinks the study of the development of automatic perception is particularly important for understanding the apparently automatic emotion responses.

Mandler also underscores the importance of the study of the development of values. He believes that how and when people experience particular emotions such as anger, fear, or sadness is determined in part by cultural values. Because Mandler believes that emotion experience depends on the registration or perception of visceral arousal, he advocates the study of the development of the perception of visceral changes innnervated by the autonomic nervous system. He thinks that different thresholds for visceral perception may account for different types of maldevelopment and that differences in sympathetic-parasympathetic balance may be a source of differences in temperament.

Kagan (1984) has made an extensive statement on emotion in human development. His position is similar to Mandler's and to Piaget's in some respects. Like Mandler, he believes that evaluation plays a crucial role in determining the quality of emotion that is experienced. Unlike Mandler, he believes that *feeling tone* can change even though it is undetected and thus unlabeled. Yet, according to Kagan, detection of the feeling tone is of extreme importance for the subsequent emotion state. Kagan, in apparent agreement with Piaget and differential emotions theory, stated that "perceived changes in state might be regarded as motivational and predictive of changes in thought and action" (pp. 6–7). Kagan differs from both Piaget and differential emotions theory in his view of emotions as transient. This can be seen as one way of relegating emotions to relatively unimportant roles in development.

A distinct feature of Kagan's position is his recognition of two types of emotions or feelings and his emphasis on the difference in undetected feeling tone defined by biological processes and feeling tone that follows from evaluative processes and is detected. He believes the two psychological states deserve categorically different names.

For Kagan, the feelings of importance are those that are detected, those that follow cognitive evaluation or judgment. The development of such feelings is explained in terms of cognitive development, and cognitive capacities define emotional capacities. Kagan's approach seems to be correct in some instances, as when he notes that the infant cannot protest the loss of an object until he or she can recognize its absence. He is less obviously correct when he says that changing anger to frustration requires the cognitive ability to relate incentive events to schemata. A study by Stenberg, Campos, and Emde (1983) led them to conclude that the 4-month-old child's objectively coded anger expression to arm restraint was accompanied by behaviors indicative of anger feeling or motivation. If anger feeling did occur, can it reasonably be attributed to the cognitive comparison processes described by Kagan?

Kagan advocates abandoning the abstract emotion terms of common language in favor of labeling feeling-event occurrences that show some regularity and coherence. Thus, rather than joy and distress as names of emotion categories, Kagan prefers "joy of understanding," "distress to physical privation," and other couplings of feelings with specific incentive events. This scheme implies that the *feeling* of joy may differ with different incentive events.

There appears to be merit in Kagan's approach to designating emotions. His system offers maximum specificity in linking incentive events, feelings, and behavior. There may be a problem, however, in deriving a complete associative network for a given emotion and arriving at a generalizable description. Joy can be associated with a wide variety of events, and, to paraphrase an old adage, one person's joy may be another person's grief. And, if we agree with Piaget that interest is an emotion and with differential emotions theory that one can become interested in virtually anything at all, we would have to expect Kagan's system of naming interest-event associations to result in a very long list.

There are no cognitive evaluations of incentives and no internal feelings during the first 4 to 6 months of life, according to Kagan. In contrast, differential emotions theory attributes to young infants specific feeling states congruent with the discrete facial expressions that they encode (Izard, Huebner, Risser, McGinnes, & Dougherty, 1980). Emprirical research bearing on this controversial issue is just beginning. Of relevance here is the Stenberg et al. study (1983) that showed that arm restraint elicited different facial expressions and different behavior, suggesting differences in underlying feeling/motivational states in 2-, 4-, and 7-month-old infants.

Whether or not Kagan (1984) is correct that emotional development is essentially epiphenomenonal, a function of cognitive development, he has raised interesting issues and discussed a number of plausible cognition-emotion sequences in development. Some of his examples follow. Object permanence enables anxiety to the unfamiliar in the 8-month-old child. Ability to recall the mother's former presence, relate this image to the current situation, and hold this information in consciousness a few seconds enables the toddler's emotion reactions to separation. The cognitive capacity to recognize that one has a choice enables the reaction of guilt in 4-year-olds. The ability to seriate the self with others enables the 6- or 7-year-old to experience pride and humility. And formal operations, or the cognitive competence to question the logic and consistency of existing beliefs, enables what Kagan calls the special feeling state of dissonance.

EMOTION EXPERIENCE AS A FUNCTION OF ATTRIBUTION PROCESSES

A different approach to the study of emotional development is being developed by Weiner and Graham (1984). Their perspective is that of the cognitive social psychologist with primary interest in attributional processes. They focus chiefly on emotions that they consider to be intrinsic to social motivation—anger, guilt, pity, and pride.

They maintain that such emotions typically are consequences of attributions about causality. That is, the way people feel about a social event depends on their interpretation of its cause. Although this seems similar to the arousal plus cognition model of emotion activation (Mandler, 1975; Schachter & Singer, 1962), it is quite different. Weiner is explicit in his belief that neither feeling pride after a self-ascription for success nor feeling gratitude following success attributed to the volitional help of others requires a state of arousal that is interpreted prior to the emotion experience. Such feelings are apparently independent of arousal, according to Weiner.

To understand the sources of the social emotions, we must understand causal attributions. Weiner holds that certain situations trigger a causal search, especially those in which an outcome is expected (success or failure) or a desire has not been fulfilled (an interpersonal rejection). Weiner's taxonomy of causes can be described by three dimensions—locus of control (internal-external) after Rotter (1966), stability (relative endurance) after Heider (1958) and controllability (the actor has a choice).

Although Weiner holds that feelings are guided by causal perceptions, he recognizes that emotions vary in the extent to which they are cognitively mediated. Some emotions, like joy and sadness, are viewed largely as a direct function of the outcome of actions or events. When explaining how Peter felt after a performance that he knows was good due to luck, more 6-year-olds than 10-year-olds will say happy. Weiner holds that an outcome-dependent emotion is typically intense and of short duration. Greater frequency of such emotions in 6-year-olds is consistent with the notion that younger children are more labile emotionally. He suggests that cognitive growth adds richness to emotional life while dampening the intensity of specific emotion experiences.

Children aged 5, 7, and 9 gave different explanations of a teacher's anger on learning that Peter failed a test. Only 77% of the 5-year-olds attributed the anger to Peter's lack of effort, whereas 89% of the 7-year-olds and all the 9-year-olds chose this explanation. When explaining why the teacher felt pity on learning of Jack's failure, 50%, 62%, and 72% of 5-, 7-, and 9-year-olds respectively explained it on the basis of low ability (Weiner, Graham, Stern, & Lawson, 1982). The pity-ability linkage showed a developmental trend in a study of 9- and 11-year-olds and college students (Weiner et al., 1982).

The emotions of pity, anger, and guilt also are linked differentially to the dimensions of locus, stability, and controllability, and these linkages show developmental trends. For example, 6- to 7-year-olds may ascribe guilt for accidental outcomes, whereas 9- and 11-year-olds acribe guilt for intentional wrongdoing. Perceived controllability also influences cognitions of anger and pity, but developmental trends for these feelings have not been demonstrated.

The locus of causality is important to the ascription of pride, and this locus-pride linkage changes with age. Although some 6-year-olds attribute pride to internal causes or self-initiated actions, there is a marked increase in the percentage of such attributions with increasing age.

Wiener speculates that the locus dimension might be the earliest to develop, following the development of the infant's ability to distinguish the self from the not-self. After the development of this dimension, cognitive processes can mediate pride or related emotions. The next dimension to emerge is the stability dimension, which precedes feelings of optimism, pessimism, and depressive affects. Last to develop is the dimension of controllability and the associated principles of justice and "ought," the antecedents of feelings of guilt.

Weiner notes, however, that young children may report feelings of guilt in response to accidental events. Zahn-Waxler, Radke-Yarrow, and King (1979) showed that certain 1½ - 2½-year-olds tended to make reparations for mother's distress when the source of distress was quite independent of the child. So what develops in emotion-attributional processes is the linkage or union between the concept of controllability and the feeling of guilt. This is similar to the differential emotions theory notion that the ontogeny of emotions is completed in infancy and that much of what is called emotional development is the development of emotion-cognition linkages or affective-cognitive structures. Much of Piaget's theory of emotional development apears to me to be concerned with the development of such structures.

The theoretical approaches of Mandler, Kagan, and Weiner have some important common features. They see most, if not all, emotion experiences as time limited (often brief) and transient phenomena. Development in the emotion domain is considered to be dependent on development in the cognitive sphere. Their emphasis is on emotion as response. These features of cognition-primacy theory tend to relegate emotion to a minor role in human development.

EMOTIONS AS ORGANIZERS AND MOTIVATORS OF ADAPTIVE PROCESSES

Research on the problem of the emotion-cognition interface should move more expeditiously if we do not get stuck on the notion that cognition must necessarily precede all changes in emotion states. Piaget, as Cicchetti and Hesse (1982) note, and several other theorists (Izard, 1977; Zajonc, 1984) believe that emotion can be a function of untransformed sensory input. Emotion results from several types of cognitive processes. Comparison of perceived and stored images that lead to a match typically may result in positive emotion whereas discrepancy may lead to either positive or negative emotion, depending on its magnitude and the context. Complex appraisal processes that go beyond the physical properties of the stimulus also activate emotion (Hoffman, 1983) as do memory, anticipation, and motor acts. It is important to remember, however, that for Piaget and for differential emotions theory, the emotion activation issue is concerned not with triggering emotions in an affectless consciousness but with changing the intensity or quality of whatever emotion is ongoing; for some emotion is always present in consciousness.

In marked contrast to the theories just discussed are those that consider emotions as continuing significant influences in development. Two such theories are differential emotions theory (Izard, 1971, 1977, 1978) and organizational theory (Emde 1980; Sroufe, 1979). In addition, Campos and Barrett (1983), Ciccheti and Hesse (1982), Field (1982), Malatesta and Haviland (1982), Hoffman (1978, 1983), Hoffman and Thompson (1980), Lewis, Sullivan and Michalson (1983), and others have contributed to the development and extension of these theories at both the conceptual and empirical levels. The theoretical positions of these investigators differ in some particulars. Those who identify more closely with differential emotions theory place more emphasis on the biological/genetic contributions to emotional development, the existence of emotion states that are defined by neurochemical/sensory processes rather than by cognition, the social-signal value of discrete emotion expressions in early infancy, the correspondence between these early expressions of specific emotions and specific emotion feelings, and the cue-producing and motivational functions of these feelings.

Although the significance of these differences between the theories must await advances in empirical research, differences may be less important than the similarities. The theories agree on a number of premises. Perhaps the most important of these is the assumption that each of the discrete emotions has unique motivational, adaptive, and organizational functions in human development. There is now substantial evidence that emotions organize and motivate intrapychic and interpersonal processes (for summaries, see Campos & Barrett, 1983, and Izard & Saxton, in press). Campos, Emde and their colleagues (Klinnert, Campos, Sorce, Emde, & Svejda, 1983; Sorce, Emde, Campos, & Klinnert, 1981) have presented striking data demonstrating how the social signal value of adults' emotion expressions regulate infants' behavior. They showed that 1-year-old infants on the starting board of the visual cliff look to the mother or other adult for emotion information, and their behavior indicates that they use the information differentially in emotion-specific expressions. When mothers posed a fear face, none of 17 infants crossed the deep side of the cliff. When mothers posed a joy face, 15 of 19 infants crossed the normally fear-eliciting deep side. Only 11% crossed when mothers posed the anger expression, whereas 75% crossed when mothers posed interest expressions. When mothers posed sadness (a contextually inappropriate expression), an intermediate number, 33%, of infants crossed, and these infants showed signs of vascillating over whether or not to cross.

In situations of this sort, I believe that two motivational conditions are operative—intrapsychic and social. The intrapsychic motivation comes from emotion-induced emotion, or emotion contagion. An example from the studies just cited would be mothers' fear expression's inducing or enhancing fear feelings in the infant. Thus, the infant's own fear prevents crossing the fear-eliciting deep side of the cliff. It also is possible that the mother's fear expression serves as a danger signal or conditioned stimulus for avoidance. Eventually such avoidance can be performed without the experience of fear. In infancy, however, I believe that emotion-induced emotion is more the rule than the exception because of the adaptive advantages of redundancy in motivational systems during this period of development. That is, in situations like that simulated by the visual-cliff experiment, both emotion as feeling state or subjective experience and emotion expression as socioemotional signal are operating to motivate adaptive behavior.

In the foregoing visual-cliff experiment, infants who saw their mothers expressing sadness vascillated about crossing the deep side. This vascillation may constitute indirect evidence of emotion contagion. The experimenters considered sadness expression contextually inappropriate in the experimental situation. It is reasonable to infer that this expression did not provide the infants with unambiguous information, yet many vascillated, and about one third crossed to the mother. It also seems reasonable to infer that the infant's own sadness, activated by mother's sadness expression, provided the motivation for the crossing or approach to the mother. Emotion contagion is the most parsimonious explanation of the vascillation and the crossing/approach behavior, because explaining this behavior as being based on the social signal system requires us to assume that the infants have learned of their capacity to alleviate mother's sadness and that the desire to do so overrides the fear of heights.

In our own laboratory we also have found evidence consistent with the premise that each emotion organizes and motivates infant's behaviours. In one study we (Shiller, Izard, & Hembree, in preparation) used the Ainsworth Strange Situation procedure to examine emotion expression during separation. We found marked individual differences in infants' emotion expression styles, on both quantitative and qualitative dimensions. Typically, infants who showed mainly interest continued to explore and play with the toys made available at the beginning of the procedure. Infants who showed predominantly anger often shook or pushed against the plexiglass barrier-wall or gate through which the mother had exited, and some threw toys and tried to climb over it. Some kicked it. Infants who showed predominantly sadness did not exhibit as much of the foregoing protest-type behaviors. They were less active and sometimes passively leaned their head on their arms, suggestive of a temporary giving up or a feeling of hopelessness.

In another study (Langsdorf, Izard, Rayias, & Hembree, 1983), we measured facial indicators of interest, heart rate, and visual fixation or attention as 2-, 4-, 6- and 8-month-old infants were presented, in random blocks of trials, a live human face, the face of a mannequin, and an inanimate object with scrambled facial features. For all stimuli there was a large stimulus effect on all variables for all ages. More important, in a regression analysis with age, interest, and heart rate as predictors of attention, interest was the only significant predictor of attention to all three stimuli. We interpreted these findings as support, although not direct evidence, of interest as an organizer and motivator of attention. In theory we, like Piaget, see interest as emotion. Piaget saw it as the energetics or affective aspect of assimilation and accommodation. I view it as the motivating condition that accounts for the selective perception and preferential attending that characterizes the human being from birth.

Lewis, Sullivan, and Michalson (1983) like Piaget, see emotion and cognition as neither separate nor independent aspects of behavior, but as parts in a Bach fugure. Lewis et al. report an interesting contingency learning experiment to support their conception of the emotion-cognition interface. The arm pull of 6-month-old infants was rewarded with a slide of a happy baby accompanied by the theme song of Sesame Street. Arm pulls were recorded on-line, and attention, facial, and vocal behaviors were videotaped. Of special interest to me were the facial behaviors, analyzed with the Maximally Discriminative Facial Movement Coding System (Izard, 1979a). The researchers found that interest and surprise peaked during the acquisition phase of the experiment and that enjoyment peaked at assymtote. These aspects of their results are consistent with the assumption of differential emotions theory that interest organizes and motivates constructive behavior. The increase in joy at assymtote is consistent with our theory as well as that of others, including Weiner and Graham (1984), who described joy as an outcome-dependent emotion.

Lewis's fugue analogy seems intended to convey the interactive nature of the emotion-cognition relationship. The idea that emotion, cognition, and motor activity influence each other reciprocally is an integral aspect of differential emotions theory. This theory emphasizes, in addition, the assumption that emotions are the primary motivations for cognition and action. Cognition and action, however, can amplify or attenuate emotion, and they can inhibit one emotion while activating another. The seeming paradox here is that *the regulation of emotions achieved through cognition and action is itself motivated and regulated by emotion.* I expect this will not sound too strange at this symposium because Piaget spoke of the will as regulation of regulations.

Sroufe (1979) and his colleagues (e.g. Sroufe, Schork, Motti, Lawroski, & LaFreniere, 1984) have made significant contributions to our understanding of emotional development, and they have reported data in support of the thesis that emotions organize and motivate adaptive behavior. In particular, their research has demonstrated an important role for emotions in the development of social competence. Their observations of preschool children led Sroufe et al. to conclude that emotions and emotion expression styles "play an important role both in attaining leadership status in the group and in promoting and sustaining interaction" (p.1).

Sroufe et al. discussed several conceptual links between social competence and affect. First, they argued that positive affect expressions serve affiliative and communicative functions, both of which can contribute to rewarding and effective interactions. Second, they held that emotion expressions regulate interactions by influencing the pacing, turn-taking, and termination of social exchanges.

Finally, they maintained that positive emotion expression is contagious and socially bonding and that it invigorates social interactions.

Findings from an observational study of preschool children by Sroufe et al. were consistent with their assumption regarding the role of emotion expressions in social competence. They found strong correlations between observers' ratings of children's affective expressions and independent teacher rankings on social competence (Rho $= .76, p < .001$). This correlation reflects a relationship between concurrent measures, but ratings of positive emotion expression on the same subjects at 2 and 5 years of age correlated .47 ($p < .03$), showing substantial stability in expression style over a 3-year period.

PIAGET'S THEORY OF EMOTION: COGNITIVE OR DYNAMIC?

Piaget's theorizing about emotions does not fall easily into either of the two types of theory I have discussed. He considered the separation of emotion and cognition as artificial, merely a theorist's ploy "for convenience of exposition " (Piaget, 1981, p. 25). This is similar to some cognitive theories of emotion. However, he saw emotions as the energy source for intellectual functioning, and if we equate the concept of "energy source " with motivation, then his theory of emotion is not a cognitive one but rather a dynamic theory, more like differential emotions theory.

Yet, Piaget repeatedly insisted that emotions could not generate or modify the structures of behavior. One might infer from this categorical denial of a role for emotion in determining behavioral structures that Piaget thought emotion to be of little significance for cognitive development. But Piaget (1981) put it this way:

> Let us recall in this regard that if affectivity cannot modify structures it still constantly influences their contents. For example, it is *interest*, therefore, affectivity *that makes the child decide* to seriate objects and *decide* which objects to seriate. (p. 10, italics added)

This appears to be a clear enunciation of the principle that emotion functions as motivation for cognitive processes and for the selection of their contents, matters of great consequence in the formation of values, goals, and the personality.

Piaget enunciated three more specific propositions that seem to attribute significance to emotions as continual influences in developmental processes. First, he noted that "feelings of success or failure" could facilitate or inhibit learning. I believe that feelings of success can be subsumed under the emotion of enjoyment, and that feelings of failure correspond to one or more negative emotions, particularly shame, sadness, or anger. There is substantial empirical evidence that these emotions do indeed influence learning and memory as well as prosocial and moral behavior, but this evidence throws little light on the problem of the development of emotion-cognition relationships (Bower, 1981; Fry, 1975; Laird, Wagener, Halal, & Szegda, 1982; Moore, Underwood, & Rosenhan, 1983).

Second, Piaget (1981) said that "affectivity constantly influences perceptual activity. Different subjects will not perceive the same elements of a complex figure, their choices being inspired by different *interests*; nor will children perceive the same details" (p. 6, italics added). Third, Piaget said that *affectivity is constantly at work in the functioning of thought* (p. 7). Although these three statements alone seem to be enough to have inspired a great deal of research on the relationship of emotion and cognition, they did not.

But why did these propositions that seem so tantalizing fail to generate research in the Piagetian tradition? There are many possitibilities. I have discussed some of them elsewhere as they relate to the larger issue of the general paucity of empirical research on emotions, but that discussion may not be relevant here, especially in trying to explain Piaget's own tendency to neglect this area. Remember, he said that subjects perceive different elements of a complex figure according to their interest. So when Piaget looked at the complex human organism, the aspect of emotion or affectivity simply did not interest him nearly as much as the emergence of cognitive structures of the mind.

I believe that the three foregoing Piagetian propositions on emotion-cognition relationships are essentially the same as three of the propositions of my differential emotions theory (Izard, 1977, 1979b), and I think they are highly important to our understanding of important aspects of development. I shall discuss two of these propositions briefly.

Emotion as a Determinant of Selective Perception.   Piaget asserted that, when confronted with a complex object, the emotion of interest determines which aspects of it we perceive. I agree. More broadly, I have maintained that some emotion is always at work in focusing as well as in maintaining perceptual-attentive processes. Negative as well as positive emotions can perform this function.

I do not want to be misleading in the estimate of the extent of the agreement between Piaget and differential emotions theory regarding the role of emotion in perceptual selectivity. Piaget said so little about the specifics of emotion as motivation or cause of cognition and behavior that it is difficult or impossible to determine his position on particular aspects of this issue. In any case, I shall try to make clear my own position on emotion-as-determinant of selective perception by describing a couple of relevant experiments. One of the experiments examined the effects of induced joy and anger on stereoscopic perception, and the other investigated the relationships of interest to the visual fixation of face-like stimuli.

Izard, Wehmer, Livsey and Jennings (1965) examined the effects of inter-personally induced positive and negative emotion on soldiers' stereoscopic per-ception of photographs of joyful and angry faces and of friendly and hostile interpersonal encounters (scenes). The joy-induction procedure consisted of warm, friendly responses from the experimenter (an officer with the rank of captain), and the anger-induction of curt, critical responses from the experimenter. The picture stimuli consisted of 26 pairs of facial expressions, one happy and one angry, and 22 pairs of interpersonal scenes, one friendly, one hostile. The paired emotion stimuli were presented stereoscopically, such that an anger expression or hostile scene was presented in the visual field of one eye and a joy expression or friendly scene to the other eye. Right and left presentations and valence of stimuli were counterbalanced and special techniques were used to control for differential visual acuity and convergence of the eyes. The negative emotion-induction treatment caused subjects to see significantly more angry faces and hostile scenes than did the subjects in the positive emotion induction group. Apparently the induced emotion determined the direction of the resolution of the binocular rivalry created by the stereoscopic presentation and led to emotion-congruent perceptions.

Emotions, Attention, and Learning.   Piaget (1981) was explicit in his state-ments regarding the affective components of the processes of assimilation and accommodation. He defined the cognitive aspect of assimilation as understanding and the affective aspect as the emotion of interest. The interest in this case appears to be an integral part of organismic functioning, for Piaget explained interest as assimilation to the self, after Dewey. Piaget defined the cognitive aspect of accommodation as the adjustment of schemas to match phenomena and the affective aspect as interest in novelty or in the novel aspects of the object.

It seems that Piaget has defined two types or sources of interest activation—the biological and the ecological. First, interest is a genetic characteristic of the organism. It initiates and sustains exploration and is a major wellspring of the organism's activity and goal-directedness. Second, the novelty, movement, and change observable within the organism's ecological niche provide specific incen-tive events or elicitors of interest. Alternatively, these incentive events that characterize the ecology may be seen as constraining factors in the canalization of interest expression and in the development of individual differences. All this is quite consistent with the several contemporary theories that conceive of emo-tion as motivational and adaptive.

Piaget (1981) also recognized individual differences in the direction or invest-ment of interest. He noted, as have all parents and educators, that those who are eager and enthusiastic learn more easily.

A decade after Piaget's Sorbonne lectures on affectivity and intelligence and unaware of their existence, my students and I (Izard, Nagler, & Fox, 1965), inspired by differential emotions theory, conducted a series of experiments on affect and learning. I believe the results and the theoretical framework that guided them are consistent with Piaget's position.

One of these studies compared the effects of intrinsic interest and positive and negative background affect on learning. We hypothesized that task-intrinsic interest and background positive affect would facilitate involvement in the learning task and that background negative affect would be disrupting.

The affective stimuli were twenty 5 × 7 chromatic facial photographs, ten with extremely high and ten with extremely low ratings on a 12-point pleasantness scale. The high positive affect pictures were of attractive young women expressing interest or enjoyment. The negative affect pictures were of hospital patients with advanced untreated facial carcinoma.

The subjects were male college students from introductory psychology classes. The learning task was to pair ten CVC trigrams, under three conditions. In the intrinsic-interest condition (described as the no-picture control group in the original publication), the affect was assumed to be interest intrinsic to the experimental situation, which included the encouragement of a warm, friendly experimenter. In the positive affect and negative affect conditions the CVC trigrams were presented at the base of either the high positive or high negative affect pictures.

On a given trial, each trigram pair appeared on two copies of the same photograph, but trigram-photograph assignments were randomized across trials to prevent subjects from associating a trigram pair with a particular picture. The stimulus half of the picture/trigram pair was exposed for 2 sec followed by a 2 sec exposure of the response half of the pair. There were four randomizations of the picture/trigram pairings repeated twice, resulting in one familiarization trial and seven learning trials. The results generally confirmed our hypothesis.

The no-picture condition, which we now interpret as the intrinsic interest condition, facilitated learning most, the positive picture or positive affect condition next most, and the negative affect condition least. The intrinsic interest and positive affect learning curves did not differ significantly from each other, but both were significantly higher than those for the negative affect condition.

We replicated the picture/trigram experiment in a within-subject design, using four levels of affective stimuli and both male and female subjects. The results further confirm our hypothesis, and they are consistent with Piaget's proposition regarding affect and learning.

Almost 30 years after the Sorbonne lectures on affect and intelligence and about 20 years after the foregoing experiments, the effects of emotion on perception, learning, and memory became a topic in experimental cognitive and social psychology. Recent research in this area has been summarized by Bower (1981; Bower & Gilligan, 1984) and by Zajonc (1980; Zajonc & Markus, 1983).

AFFECTIVE-COGNITIVE STRUCTURES AND
PERSONALITY DEVELOPMENT

It is unnecessary for me to detail systematically the contributions of Piaget to the study of emotional development. Cicchetti and Hesse (1982) already have published an extensive account of Piaget's contributions to emotional development in the sensorimotor period. They have presented a cogent account of event-emotion expression relationships in this period of development. Their systematic analysis identified four types of situations that led Piaget to identify specific emotions in his children: proprioceptive-kinesthetic reactions, recognition of similarity, competent behavior, and recognition of discrepancy. Only proprioceptive-kinesthetic reactions were judged to elicit emotion in a reflex-like manner apparently independent of cognitive mediation. Because all other types of eliciting situations involve cognitive and/or instrumental motor acts, a careful study of Ciccheti and Hesse's integrative analysis should sharpen the ability to monitor both major shifts and nuances of cognitive development.

Cicchetti and Hesse (1982) also discuss Piaget's contributions to a developmental theory of emotions. What they have done so far is to specify in precise detail the observed relationships between cognitive and cognitive-motor processes as antecedents on the one hand and emotion expressions as consequences on the other. What remains to be done is an equally comprehensive analysis of Piaget's thinking on emotions as antecedents or causes.

I believe we would do both Piaget and behavioral science an injustice if we did not seek to understand better the role of each of the emotions in cognition and action. Emotion expressions can be well used as criteria for cognitive attainments, as Piaget and others have shown (Haviland, 1976; Ramsay & Campos, 1978), but this is only a small part of the emotion domain. Further, this use of emotion expressions as markers can be misleading. *Emotion is never merely response.* When emotion serves a response function, and it often does, it simultaneously serves as stimulus or motivation: Its experiential/feeling component motivates the individual and its expressive component influences the behavior of the observer.

In this chapter, I have expressed some of my ideas on emotion-as-motivation in relation to Piaget's thinking. Let me develop one more of my impressions. Piaget stoutly and repeatedly maintained that affectivity did not shape or alter cognitive structures, and vice versa. Yet he was emphatic in his distinction between structure on the one hand and energetics or functioning on the other. This idea of the energetic aspects of behavior is close to my conception of the emotions, defined as motivational phenomena with broad and profound functions in cognitive and personality development. Piaget (1981) said that these "energetic aspects are the interests, efforts, and intraindividual feelings that regulate behavior" (p. 74). This statement, minus the one word "efforts," can be found in the writing of a number of investigators who contribute to differential emotions theory or the organizational theory of development, both of which, to my knowledge, were derived independently of Piaget. And, of course, Piaget's major statement on emotional development could not have been influenced by these theories of emotion, for his work preceded them.

The notion I develop may provide a bridge between Piaget and contemporary emotion theory. In *Intelligence and Affectivity*, Piaget's 1953-1954 Sorbonne lectures, several stages of affective development are described. The stages range from hereditary organizations that may include instincts or reflexive affects to idealistic feelings that come after the emergence of formal operations and that "define the personality" (1981 p. 70). In the language of differential emotions theory, Piaget's stages of affectivity are not stages in the development of emotion processes proper, but stages of the emergence of increasingly complex affective-cognitive structures that do indeed define the traits and characteristics of the individual personality. I have defined affective-cognitive structures as bonds between specific emotion feelings on the one hand and images, symbols, thoughts, and memories on the other. I can find an apparently strong similarity between this definition of affective-cognitive structure and Piaget's concept of affective structure, which he defined as "feeling intellectualized". He restricted the concept, however, to the social domain, arguing that "affective structures become the cognitive aspect of relationships with other people" (1981, p. 74).

I hasten to emphasize that Piaget did not use the term *intellectualization* in the way it is used in the psychoanalytic tradition. As a defense mechanism, intellectualization inhibits or attenuates the emotion that would normally occur in a given situation by a rational explanation that divests the situation of personal significance. Because of the relatively common use of intellectualization to describe this process, a more appropriate term for describing how feeliings organize and merge with images and symbolic processes (thought) to form personal values and goals might be *emotionalization*. This term places the emphasis on emotion as an organizing, motivating condition. Emotionalization, defined as the process of bonding emotion feeling with images, symbols, and thoughts, and affective-cognitive structures, defined as the end products of this process, provide part of a conceptual framework for studying the processes of trait formation and personality development.

I see the fundamental emotions as products of evolutionary-biological processes, as primarily determined by biogenetic and maturational processes. Some affective-cognitive structures may be so determined, but most of them are learned, and the learning or affective-cognitive processes that produce these structures are of inestimable significance in human development. I also think that experts in cognitive development who believe this can be among the frontrunners who will make the giant step toward a more unified theoretical approach to the immensely challenging search for the origins and development of affective-cognitive structures.

ACKNOWLEDGMENTS

The work for this paper was supported by NSF Grants BNS 811832 & BNS 8410586.

REFERENCES

Bower, G. H. (1981). Emotional mood and memory. *American Psychologist, 36*(2), 129–148.

Campos, J. J., & Barrett, K. C. (1983). Toward a new understanding of emotions and their development. In C. Izard, J. Kagan, & R. Zajonc (Eds.), *Emotions, cognition, and behavior*. New York: Cambridge University Press.

Cicchetti, D., & Hesse P. (1982). Perspectives on an integrated theory of emotional development. In D. Cicchetti, & P. Hesse (Eds.), *Emotional development* (pp. 3–48). San Francisco: Jossey-Bass.

Emde, R. (1980). Toward a psychoanalytic theory of affect. In S. Greenspan & G. Pollock (Eds.), *Psychoanalytic contributions toward understanding personality and development*. (Vol. I). Atlanta: National Institute of Mental Health.

Field, T. (1982). Affective displays of high-risk infants during early interactions. In T. Field & A. Fogel (Eds.) *Emotion and early interaction* Hillsdale, NJ: Lawrence Erlbaum Associates.

Fry, P. S. (1975). Affect and resistance to temptation. *Developmental Psychology, 11*, 466–472.

Gilligan, S., & Bower, G. H. (1984). Cognitive consequences of emotional arousal. In C. Izard, J. Kagan, & R. Zajonc (Eds.), *Emotions, cognition, and behavior* (pp. 547-588). New York: Cambridge University Press.

Haviland, J. (1976). Looking smart: The relationship between affect and intelligence in infancy. In M. Lewis (Ed.), *Origins of intelligence* (pp. 353-377). New York: Plenum Press.

Heider, F. (1958). *The psychology of interpersonal relations* New York: Wiley.

Hoffman, M. L. (1978). Empathy, its development, and prosocial implications. In C. B. Keasey (Ed.), *Nebraska symposium on motivation: Vol. 25* (pp. 169–218). Lincoln University of Nebraska Press.

Hoffman, M. L. (1978). Empathy, its development, and prosocial implications. In C. B. Keasey (Ed.), *Nebraska symposium on motivation: Vol. 25* (pp. 169–218). Lincoln: University of Nebraska Press.

Hoffman, M.L., & Thompson, R. (1980). Empathy and the development of guilt in children. *Developmental Psychology, 16*, 155–156.

Izard, C. E. (1971). *The face of emotion* New York: Appleton-Century-Crofts.

Izard, C. E. (1977). *Human emotions*. New York: Plenum Press.

Izard, C. E. (1978). On the ontogenesis of emotions and emotion-cognition relationships in infancy. In M. Lewis & L. Rosenblum (Eds.), *The development of affect* (pp. 389–413). New York: Plenum.

Izard, C. E. (1979c). *The maximally discriminative facial movement coding system (max)*. Newark, DE: University of Delaware, Instructional Resources Center.

Izard, C. E. (1979b). Emotions as motivations: An evolutionary-developmental perspective. In R. A. Dienstbier (Ed.), *Nebraska symposium on motivation*. Lincoln: University of Nebraska Press.

Izard, C. E., Huebner, R. R., Risser, D., McGinnes, G., & Dougherty. L. (1980). . The young infant's ability to produce discrete emotion expressions. *Developmental Psychology, 16*(2), 132–140.

Izard, C. E., Nagler, S., Randall, D., & Fox, J. (1965) The effects of affective picture stimuli of learning, perception and the affective values of previously neutral symbols. In S. S. Tomkins & C. E. Izard (Eds.), *Affect, cognition, and personality* (pp. 42–70). New York: Springer.

Izard, C. E., & Saxton, P. (in press). Emotions. In W. Estes, R. Hernstein, G. Lindzey, D. Luce, & R. Thompson (Eds.), *Steven's handbook of experimental psychology*. New York: Wiley.

Izard, C. E., Wehmer, G. M., Livsey, W., & Jennings, J. R. (1965). Affect, awareness, and performance. In S. S. Tomkins & C. E. Izard (Eds.) *Affect, cognition, and personality* (pp. 2–41). New York: Springer.

Kagan, J. (1984). The idea of emotion in human development. In C. E. Izard, J. Kagan, & R. Zajonc (Eds.), *Emotions, cognition, and behavior* (pp. 38–72). New York: Cambridge University Press.

Klinnert, M., Campos, J., Sorce, J., Emde, R., & Svejda, M. (1983). Emotions as behavior regulators: The development of social referencing. In. R. Plutchik & H. Kellerman (Eds.), Emotion: Theory, research and development. Vol. 2: *Emotions in early development* (pp. 57–86). New York: Academic Press.

Laird, J. D., Wagener, J. J., Halal, M., & Szegda, M. (1982). Remembering what you feel: Effects of emotion on memory. *Journal of Personality and Social Psychology*, *42*(4), 646–657.

Langsdorf, P., Izard, C. E., Rayias, M., & Hembree, E. A. (1983) Interest expression, visual fixation, and heart rate changes in 2- to 8-month-old infants. *Developmental Psychology, 19*, (3), 375–386.

Lewis, M., Sullivan, M. W., & Michalson, L. (1983) The cognitive-emotional fugue. In C. Izard, J. Kagan, and R. Zajonc (Eds.), *Emotions, cognition, and behavior* (pp. 264–288). New York: Cambridge University Press.

Malatesta, C. Z. & Haviland, J. M. (1982). Learning display rules: The socialization of emotion expression in infancy. *Child Development. 53*, 991–1003.

Mandler, G. (1975). *Mind and emotions*. New York: Wiley.

Mandler, G. (1982). The construction of emotion in the child. In C. E. Izard (Ed.), *Measuring emotions in infants and children* (pp. 335–343). New York: Cambridge University Press.

Moore, B., Underwood, B., & Rosenhan, D. L. (1983). Emotion, self, and others. In C. Izard, J. Kagan, & R. Zajonc (Eds.), *Emotions, cognition, and behavior* (pp. 464–483). New York: Cambridge University Press.

Piaget, J. (1981). *Intelligence and affectivity*. California: Annual Reviews.

Ramsay, D., & Campos, J. (1978). The onset of representation and entry into stage 6 of object permanence development. *Developmental Psychology, 14*, 79–86.

Rotter, J. B. (1966). Generalized expectancies for internal versus external control of reinforcement. *Psychological Monographs, 80*, (1, Whole No. 609).

Schachter, S. , & Singer, J. E. (1962). Cognitive, social, and physiological determinants of emotional states. *Psychological Review, 69*(5), 379–399.

Shiller, V. M., Izard, C. E., & Hembree, E. A. *Patterns of emotion expression during separation.* Manuscript submitted for publication.

Sorce, J., Emde, R., Campos, J., & Klinnert, M. (1981, June).*Maternal emotional signalling: Its effect on the visual cliff behavior of one-year-olds.* Paper read at meeting of the Interamerican Congress of Psychology, Santo Domingo, Dominican Republic.

Sroufe, L. A. (1979). Socioemotional development. In J. Osofsky (Ed.), *Handbook of infant development* (pp. 462–516). New York: Wiley.

Sroufe, L. A., Schork, E., Motti, F., Lawroski, N., & LaFreniere, P. (1984). The role of affect in social competence. In C. Izard, J. Kagan & R. Zajonc (Eds.), *Emotions, cognition, and behavior* (pp. 289–319). New York: Cambridge University Press.

Stenberg, C., Campos, J., & Emde, R. (1983). The facial expression of anger in seven-month-old infants. *Child Development, 54*, 178-184.

Weiner, B., & Graham, S. (1984). An attributional approach to emotional development. In C. Izard, J. Kagan & R. Zajonc (Eds.), *Emotions, cognition, and behavior* (pp. 167–189). New York: Cambridge University Press.

Weiner, B., Graham,. S., Stern, P., & Lawson, M. E. (1982). Using affective cues to infer causal thoughts. *Developmental Psychology, 18*, 278–286.

Zahn-Waxler, C., Radke-Yarrow, M., & King, R. A. (1979). Child rearing and children's prosocial initiations towards victims of distress. *Child Development, 50,* 319–330.

Zajonc, R. B. (1980). Feeling and thinking: Preferences need no inferences. *American Psychologist* 35(2), 151–175.

Zajonc, R. B., & Markus, H. (1984). Affect and cognition: The hard interface. In C. E. Izard, J. Kagan & R. Zajonc (Eds.), *Emotions, cognition, and behavior* (pp. 73–102). New York: Cambridge University Press.

Zajonc, R.B. (1984) Feeling and thinking: Preferences need no inferences. *American Psychologist,* 35(2), 151–175.

4

Notes Toward a Co-constructive Theory of the Emotion-Cognition Relationship

Robert H. Wozniak
Bryn Mawr College

Our understanding of the developing relationship between emotion and cognition is still primitive. Although there undoubtedly are many reasons for this, two are especially relevant to the argument presented in this chapter. First, with only a few exceptions (Emde, Gaensbauer, & Harmon, 1976; Izard, 1978, 1979, 1980; Kagan, 1978; Lewis & Brooks, 1978; Sroufe, 1979; Thomas & Chess, 1980; Weiner, Kun, & Benesh-Weiner, 1980), theorists of emotion have been notorious for ignoring issues of development; and developmentalists have been equally notorious for avoiding something as raw and unrefined as emotion. Many developmentalists encountering the word *affect* still mentally transform it into *socialization* and assume that studying parent-child interaction is somehow equivalent to studying the development of affect. Those who are a bit more modern perhaps think of affect as *social cognition*. Others equate affect with *self* or a personality subsystem like the *id* and still others with *motivation*—but only a courageous few have taken *human emotionality* as the core meaning of the term affect and focused on human emotionality in its development.

Second, although there certainly is no shortage of research or theory on the development of cognition, there is still considerable disagreement and even confusion among psychologists over how the term *cognition* should be theoretically construed. As will become evident, the term cognition has been subjected to a number of very different interpretations in various contexts by different, and occasionally even by the same, theorists. This, coupled with a parallel problem encountered in specifying what is meant by *emotion*, makes it difficult even to make sense of a question such as, "how does the relationship between emotion and cognition develop?" Indeed, if anything is to be made of such a question, it must be within the context of a broader theory that first addresses the nature of cognition and emotion respectively.

The problem with this type of broad theory, however, is that it depends in turn on a commitment to one or another view of the nature of psychological reality and the nature of psychological explanation—commitment to assumptions about the way the world is and about what psychology is or should be. Commitments of this sort, of course, are not strictly theoretical, but metatheoretical. They are the sort of commitments that are tacit in all psychological theory but that psychological theorists rarely if ever make explicit.

Yet, if confusion about what is to be meant by terms like cognition and emotion is to be avoided, some explicit characterization of metatheoretical commitments seems to be a necessity. We need, in other words, reasoning of the following sort: Given that this is the way the world (human and nonhuman, mental and physical) is organized and that this is the nature of the psychologist's task, then this is the general form that theoretical explanation ought to take. Within the context of this form of general theory, here is a way to make consistent sense of the terms cognition and emotion. Given that this is what we mean by cognition and emotion, here is a theoretical specification of the nature of cognitive and emotional psychological structures and processes, of the way in which these structures and processes might be related, and of the way in which developments in one might be reflected in the other.

This is a large task. To provide a framework that makes consistent sense of questions about the relationship between emotion and cognition, we need a theory broad enough to give theoretical meaning to the terms cognition and emotion. If we are to make that theory reasonably clear and consistent, we need to characterize the metatheoretical principles on which it is based in a way that answers the seldom-asked question, "What kind of a theory is this?"

It would be optimistic indeed to think that this could be adequately accomplished within the framework of a single chapter. Still, it is possible to indicate, in at least a preliminary way, some general ideas about the requirements for potentially adequate psychological theory that I have been developing over the past few years (Wozniak, 1975, 1981, 1983) and within that framework to discuss both the range of theoretical meanings that might accrue to terms like cognition and emotion and the sense that can and cannot (given the framework) be made of questions about the developing relationship between cognitive and emotional structures and processes. Following this, in order to indicate the potential value of this sort of analysis for the clarification of claims that theorists of emotion and cognition make, I will briefly and critically discuss one recently articulated and influential view of the development of the relation between emotion and cognition: the differential emotions perspective of Izard (1977, 1978, and chapter 3 in this volume).

CO-CONSTRUCTIVE METATHEORY

Metatheory is, of course, the theory of theories—theoretical method. Metatheoretical discourse attempts to provide an analysis of how theory has been, is, or might be constructed. Metatheoretical statements represent basic commitments about the nature of reality and the nature of science which theorists embed (usually tacitly) in theoretical constructs. Specific metatheoretical statements themselves are not presumed to be directly testable. This should not, however, be taken to mean that they are totally immune to confirmation. On the contrary, indirect confirmation of metatheoretical commitments is inherent in the extent to which theories embodying those commitments are themselves confirmed.

Metatheoretical analysis in psychology begins with the question of what constitutes proper subject matter for psychological science. Historically, this question has had a varied and interesting succession of answers. For James (1890) and many of his contemporaries, the answer would have been "consciousness" or "consciousness as experience". For Freud (1913) and, in an even more extreme form for certain contemporary analytic theorists (Lacan, 1968; Schafer, 1978), the answer would have been "symbolic discourse". For Watson (1919) and many of those who followed him, the answer was "behavior". For Piaget (1950), one can persuasively argue that the answer would have been "mental structure," and for Gibson (1979), the answer would have included the "affordances for action" that are provided by the structure of the environment.

The problem is that none of the foregoing were quite right, because they were all right. Experience, symbolic discourse, and behavior, or, as it is better termed, *action* must certainly constitute the "that which is to be explained" for psychological science. How is experience organized? How is it that two people present at the same event can experience it differently? How is a symbol system like language organized? How does language differ in function from mental imagery? How is action organized? How do people's actions reflect the psychologically effective structure of the environment? A psychology that cannot at least in principle be brought to bear on questions such as these is hardly a psychology at all.

How, then, is explanation to be achieved? The answer, and this is quite clearly a metatheoretical commitment, must involve both mental structure and ecological structure, the structure of the mind and the psychologically effective structure of the objects and events that form the physical and social context for experience, symbolic discourse, and action.

The argument, in other words, is that experience, symbolic discourse and action are co-constructions that arise (in the here and now) in the interaction of mental structures and mental acts with physical/social objects and events and (ontogenetically) from the interaction of mind with physical/social reality. The system that is being proposed is generally represented in Fig. 4.1.

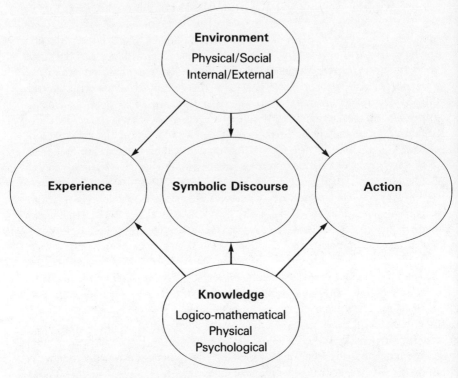

FIG. 4.1

Before briefly considering each of the elements in this representation, a ... general assumptions inherent in this form of explanation should be made explicit. The first has to do with the stream-like character of experience, symbolic discourse, and action. James provided the classic description of the "stream of consciousness" and, without arguing the point here, I would simply like to note that the same general flow, unfolding over time in a continuous or nearly continuous fashion, can be said equally to characterize symbolic discourse and action.

In addition, however, the streams of experience, symbolization, and action also are characterized by internal structure. They are organized; and that organization both exists in and changes over time. Experience may consist of a flow, but that flow is one of objects and events. That symbolic discourse depends intimately on internal structure is evident from a comparison of the meaning of a sentence such as "the dog chased the cat" with that of a sentence such as "the cat chased the dog". Similarly, actions such as tying a shoe or writing a signature unfold in time in a very precise sequence of movements closely tailored to the support provided by the structure of objects and events being acted on.

The descriptive problem for psychology, then, is adequately to characterize over time the dynamic structure and changes in dynamic structure in experience, symbolic discourse and action. The explanatory problem is one of accounting for this structure and change in structure. To do this, we need to understand both the structures and processes of the mind and the structures and processes of psychologically relevant (*ecological*) physical and social reality.

The *constructivist* program of Piaget (Piatelli-Palmarini, 1980), and to a certain extent contemporary cognitive psychology (e.g., Rumelhart, 1980; Rumelhart & Ortony, 1978) have addressed the first problem. It is much less controversial now than it once would have been to claim that, to experience a camera as something that can take a picture, we must know something about light, lenses and film; or that to understand English, we must know the syntactic rules that govern spoken English; or that to tie a shoe, we must know how to move our fingers in relationship to the laces. Knowledge (as structure) and knowing (as process), in other words, now are taken by many (if not all) psychologists to be acceptable constructs relevant to the explanation of psychological phenomena.

The ecological program of Gibson (1966, 1979) has addressed the second problem. To experience a camera visually as affording picture taking, we must detect over time the higher order invariant structure in the light to the eye bearing a regular (and hence informative) relation to certain properties of the camera, properties which themselves are a function of the structure of the camera. To understand spoken English, we must extract over time the higher order patterns informative about certain symbols that have been coded into the sound stream by the speaker. To tie a shoe, we must detect the properties of laces that will support that action, properties such as their flexibility, solidity, and small diameter in relation to that of the fingers.

Physical and social structures and processes, in other words, support properties of physical and social objects and events. These properties are in turn broadcast in the higher order invariant relationships over time that exist in patterned energy to the receptor and are experienced by the organism as objects and events affording actions of various sorts. The psychologically relevant properties of physical and social structures, then, also must be taken to be acceptable constructs relevant to the explanation of psychological phenomena.

Now, for purposes of psychological explanation, it is necessary to treat our concepts of both cognitive structure and process (knowledge and mental acts of knowing) and physical and social structure and process (physical and social objects and events) as hypothetical constructs (Hempel, 1966). Here "hypothetical construct" refers to a concept of an entity or process assumed to exist, to underlie the organization and change in organization in experience, symbolic discourse, and action, and about which we theorize. Neither the underlying structure and processes of knowledge (i.e., concepts and interpretive processes) nor those of the physical/social world (i.e., properties of physical and social objects and events and higher order invariants informative about those properties) are directly given, in other words, *in* experience. They are in-principly non-conscious, known only by inference *from* experience, the experience of objects and events, the experience of experience itself, of symbolic discourse and of action, our own and that of others.

The explanatory problem for psychology, then, becomes one of developing adequate theories of knowledge and knowing and of the psychologically relevant structures and properties of the environment and of showing how they interactively co-determine or co-construct experience, symbolic discourse and action. A program of this sort is partly compatible with and partly larger than either the constructivism of Piaget or the ecological approach of Gibson.[1] In an adequate discussion of this formulation of the problem, many issues would need to be

---

[1]It is important to point out here that neither Piaget nor Gibson would have had much sympathy with this use of their work. Piaget's interest, as he often stressed, was not strictly speaking psychological at all, but genetic epistemological, an interest in the historical and ontogenetic development of the rational thought processes and structures underlying those processes that guarantee the progressive approximation to valid knowledge that is achieved by science. For this program, structure and change in experience, symbolic discourse and even action (if one excludes the very general sensorimotor actions that are the precursors of logic) were, for Piaget, of scant relevance. Gibson rejected any attempt to intrude cognition into his theory of "direct perception". This rejection derived, in my view, partly from an unwillingness to draw a distinction that I consider to be essential and partly from a faith in ultimate physiological reduction that I do not share. The distinction is that between two very different senses in which cognitive processes might be said to operate in perception—at the level of detection and at an executive level. Gibson's theory was specifically formulated in opposition to the Helmholtzian view that perception is based on cognitive processes of unconscious inference. From this point of view, it is assumed that very low-order sensory features are detected by the perceiver and then inferentially operated upon to yield complex perception. By contrast, from a Gibsonian perspective, complex perception is assumed to be direct in that higher-order invariants in stimulus flux over time which are regularly related to (i.e., informative about) complex properties of the environment are detected without the necessity of any inferencing process. Although the burden of proof that such invariants can be specified for all important higher order properties lies with the "direct perception" theorist and as yet is still largely a promissory note, a number of very impressive gains in this direction have been made and I find myself in general agreement with Gibson that this is the right approach to take. There is, however, another issue. What is the mechanism in the organism responsible for directly detecting higher-order invariants over time? Gibson's answer to this question appears to have been to assume that such detectors would be found eventually in the nervous system and to relegate all attempts to account for detection psychologically to the status of mythologizing. For reasons that can not be discussed here (but see Margolis, 1984, for an excellent discussion of problems intrinsic to reductionism), I believe that all attempts at physiological reduction are bound to fail and that a psychological theory of the detection mechanism is essential. This is, of course, where cognition enters the explanation. To the extent that the detection of higher-order invariants is context sensitive, the perceiver's knowledge serves an executive function. The perceiver uses contextual information (e.g., knowledge of what has just occurred) to generate expectations (predictions about what is likely to occur next) which tune the detection mechanism to certain higher-order invariants and not to others. In my view, the operation of this sort of cognitive process is perfectly compatible with a view of "direct perception" formulated contra-Helmholtz and the postulation of some such process will be essential to any account of the construction of experience.

addressed. What, for example, is meant by social structure and how social structure is broadcast in the light to the eye (cf., McArthur & Baron, 1983, for an interesting discussion of this issue)? What is the logical status of explanatory constructs such as *cognitive structure, cognitive process,* or *affordance* that can be said partly to determine the form of experience or action but can hardly be said to cause it? Or how exactly does this form of explanation differ from traditional hypothetical construct (e.g., Hull) and nonconstruct (e.g., Skinner) views in psychology? For purposes of this chapter, however, it is more important to push ahead to a slightly more detailed consideration of the nature of experience, symbolic discourse, and action in order to prepare the basis for a discussion of how to make one kind of sense of questions about the relation between cognition and emotion.

Experience as Consciousness

Suppose a newborn baby girl, an average adult, and a skilled forester all were gazing at the same tree from approximately the same spatial position. In one sense, we might say that they would all see the same "thing," i.e., the tree. But, in another sense, most would agree that they would not "see" the same thing at all. Based on what we now know of the rather highly developed state of the newborn's visual abilities (Cohen, DeLoache, & Strauss, 1979; Spelke & Gibson, 1983), we would probably be willing to believe that the baby girl is able to see shapes of leaves, movements of branches, textures of bark and leaf, variations in brightness of tree and sky, and that quite possibly she may even be able to perceive the match between subtle changes in these visual features and the soft murmur made by the leaves as they shift back and forth in the breeze.

We believe, however, that there is information in the light to the infant's eye that specifies much more than this. Type of tree, oak or apple, presence or absence of fruit or acorns, and time of year in buds or reddening foliage are all potentially detectable elements of the stimulus array. Yet we would be much slower to assume that the infant can detect this information (i.e., that she can attend to these variables of stimulation). The average adult, on the other hand, can; and the forester can detect even more. The age and health of the tree, the particular subvariation of oak or apple, the type of bark, and numerous other more subtle features may be detected by someone with a forester's skill and experience (see Gibson, 1969, for evidence concerning the occurrence of this type of peceptual development).

This is, of course, the important point. The light to the eye is rich in potential information, rich in structure bearing a regular relation to numerous properties of the environment. That information is in the light to and potentially detectable by infant, adult and forester—yet it is not by itself a sufficient condition for experience. The perceiver also must have developed, in experience, the capacity to detect that information. That capacity is best understood as a cognitive capacity, one dependent on the development of a conceptual system and processes in which information from and about the environment is actively interpreted, assimilated to appropriate concepts, and thereby given meaning. Perceiving, in other words, can be thought of as a process of the co-construction of experience in which the environment provides a *figurative* component (form), dependent on structure over time in the stimulus flux, and the mind provides a *conceptual* component (meaning), dependent on the structure of knowledge and knowing processes.[2]

Although I discuss this in much more detail later, the relevance of this analysis for a consideration of emotion is evident from the fact that emotion is, among other things, a form of experience. We feel ourselves grow angry. We feel ourselves become disgusted. We feel ourselves overcome with joy. As with all experience, then, emotional experience must be understood in terms of both form and meaning, figurative and cognitive components.

Symbolic Discourse

In addition to experiencing the world, human beings also generate symbols to stand for it, symbols that take the form of words or mental images. Piaget and Inhelder (1969) referred to the mental activity of symbol generation as semiotic activity. Symbolic discourse is the product of such semiotic activity. The function of symbolic discourse is representational. Two of the most important characteristics of symbols are implied in the term *representation*. Symbols represent objects and events in experience. Symbols, in other words, are entities that stand for something other than themselves. And symbols have the capacity to *re*-present objects and events, that is, to bring back to awareness objects and events not currently present to the senses. When I reflect on the breakfast I ate this morning, I am aware of details of the event through words and/or mental images standing for them, even though the event itself is no longer directly available to experience.

Like experience, symbolic discourse also has figurative and cognitive components, form and meaning. The figurative component of a spoken word is auditory and phonemic; of a written word, visual and orthographic. The figurative component of a nonlinguistic mental image is modality specific sensory content stored from past experience (stored patterns of light, sound, etc.). The semiotic act of symbol generation involves retrieving that figurative content and assimilating it to the same conceptual structures that provide the basis for the meaning

---

[2]To reiterate, neither the information in the stimulus flux from the environment nor knowledge are themselves in experience, i.e. we are not and cannot be directly aware either of higher order invariants or of what we know—both information and knowledge are hypothetical constructs contributing to the explanation of experience but are not themselves experienced.

of the objects and events for which the symbolic discourse stands (cf., Furth, 1969, on Piaget's "double constitutive bond" theory of symbolic reference). In fact, it is presumably just because the products of semiotic activity can be given most, if perhaps not quite all, of the meaning of the objects and events they stand for that they are able to function as symbols. The word "chair," for example, shares much of the meaning that is attributed to that class of objects in the world on which we routinely sit.

What critically differentiates symbolic discourse from experience is the fact that, in the semiotic act of constructing symbols, not only the cognitive, but also the figurative, component of the symbol can be generated by the symbolizer from within. By contrast, in the co-construction of experience, the figurative component is provided by the environment and the conceptual component by the perceiver. This is a simple point, but its force is far reaching. It is part of the explanation for why human beings can, on a beautiful sunny day, imagine or tell themselves or others that it is raining while they are unable to go to the window, look out, and see the rain.

This analysis, too, is crucial for an understanding of the sense that can and cannot be made of questions about the relationship between cognition and emotion. What we tell ourselves or imagine can, quite apart from whether or not the content of the message bears a strong relationship to any objective state of affairs, affect our emotional state. If I imagine myself failing to complete this chapter, for example, I can rapidly make myself anxious. If I then tell myself that I have finished chapters before and that there is no reason at all to suspect that I won't finish this one, I can reduce, if not eliminate, that sense of anxiety; and if I add, whether or not it is true, that the chapter seems to be going quite well, I may even be able to turn that anxiety into joy.

As is well known, many contemporary psychologists (e.g., Beck, 1976; Mahoney, 1974; Meichenbaum, 1977; Weiner & Graham, in press) refer to self-statements and images of the above sort as *cognitions*. If the problem of the relationship of cognition to emotion is taken to be nothing more than a problem of the relationship between cognition*s*, as internal symbolic discourse, and emotion, then we can certainly formulate a limited but straightforward and relatively unambiguous set of descriptive questions about what classes of self-statements or mental images in what situations tend to be related to what emotional states. This seems to me, in fact, to be pretty much the class of questions addressed by a number of contemporary theorists, particularly those who share an attribution theoretical approach to emotion-cognition relationships (Dweck & Goetz, 1978; Weiner & Graham, in press).

The problem with this formulation, from the metatheoretical perspective being developed here, is that it is a severly restricted approach that ignores the fact that cognition can be taken in a different and much deeper sense to mean internal, nonconscious knowledge structures and processes in the subject. It therefore leaves open the much deeper question of the role of knowledge in the determination of both symbolic discourse (self-statements and images) and emotion.

Action

Finally, in addition to experiencing and constructing symbols that stand for the world, human beings are able to act on it. Action in this context does not mean nor is it reducible to movement. Action here refers to a system of hierarchically patterned sequences of movement organized in relation to some end. That end or goal may be conscious or nonconscious. Such actions as painting a house or going to buy food at the grocery store generally are organized in relation to conscious goals but more automatic actions such as dipping the brush into the paint or turning the key in the ignition typically are organized in relation to end states of which we are not, and in some cases may not even be able to be, aware. End states toward which action is organized furnish expectations against which the success of the action can be evaluated (cf., Miller, Galanter, & Pribram, 1960, for a discussion of this issue). The cognitive component of action includes specification of possible end states. It also may be presumed to include knowledge of the general structure or scheme for action and some specification of the range of variation in action necessary and permissable under different environmental conditions.

Action itself, however, like experience and symbolic discourse, is a co-construction. The actor provides the schemes and goals. The environment provides the physical and social support for action. As Gibson (1979) put it, the environment has properties that afford human beings certain actions and not others. A solid surface that will resist a force of a few hundred pounds or more and a medium consisting of air will afford walking and standing but will not afford swimming. A liquid medium, on the other hand, affords swimming but not walking or standing.

The relevance of action to emotion is at least two-fold. First, as Gibson[3] and others have suggested, action and experience, although logically separable, are psychologically a single system. Actions are guided by experience. Experience, in turn, is a function of the operation of perceptual systems which act to maximize the detection over time of higher order invariants in the stimulus flux.

Second, in addition to being experiential, emotion also is expressive. Emotional expression serves the dual function of social communication of affect (as, for example, in facial expression) and preparation for adaptive action (fight, flight, procreation, etc.) Of particular importance for the understanding of emotion is the obvious fact that, in emotional expression, the human body itself is

---

[3]Gibson would not have used the term experience here but would have referred to action and *perception*.

a rich source of patterned stimulation. It seems reasonable that there may exist in that stimulation higher order invariants over time bearing a regular relationship to, and hence informative about, internal bodily states and processes organized around action. If so, to the extent that they are detected, they will contribute to experience. We will feel ourselves prepare to act and then act. It may plausibly be argued (Arnold, 1960; Izard, 1977; James, 1890; Tomkins, 1962–1963) that the relatively discriminable phenomenology of the more clearly differentiated emotional states reflect variations in the perception of bodily states of preparation for action, and social signaling through facial expression, more or less correlative to variation in emotional reaction.

Knowledge and Environment

Although both have figured prominently in our previous discussion of experience, symbolic discourse, and action, *knowledge* and *environment* are complicated constructs, and much more could be said of them than has been said or could be incorporated within this chapter. Nonetheless, there are two distinctions concerning environment and two concerning knowledge that must be drawn before turning to the question of how the nature of emotion and its relationship to cognition can be construed from within this metatheoretical framework.

With respect to environment, the first distinction of importance for our purposes is that between the physical and the social. This distinction in turn seems to rest on our inferences concerning the presence or absence in environmental objects and events of mental states—subjectivity. Although we have direct experience only of our own subjectivity, there are objects such as other people, and at least some animals in our environment, to which we seem irresistibly predisposed to attribute a subjectivity of their own. Such objects (or more properly *subjects*) and events involving those objects constitute the social environment.

By contrast, there is a much larger class of objects and events to which we do not attribute subjectivity. These objects, such as chairs, and events, such as the rising of the sun, constitute the physical environment. This distinction is important for an understanding of cognition and emotion because there seem to be certain human emotions (e.g., shame or guilt) that may be uniquely a function of experienced or symbolized events having to do with the social rather than the physical environment.

The second distinction is between the external and internal environment. The external environment consists of objects and events that in experience we localize outside our bodies. People talking, animals running, tables standing next to chairs are all part of the external environment. The internal environment, on the other hand, consists of objects and events that are experientially localized within our bodies. Our fingers moving, our muscles flexing, our teeth aching, our stomach growling, and our anger rising are all part of the internal environment.

The implication of this distinction for emotion is obvious. Emotion is, among other things, an internally localized experience.

Knowledge, as it is used here, may be thought of as a structural mental code embodying information about the environment. Knowledge is both given in the human biological endowment and extracted from experience. With respect to knowledge so defined, there also are two critical distinctions to be drawn. The first of these distinctions has to do with the broad classes into which knowledge can be divided in general and complimentary correspondence with classes of environmental objects and events.

Borrowing from and slightly adapting a taxonomy proposed by Piaget and Inhelder (1969), I would distinguish among the following broad classes of knowledge structures: (a) logico-mathematical knowledge; (b) physical knowledge; and (c) psychological knowledge.[4] And although it is clear that a full explication of this distinction (cf., Piaget & Inhelder, 1969, and Wozniak, 1983, for somewhat more extensive discussions) is beyond the scope of this chapter, I will briefly discuss the basic sense of this taxonomy as it relates to the treatment of emotion and cognition to follow.

Logico-mathematical knowledge is methodological knowledge. It organizes a set of rational procedures that the developing human being can bring to bear on the interpretation of experience, symbolic discourse, and action. Logico-mathematical development through major stage transitions of the sort described by Piaget sets boundary conditions on the form that experience, symbolic discourse and action can take. This may be presumed to be as true for emotional as for any other sort of experience.

Physical knowledge is knowledge of the objects and events of experience *as objects*, that is, apart from any subjectivity which we do or do not attribute to them. Physical knowledge is derived from the consistencies encountered in experience with the objects and events constituting the physical environment.

Psychological knowledge, on the other hand, is knowledge of the subjective states of those objects and events to which we do attribute subjectivity, including ourselves. Psychological knowledge is derived from the consistencies we find in the symbolic discourse and actions of others and from the patterns we encounter in our own subjective states of experience of, symbolic discourse about, and action in the environment. Psychological knowledge also is, therefore, knowledge of our own consistency as selves operating in a physical and social environment.

As human beings develop and increase the range and depth of their physical and psychological experience, their knowledge of the external physical and social environment, of their bodies, and of themselves as experiencers, symbolizers, and actors undergoes continuous refinement. As we shall see, there is reason to

---

[4]A fourth type of knowledge, social knowledge, knowledge of the collective behavior of persons in relation, also can be distinguished. This distinction, however, is not essential for the present discussion.

argue that both the nature of emotional experience and the conditions under which emotional reactions occur are heavily influenced by such development.

The second distinction concerning knowledge is between knowledge structure and knowing process, mental structure and mental act. Although this too is a very complicated and theory-laden issue (inasmuch as what is process at one level of a system may be a structural element at another), at least one aspect of the issue relevant to the analysis of emotion and cognition to follow must be briefly discussed. As indicated earlier, from the metatheoretical standpoint being described here, experience, symbolic discourse, and action are co-constructed in the interaction between mind and environment. Both mind and environment, in other words, are assumed to be active determinants of experience, symbolic discourse, and action.

On the mental side, this activity might be thought of as being constituted by at least two kinds of knowing processes or internal mental acts. One might be termed *constitutive* and the second *evaluative*. Both constitutive and evaluative mental processes are organized in relationship to the subject's knowledge. Constitutive processes are those in which patterned information, provided by the external and internal environment, is referred to underlying structural codes in order that an object or event be identified or recognized for what it is and discriminated from other objects or events. What is normally thought of as the *objective* meaning of experience, in other words, is given by constitutive mental acts organized in relation to knowledge about objects and events as they exist in independence of the knower. These structures and processes seem to me to be just the structures and processes on which most of contemporary cognitive psychological research is focused.

Evaluative mental acts also are conceived to be processes in which patterned stimulation provided by the internal and external environment is referred to underlying structural codes, i.e., to knowledge. But evaluative processes refer this information not to concepts of objects and events in themselves but to concepts of objects and events as they relate to the self. Concepts of this sort might be termed *values*. Evaluation processes refer information from the environment to value structures and yield not the identification or recognition of the object or event for what it is, but the meaning of the object or event for what it is-for-me. Evaluation is, in other words, a process of appraisal of the potential of an environmental object or event to bring me pleasure, to satisfy my need, to insult me, to threaten me with harm, or even to kill me. Evaluation processes might be presumed to yield what is sometimes called the *subjective* meaning of experience.[5]

Now the general shape that the discussion of emotion and its relationship to cognition takes should be obvious. Emotion depends intimately on evaluative

---

[5]Mandler (1982) has employed the terms *descriptive* and *evaluative* to refer to processes very similarly distinguished.

processes. Evaluative processes in turn depend directly on our values—our knowledge of the potential that internal bodily and external physical and social objects and events have for our selves—and indirectly, therefore, on our developing knowledge of the environment and of our selves. As knowledge and values develop, evaluations change. What may have terrified us at age 4 may excite us at 14 and make us angry at 40.

In this deep sense, emotion as experience and as expression is, like all experience and expression, a co-construction. To this co-construction, the environment contributes patterned stimulation informative about the properties of internal and external objects and events. The developing mind contributes evaluative and constitutive meaning through the operation of mental acts which refer environmental information to relevant cognitive structures. These structures code our knowledge of the physical and social environment, of our bodies, of our subjective states, and of the potential which external and internal environmental objects and events have for our selves.

EMOTION AND COGNITION

Historically, the psychological literature on human emotion has been organized around six more or less closely related issues: (a) the nature of emotion in general; (b) the taxonomy of discriminable emotions in particular; (c) the relation between emotion and motivation; (d) the adaptive function of emotion; (e) the typical range of variation in emotion among individuals and across the life-span; and (f) the nature of emotional pathology and the effects of psychotherapeutic intervention. Theory and research relating to issues b through f depends in large measure on the theoretical perspective taken with respect to the issue a. For this reason, and because the purpose of this chapter is to set out one such perspective as a basis for considering developing emotion-cognition relations, I will concentrate here on the question of the nature of emotion. Such a consideration is theoretically prior to, and therefore directly relevant for, any discussion of the remaining issues.

What do we mean when we talk about emotion? What is a question about the developing relationship between emotion so described and cognition about? As has long been argued (Arnold, 1960; Beebe-Center, 1932; Izard, 1980; James, 1890; Titchener, 1908; Tomkins, 1962–1963, 1965), human emotion, whatever else it might be, is first and foremost a particular kind of experience. We experience anger, we experience fear, we experience joy, and we experience disgust. But emotion is not at all like the experience of a chair or a table, experiences that we localize in the external environment. Emotion is an internally localized experience. We experience emotion as existing inside, rather than outside, our bodies. We experience anger, fear, joy, disgust inside ourselves. Furthermore, as with all experience, emotion unfolds over time. Anger, fear, joy, disgust, and so on arise within us and gradually fade away.

Finally, like experience, emotion is extremely complex, with at least three logically separable components. One component is the experience of a precipitating object or event. As Arnold (1960) has convincingly asserted, none of the previously mentioned criteria (experience, internally localized, varying in time) would distinguish emotion from numerous other feeling states such as hunger, thirst, satiety, pain, or pleasure. Although it is beyond the scope of this discussion to argue the point in detail, emotion may plausibly be distinguished from feeling states like those mentioned by the fact that, although feeling states are precipitated by and monitor the functioning of the organism, emotions are occasioned by objects and events and monitor the potential of those objects and events to bring pain, pleasure, threat, death, and so on to the self. In other words, whereas feeling states are function oriented, emotions are object/event oriented. We are afraid of X, angry at X, joyful about X and disgusted at X where X may be an external (e.g., a man with a gun) or an internal (e.g., rapid growth of a lump in the neck or pain itself) object or event in experience.

Now, what sense does it make to talk about the experience of the precipitating object or event as a *component* of emotion? The answer to this question appears to lie in the co-constructed nature of experience as previously discussed. Like all experience, the experience of the object of an emotional reaction is a joint function of figurative input from the environment (internal or external) and cognitive interpretation by the experiencing subject. Part of that interpretive process may be conceived to involve nonconscious mental acts of evaluation, of tacit appraisal of the potential that the object or event has to benefit us or to bring us harm. This evaluation is part of the very process of constructing the experience of the object or event. The object or event, in other words, is not on this account presumed to be perceived and then appraised but to be appraised in the act of being perceived, in the act by which experience is co-constructed. A snarling doberman is not first experienced as a snarling doberman and then as something to fear, but is from the first experienced as a "snarling-doberman-of-which-we-are-afraid." To talk about the experience of the emotion-precipitating object or event as a component of the total emotional experience itself, then, makes sense because that object or event is, from the outset, experienced affectively, as evaluated.

Furthermore, it might be presumed that the particular emotion precipitated by the object or event will be a function of this initial evaluation process. An event that is experienced as threatening, an object that is experienced as bringing pleasure, and a person who is experienced as insulting will elicit very different emotional reactions from the experiencing subject. From this perspective, it now should be clear how cognition as knowledge and as knowing might be expected to interact with emotion. Knowledge guides and constrains mental acts of evaluation.[6] Development in object/event and self-knowledge will change our values and, as our values change, our evaluations of environmental objects and events will change. As evaluations change, the direction and intensity of emotional reactions will change as well. To paraphrase an earlier line, the dog that frightened me at 4 and brought me pleasure at 14 may annoy me at 40.

In addition to the emotional experience of the precipitating object and event, however, there are at least two other important components to the experience of emotion. In an emotional reaction, the initial object/event evaluation is routinely followed by experienced changes in bodily arousal and by experienced changes in bodily expression.[7] We experience ourselves preparing for adaptive action. Threatened, we feel our hearts begin to pound, our faces pale and our attention become highly focused. We also experience ourselves assuming a particular expression. We feel our eyes widen, our mouths drop, and our bodies begin to pull back from the threatening object.

Again, as with any experience, this component of the total emotional experience also is co-constructed, a joint function of figurative information from the body and cognitive interpretation by the experiencing subject. Thus, the relatively discriminable phenomenology of different emotional states is presumed to reflect the joint interaction between variations in the temporal pattern of arousal and expression and constitutive and evaluative mental processes dependent in turn on the individual's developing knowledge of bodily states and values concerning emotional experience itself.

This last seems to me to be an important and often overlooked point. Just as the object/event that precipitates emotion is evaluated in the co-construction of the experience of that object/event, so too are internal bodily events (experienced as the temporally unfolding emotional reaction) evaluated in the process by which the experience of that emotional reaction is co-constructed. Emotion itself, in other words, can and does function as an event for further evaluation. And because certain evaluations lead to emotion, emotion, on this account, can beget further emotion.

Whether or not emotion does beget emotion, of course, depends on the outcome of the evaluation that occurs in the co-construction of the emotional experience. That evaluation in turn depends on the individual's knowledge of

---

[6]Of the many theories of emotion currently in the field, the theory to which this view is most closely akin is undoubtedly that of Mandler (1975, 1982). Nonetheless, there are a number of important differences between Mandler's views and those being proposed here. Although a detailed discussion of these differences would be out of place in this chapter, it is noteworthy that two of the most important of these differences have to do with our respective treatments of the role of physical arousal in emotion and the nature of values and evaluation processes.

[7]The use of the terms "*experienced* changes in bodily arousal" and "*experienced* changes in bodily expression" is deliberately meant to reflect both a mind-body view that assumes the existence of mental events in regular concomitance with but not identical to physiological events and a metatheoretical view of psychological explanation based on the irreducibility of psychological to physiological language.

his or her own emotional states and of the potential that those states as bodily events have to bring harm, benefit, and so on to the self. If, for example, a child learns that anger expressed in a social environment has the potential to lead to consequences that are threatening or positively damaging to the self, the experience of anger may itself become the precipitating event for fear. If the child learns to evaluate the experience of fear as involving a loss of self-esteem, fear may lead to shame. On this account, the potential interrelationships that might exist among emotional states considered as possible precipitating events for further (and not necessarily the same) emotional states is obviously huge in number. This fact could help explain some of the wide variation in the symptomatology of emotional pathology.

From this perspective, then the term emotion is used to refer to a well-organized transformation in experience over time. This transformation begins with the experience of an environmental object or event evaluated as potentially harmful, pleasurable, and so on to the self. It continues as a pattern in internally localized experience (of bodily arousal and expression) the direction of which is determined by the precipitating evaluation. This internal event, as experienced, then functions itself as an occasion for further evaluation.

The processes of evaluation, which are not themselves experienced, are components of a cognitive system, knowledge structures and knowing processes, which contribute to the co-construction of experience, symbolic discourse, and action. On this account, the processes that are designated by the term emotion are presumed to be dependent on the structures and processes that we call cognition and development of cognition should have direct implication for the development of emotionality.

Before leaving discussion of the co-constructed nature of emotional experience, one final point should be made. An emotion precipitating object or event need not be present in the here and now in experience. Symbolic discourse can and frequently does function to precipitate emotional reaction. For those who fear ascent to the speaker's platform, sudden recall in words or images of an upcoming speaking engagement may bring on as much, or more, anxiety than will the occasion itself. A remembered public humiliation may precipitate as strong a sense of shame as did the original event; and anticipation of seeing a long absent loved one may be as joyful as their eventual appearance.

DIFFERENTIAL EMOTIONS THEORY: A CRITIQUE

That the view just outlined is by no means uniformly accepted is clearly indicated by the rather different acount of emotion-cognition relations embedded in the differential emotions perspective described by Izard in chapter 3 in this volume. Having sketched out the broad outline of a co-constructive approach to emotion, I will now employ it as a framework for a critique of differential emotions theory. Although much in the differential emotions point of view is compatible with the notion of emotion as co-constructed experience, there are important differences between these views. In clarifying the basis of these differences, I suggest that they stem from the fact that certain postulates of differential emotions theory seem to me to be either unnecessary or theoretically counter-productive.

Because the positions of differential emotions theory are well known and are described in this volume by Izard himself, no systematic summary of the basic postulates of the theory or the position taken by Izard on cognition-emotion relations is undertaken. Instead, I begin by calling attention to those postulates with which I find myself in general agreement. Following this, I examine three critical claims that Izard makes about emotion and its relation to cognition that do not seem to me to be fully defensible. Together, in fact, these claims form a sort of skeleton, implicit in the logical structure of differential emotions theory, which needs to be taken out of the closet and, with all due respect, laid to rest. In that discussion, as appropriate, I make reference to Izard's chapter in this volume. I then conclude by briefly pointing the way to the *Golden Future* of theory and research in this area as I see it.

Claims Defensible and Controversial

In the chapter included in this volume, and in his other theoretical writings, Izard (1977, 1979) presents a persuasive case for the existence of a set of discrete emotion systems and for the claim that each of these systems consists of neurophysiological processes, feeling states subjectively experienced, and expressions (especially facial expressions) functioning as socio-emotional signals and as sources of reafference that differentiate the discrete emotions. Izard (Chap. 3) also asserts, and I generally agree, that the "emotions organize and motivate intrapsychic and interpersonal processes" (p. 26) that emotion, cognition, and motor activity influence one another reciprocally, that emotion plays a role in the development of social competence and, in fact, that emotion exerts a continuing influence on all development.

But as is often the case with a persuasive theorist, Izard uses these, his most plausible assertions, as the context for other, more controversial claims. These assertions are usually phrased in such a way as to lead readers to feel that, if they accept a part of his story, which most certainly they do, they must be led irrevocably to accept the whole. This is particularly true with respect to three critical claims.

The first such claim is Izard's assertion that emotion is not transient, that human beings exist in a continuous state of emotionality that changes only in intensity or quality, one emotion growing stronger or weaker or taking up where another has left off. The second claim is that emotion is the primary human motivational system, motivating even cognition and action. The third claim is that emotion is not primarily a function of cognitive appraisal, that cognition need not necessarily precede all changes in emotion states.

Three examples from his chapter in which these claims are persuasively, if perhaps not quite irrefutably, embedded in more plausible contexts are of note. In the first, Izard suggests that "Kagan differs from both Piaget and differential emotions theory in his view of emotions as transient. This can be seen as one way of relegating emotions to relatively unimportant roles in development" (p. 22). Clearly, implicit in this statement is a backwards inference that many an unwary reader might unconsciously draw. This inference takes the following form: Because we don't wish to downplay emotion, and because arguing that emotion is transient does just that, we ought probably to look for a way to view emotion as continuous.

The infant's perception of its mother is transient. She comes and she goes. Yet who among us would dare assign the perception of the mother an unimportant role in development just because of its transient character? I think that one's view of the developmental importance of emotions can, in principle, be completely independent of one's view of the transiency of emotional states. As is evident from the co-constructive account of emotion presented in the first part of this chapter, I completely share Izard's conviction that emotion is important. I am, however, considerably less persuaded to his view that emotion is continuous.

In the second example, Izard has written that Kagan has raised interesting issues, whether or not he is "correct that emotional development is essentially epiphenomenal, a function of cognitive development . . ." (p. 23). Again, the unwary reader, too easily accepting this equation of emotional epiphenomenalism with the notion that emotion is a function of cognitive development and wishing at all costs to reject any suggestion of epiphenomenalism, might jump to the conclusion that any view of emotion that construes it to be a function of cognition must then be rejected as well.

Need this, however, be so? Can emotional states be a function of cognition and yet function themselves to motivate action, perception, and even thought? Certainly. Izard has himself given us the formula by taking just the obverse position in his statement of the "seeming paradox . . . that *the regulation of emotions achieved through cognition and action is itself motivated and regulated by emotion*" (p. 28). That this is logically possible is true; but, then, so is it also logically possible that the regulation and motivation of cognition achieved through emotion could itself be motivated and regulated by cognition. Emotion that is a function of cognition, in other words, need not by any means necessarily be epiphenomenal.

Finally, in the third example, Izard tells us that we should "not get stuck on the notion that cognition must necessarily precede all changes in emotion states," that "emotion can be a function of untransformed sensory input" (p. 25). Yet, once again, we have the possibility of an implicit inference. If emotion can be a function of untransformed sensory input, then it seems that cognition need not "necessarily precede all changes in emotion states" (p. 25). But is this necessarily so? Could one conceive of emotion as a direct function of untransformed sensory input and yet argue that cognition nonetheless precedes all changes in emotional states? The answer to this question seems to me to be a most definite "yes". My argument turns on the already noted fact that the term cognition is a highly syncretic one which conflates a number of essentially separable meanings.

First, cognition (or, worse, the *barbarous* "cognitions") often is used to refer to internal, subjectively experienced mental processes like mental images or inner speech, i.e., to internal symbolic discourse. Clearly, as earlier suggested (in agreement with Izard), emotional states can be said to change as a function of cognition in this sense. As cognitive therapists from Coue (1922) to Meichenbaum (1977) have pointed out, a simple, assiduously repeated phrase like "Day by day, in every way, I get better and better," can achieve surprising emotional results. But here, emotion, although a function of cognition, is not a direct function of untransformed sensory input, so we must look further.

A second sense in which the term cognition is sometimes used is that of *object experience*—to cognize an object is to experience it, to perceive it. Thus, as Izard points out in his chapter, it is often held by cognitive theorists that the subjective experience of emotion follows upon the objective perception of the object of the emotion. On this view, if we were walking down the street and were suddenly confronted with a man holding a gun, we would first perceive the man holding the gun, then we would feel fear. Clearly, if such a process exists (and as so simply described, I do not believe that it does), emotional states once again could be said to be changing as a function of cognition but not as a function of untransformed sensory input.

We must, therefore, look still further. However, before we do, it is worth briefly pointing out that one common form of the cognitive appraisal approach to emotion consists of a combination of these first two senses of cognition. In this view, when confronted with a man holding a gun, we would first perceive the man holding the gun, and then *consciously* and *symbolically* interpret this perception as potentially threatening, telling ourselves something like, "Oh no! I'm going to be shot!" or imagining ourselves lying in a pool of blood, whereupon we would feel fear. Although something like this might occur under very peculiar conditions, I would agree with Izard that it is not at all likely to be the fundamental emotion process—for one thing, it's much too slow and therefore maladaptive. By the time we had acted on our fear, we might indeed be dead.

As indicated earlier in this chapter, however, there is a third, historically more accepted and, in recent years, once again common use of the term cognition. This use is in reference to internal mental structures (schemes, concepts, logical operations, and the like). These structures are presumed to organize internal mental acts of interpretation that operate with direct or, in the case of symbolization, stored, patterned sensory input to jointly co-construct experience, symbolic discourse, and action. The operation of these mental structures in mental acts is automatic and non-conscious. We open our eyes and we experience meaningful objects like chairs and trees and people. We listen to someone speak and we understand meaningful discourse—but we do not experience either the mental structures themselves or the interpretive processes by which that experience or understanding is itself constructed.

Thus, for example, our experience (our perception) of a man holding a gun is a joint construction of patterned sensory input and relevant knowledge structures to which that patterned sensory input is referred in the automatic, non-conscious and co-constructive process of interpretation. It should be fairly clear from this and from the earlier discussion that, given this perspective, it is easy to accommodate a view of emotion as experience as both a function of cognitive acts and also a direct function of untransformed sensory input.

We do not perceive a man with a gun, appraise that perception, and then become fearful. We perceive a "man-with-a-gun-of-whom-we-are-afraid". The very mental act of constructing the externally localized experience of a man with a gun is also an act of constructing the initial component of the internally localized experience of fear. Emotional experience is every bit as direct as is object/event experience. Indeed, it would have to be that way for emotion to serve the biological survival functions for which it seems to have evolved—but the fact of its directness, the fact that it is an immediate function of untransformed sensory input, makes it no less a function of cognitive structure and cognitive process, of knowledge and knowing.

As noted earlier, that cognitive structure and process may be presumed to include an evaluative component. This suggests the possibility of pursuing future research on the relationship between values development and emotion, a topic to which I return briefly in discussing the Golden Future. First, however, I will conclude this critique by rattling what I take to be a rather shaky skeleton nestling comfortably within the differential emotions theory closet.

Skeleton Rattling

At the foot of this skeleton lies *interest*. Interest, Izard argues, is an emotion and an exceedingly important one, because it allows us to make sense of the statement that emotion is continuous. After all, most of us would agree that in lay terms, at least, we do not feel ourselves to be in a constant state of emotionality. Joy is nice, but who would want to be constantly up; and anger and anxiety, it goes without saying, should, if at all possible, be restricted to appropriate occasions. In fact, if asked, most of us would report that our emotional states come and go. Mostly we don't feel particularly emotional at all until, for example, we happen to recall an unpleasant past encounter or think of a dreaded future engagement, when we may, respectively, become angry all over again or anxious at the prospect. Eventually this anger or anxiety recedes, and we go unemotionally about our business until something else triggers an emotional reaction that eventually recedes in its turn.

But if emotion is continuous, what fills in all of the phenomenal spaces between those occasional experiences that most of us consider to be emotional? The answer, of course, for differential emotions theory, is interest. Interest must be the state we are constantly in when we are not in those intermittent states called anger, fear, joy, shame, surprise, distress, contempt, disgust, or guilt. The inclusion of interest as a discrete emotion, in other words, supports the postulate of emotional continuity.

What then is the function of the continuity postulate in the differential emotions theory skeleton? Continuity, it seems to me, in turn supports the notion that emotions function as the primary human motivational system. After all, a primary motivational system must be continuous if we are not to leave the organism in a state of transient motivation. But what then is the function of the primary motivation postulate? This, it seems, supports the notion that is at the head of the skeleton, the notion that emotion is not dependent on prior cognitive appraisal because, if it were, it could no longer be considered to be the primary motivational system.

To recapitulate briefly, the logical skeleton within differential emotions theory appears to me to take roughly the following shape: If interest is an emotion, emotion is continuous. If emotion is continuous, it can function as the primary motivational system; and if emotion functions as the primary motivational system, then, clearly, emotion could not possibly depend on prior cognitive appraisal.

Now, as I have already suggested, emotion does not need to depend on prior cognitive appraisal in order still to be an immediate function of cognitive structures and mental acts—so I am not especially persuaded that differential emotions theory must be guided by the notion at the head of the skeleton. Nor am I totally convinced that the notion at the foot is strong enough to stand on. Although I am not absolutely ready to deny that interest ought to be conceived as an emotion (and, in fact, suspect that this may be partly an empirical matter), I am concerned by the fact that, at best, interest is a strange emotion—different in at least five respects from its colleagues.

1. Interest seems phenomenally to have a radically different time course from most other emotions. It is possible for interest to be sustained over long periods of time, even hours, whereas most emotional states are, indeed, much more transient.

2. Although the neurophysiological substrate of interest is complex and only partially understood, the autonomic concomitants of interest, at least in so far as interest is manifest in sustained attention, seem to be basically of a conservative character such as cardiac deceleration and decrease in heart rate variability (Porges, 1980). The autonomic concomitants of other emotions, on the other hand, tend

to have more the character of arousal as typified by cardiac acceleration, increased blood pressure, and pupillary constriction (Tarpy, 1977).

3. Cognitively, interest seems to be readily capable of direct voluntary control in ways in which anger, fear, anxiety, guilt, etc. are not.

4. Although some shifts in attention can be shown to be motivated by interest (Renninger & Wozniak, 1985), it hardly seems possible to attribute all shifts in attention (not to mention our many shifts in action) to interest. If this is true and if emotion is the primary motivational system, then the organism seems to be left in a motivational vacuum. If I am wandering aimlessly through the woods and reach up and break off a leaf, not out of any interest in that or any other leaf, and not out of anger, fear or any other obvious emotion, how is the act to be explained?

5. Interest, as Izard has himself noted, is not tied to a specific class of biologically adaptive acts such as fight, flight, approach, and so on. In fact, it often doesn't seem to be tied very closely to any acts at all, at least not physical motor acts. If, as I hope, as a reader of this chapter, you have been interested in what I have had to say, it is doubtful that you have yet to show it in your action.

GOLDEN FUTURE

So where does this take us? What is the Golden Future to which we all look forward so eagerly? Well, I am of the opinion, despite much of what I have said, that differential emotions theory is fundamentally more compatible with the general co-constructive metatheory that I have outlined than might immediately be evident. With the possible exception of interest, I very much like Izard's taxonomy of discrete emotions, his emphasis on the evolutionary biological functions that emotions have evolved to serve, his willingness to deal not only with the neurophysiological underpinnings of emotion, but with emotional experience and the reafferent and social signalling function of emotional expression. I am intrigued with his emphasis on the coding of such expression, especially facial expression as an objective index of emotional experience, and I have found his discussion of the developmental time-table for emotional expression in infancy very persuasive.

I do not believe, however, that any of the aforementioned depends in intimate fashion on the postulates of continuity or primary motivation. Nor do I believe that it depends on the denial that emotional experience, co-constructed in a mental act of interpretation of patterned sensory input organized by mental structures, is a function of cognitive evaluation—an evaluation consisting not of *secondary* appraisal, but of an automatic, non-conscious, primary appraisal that is part of the very act of constructing the immediate experience of the emotion precipitating object/event and of the emotion which that object/event occasions.

Evaluation processes so conceived depend on values. These values may be presumed to be culture-bound, family-bound and, to a certain extent, even somewhat idiosyncratic—the bases for precisely the sort of automatic, non-conscious interpretation with which psychotherapists have constantly to be concerned. The Golden Future, it seems to me, lies in studying the development of individual's values and in eventually adumbrating a theory of values development which, when combined within a co-constructive metatheoretical framework with all that is excellent in differential emotions theory, will increase our insight into the nature of emotional development.

ACKNOWLEDGMENT

The author wishes to express his appreciation to Peter Goldenthal and Mary Rohrkemper for their detailed comments on an earlier version of this manuscript and to the Clark Fund of Bryn Mawr College for providing research assistance in support of this project.

REFERENCES

Arnold, M. B. (1960). *Emotion and personality. Vol. 1: Psychological aspects.* New York: Columbia University Press.

Beck, A. T. (1976). *Cognitive therapy and the emotional disorders.* New York: International Universities Press.

Beebe-Center, J. G. (1932) . *The psychology of pleasantness and unpleasantness.* New York: Van Nostrand.

Cohen, L.B., DeLoache, J. S., & Strauss, M. S. (1979). Infant visual perception. In J. D. Osofsky (Ed.), *Handbook of infant development* (pp. 393–438). New York: Wiley

Coue, E. (1922). *Self mastery through conscious auto-suggestion.* New York: American Library Service.

Dweck, C., & Goetz. T. (1978). Attributions and learned helplessness. In J. Harvey, W. Ickes, & R. Kidd (Eds.) *New directions in attribution research.* (Vol. 2, pp. 157–179). Hillsdale, NJ: Lawrence Erlbaum Associates.

Emde, R. N., Gaensbauer, T. J., & Harmon, R. J. (1976). *Emotional expression in infancy; A biobehavioral study.* (Psychological Issues Monograph. No. 37). New York: International Universities Press.

Freud, S. (1913). *The interpretation of dreams.* London: G. Allen.

Furth, H. G. (1969). *Piaget and knowledge. Theoretical foundations.* Englewood Cliffs, NJ: Prentice-Hall.

Gibson, E. J. (1969). *Perceptual learning and development.* New York: Appleton-Century-Crofts.

Gibson, J. J. (1966). *The senses considered as perceptual systems.* Boston: Houghton-Mifflin.

Gibson, J. J. (1979). *The ecological approach to visual perception.* Boston: Houghton-Mifflin.

Hempel, C. G. (1966). *Philosophy of natural science.* Englewood Cliffs, NJ: Prentice-Hall.

Izard, C. E. (1977). *Human emotions.* New York: Plenum.

Izard, C. E. (1978). On the ontogenesis of emotions and emotion-cognition relationships in infancy. In M. Lewis & L. Rosenblum (Eds.), *The development of affect* (pp. 389–413). New York: Plenum.

Izard, C. E. (1979). Emotions and motivations: an evolutionary-developmental perspective. In R. A. Dienstbier (Ed.), *Human emotion. Nebraska symposium on motivation, 1978.* (pp. 163–200). Lincoln: University of Nebraska Press.

Izard, C. E. (1980). The emergence of emotion and the development of consciousness in infancy. In J. M. Davidson & R. J. Davidson (Eds.) *The psychobiology of consciousness,* (pp. 193–216). New York: Plenum.

James, W. (1890). *The principles of psychology.* 2 Volumes. New York: Holt.

Kagan, J. (1978). *The growth of the child. Reflections on human development.* New York: Norton.

Lacan, J. (1968). *The language of the self; the function of language in psychoanalysis.* Baltimore: Johns Hopkins University Press.

Lewis, M., & Brooks, J. (1978). Self-knowledge and emotional development. In M. Lewis & L. Rosenblum (Eds.), *The development of affect,* (pp. 205–226). New York: Plenum.

Mahoney, M. J. (1974). *Cognition and behavior modification* Cambridge, MA: Ballinger.

Mandler, G. (1975). *Mind and emotion.* New York: Wiley.

Mandler, G. (1982). The structure of value: Accounting for taste. In M. S. Clark & S. T. Fiske (Eds.), *Affect and cognition: the seventeenth annual Carnegie Symposium on cognition,* (pp 3–36). Hillsdale, NJ: Lawrence Erlbaum Associates.

Margolis, J. (1984). *Philosophy of psychology.* Englewood Cliffs, NJ: Prentice-Hall.

McArthur, L. Z., & Baron, R. M (1983). Toward an ecological theory of social perception. *Psychological Review, 90,* 215–238.

Meichenbaum, D. (1977). *Cognitive-behavior modification. An integrative approach.* New York: Plenum.

Miller, G. A., Galanter, E., & Pribram, K. H. (1960). *Plans and the structure of behavior.* New York: Holt.

Piaget, J. (1950). *The psychology of intelligence.* New York: Harcourt, Brace.

Piaget, J., & Inhelder, B. (1969). *The psychology of the child.* New York: Basic Books.

Piatelli-Palmarini, M. (Ed.), (1980). *Language and learning: The debate between Jean Piaget and Noam Chomsky.* Cambridge, MA: Harvard University Press.

Porges, S.W. (1980). Individual differences in attention: A possible physiological substrate. In B. K. Keogh (Ed.), *Advances in special education.* (Vol.2, pp. 111–133). Greenwich, CT: JAI Press.

Renninger, K. A., & Wozniak, R. H. (1985). Effect of interest on attentional shift, recognition, and recall in young children. *Developmental Psychology, 21,* 624–632.

Rumelhart, D. (1980). Schemata: The building blocks of cognition. In R. J. Spiro, B. C. Bruce, & W. F. Brewer (Eds.), *Theoretical issues in reading comprehension. Perspectives from cognitive psychology, linguistics, artificial intelligence, and education* (pp. 33–58). Hillsdale, NJ: Lawrence Erlbaum Associates.

Rumelhart, D. E., & Ortony, A. (1978). The representation of knowledge in memory. In R. C. Anderson, R. J. Spiro, & W. E. Montague (Eds.), *Schooling and the acquisition of knowledge* (pp. 99–135). Hillsdale, NJ: Lawrence Erlbaum Associates.

Schafer, R. (1978). *Language and insight.* New Haven: Yale University Press.

Spelke, E. S., & Gibson, E. J. (1983). The development of perception. In J. H. Flavell & E. M. Markman (Eds.). *Handbook of child psychology. Volume. III: Cognitive development* (pp. 2–76). New York: Wiley.

Sroufe, A. (1979). Socioemotional development. In J. D. Osofsky (Ed.), *Handbook of infant development* (pp. 462–516). New York: Wiley.

Tarpy, R. M. (1977). The nervous system and emotion. In D. K. Candland, J. P. Fell, E. Keen, A. I. Leshner, R. M. Tarpy, & R. Plutchik. *Emotion* (pp. 149–187). Monterey, CA: Brooks/Cole.

Thomas, A., & Chess, S. (1980). *The dynamics of psychological development.* New York: Brunner/ Mazel.

Titchener, E. B. (1908). *The psychology of feeling and attention.* New York: Macmillan.

Tomkins, S. S. (1962–1963). *Affect, imagery, consciousness.* 2 Volumes. New York: Springer.

Tomkins, S. S. (1965). Affect and the psychology of knowledge. In S. S. Tomkins & C. E. Izard (Eds.), *Affect, cognition, and personality* (pp. 72–97). New York: Springer.

Watson, J. B. (1919). *Psychology from the standpoint of a behaviorist.* Philadelphia: Lippincott.

Weiner, B., Kun. A., & Benesh-Weiner. M. (1980). The development of mastery, emotions, and morality from an attributional perspective. In W. A. Collins (Ed.), *Minnesota symposia on child psychology.* (Vol. 13, pp. 103–129). Hillsdale, NJ: Lawrence Erlbaum Associates.

Weiner, B., & Graham. S. (in press). An attributional approach to emotional development. In C. Izard, J. Kagan & R. Zajonc (Eds.), *Emotion, cognition and behavior.* Cambridge, MA: Harvard University Press.

Wozniak, R. H. (1975). Dialecticism and structuralism: The philosophical foundations of Soviet psychology and Piagetian cognitive developmental theory. In K. F. Riegel & G. C. Rosenwald (Eds.), *Structure and transformation: Developmental and historical aspects* (pp. 25–45). New York: Wiley.

Wozniak, R.H. (1981). The future of constructivist psychology: Reflections on Piaget. *Teachers College Record, 83,* 197–199.

Wozniak, R. H. (1983). Is a genetic epistemology of psychology possible? *Cahiers de la fondation archives Jean Piaget, 4,* 323–347.

5 On the Structure of Personality

Jane Loevinger
Washington University

Speculations on the structure of personality are ancient pastimes of psychologists. Beginning with modern psychology, there has been a trend to take the achievements in the field of measurement of intelligence as a paradigm for measurement of personality. For various reasons, this has been partly inappropriate or unsuccessful. The import of this chapter is that Piaget's work can be looked at as a reversal of this sequence. One can look at Piaget's early work as being in a cognitive-affective area closely allied to personality as a whole. Only later did he turn to purely cognitive development. Possibly in consequence, Piaget developed models more appropriate for personality than did previous investigators. The current popularity of Piagetian models for at least one group of researchers in the field of personality can be seen as a further consequence. But importation of too strict a version of late-Piagetian stage theory threatens to impoverish the study of personality structure.

ABILITY AS MODEL FOR PERSONALITY MEASUREMENT

Tests of ability are largely constructed in the format that the score is the number of right answers. This can be called the cumulative model (Loevinger, 1948). Beginning with Binet, as tests of ability became increasingly effective for various practical purposes, the model was emulated by those studying personality in various aspects. For example, the Woodworth Personal Data Sheet, worked out by R. S. Woodworth during World War I as a screening device for neurosis or psychiatric disability, followed this pattern, as do the scoring keys for the Minnesota

Multiphasic Personality Inventory (MMPI) and its derivatives and imitators. The more symptomatic answers the person checks as characteristic of him or herself, the more neurotic or maladjusted he or she is assumed to be. Although this assumption is sometimes useful, it has limitations as a general model for personality measurement. In certain instances it can lead one astray, a fact the makers and users of the MMPI have long had to contend with.

Let us take another instance, or another aspect of the problem. In picking tests for his mental age scale, Binet succeeded where his predecessors had not, in large part because he engaged in what we would now call construct validation. He demanded that the tests included in his scale discriminate not only the teacher-nominated bright from teacher-nominated dull students, but that they also discriminate average children of successive ages. Thus age became an anchorage point for mental age. That criterion is mostly unavailable in measuring personality. In general mental abilities can be assumed to be monotonically increasing functions of age during childhood and early adolescence. There may be some personality traits for which that is true, but surely no one would say that that is an assured pattern with only minor exceptions. Thus one important anchorage point is lost when moving from measurement of ability to measurement of personality, an anchorage point that contributed much to Binet's success.

THE STRUCTURE OF ABILITIES

As the measurement of ability became a commonplace, tests proliferated, each psychologist having his or her own favorite ability. That made more acute the old question as to the fundamental structure of the domain of abilities. Factor analytic methods evolved as a way of coping with this new problem. Two general models became popular. The British model assumed a single general factor plus group factors, whereas Thurstone (1938) proposed, and his American followers used, a model assuming no general factor but many group factors.

Thurstonian factor analysis and its variants have been widely practiced over a long period of time. However, the glowing programmatic utterances that characterized the early years, proclaiming that all problems of mental structure would now be solved scientifically, have lost their sheen. One problem was the difficulty in defining or estimating the communalities of the tests, needed for the initial factor analysis, a problem akin to that of the circularity of the definition of reliability (Loevinger, 1957).

Another problem turned up with the proliferation of factorial studies. The nature of this problem was exemplified for me when I remarked to Lloyd Humphreys that I knew of only one factor that regularly appeared in factorial studies without being subdivided into finer factors; that was the arithmetic factor. He replied that it did subdivide, into addition, subtraction, multiplication, and division. As Humphreys (1962) has pointed out, any factor can be subdivided indefinitely by suitable choice of new tests, so that some elements of the factor are repeated in the items of one test, other elements repeated in items of another test. This process has no limit. In the language of factor analysis, the smallest subdivisions are the *primary factors*, whereas the second order and third order factors, summarizing and cutting across several primary factors, are considered less fundamental in importance. Humphreys argues that this is a reversal of appropriate priorities.

The virtue of factor analysis, according to its proponents, lies in whatever merit the rotation of axes yields, and that is a problem that has no unique solution; so methods of rotation also have proliferated. However, there is one important criterion in rotating ability factors, and that is the so-called *positive manifold*. The positive manifold corresponds to the assumption that all tests of ability can be assumed to correlate positively with each other. That is, there are few abilities whose possession implies a lesser achievement of some other ability. This assumption of a positive manifold is again a disanalogy between measurement of ability and measurement of personality.

Along somewhat similar lines, a limitation of factor analysis is that it can only deal with rectilinear relations. Personality traits, in general, may have any kind of interrelations whatsoever, including curvilinear and even nonmonotonic ones. There is no factorial technique that can handle such complexities.

FACTOR ANALYSES OF PERSONALITY

Despite these limitations, there have been numerous attempts to factor analyze personality traits. Some of these studies have begun with vast arrays of tests and the usual advance programmatic claims that this study will, finally and for good, yield up the ultimate structure of personality. Then the study seems to fizzle out. I know of only one such program that has been carried through and resulted in a major, significant publication. That resulted in Cattell's (1965) proposal of a "universal index" of personality traits. This has been the basis of an extended research program. However, the followers of Cattell's system are not universal. Instead, each investigator outside of the relatively small group of Cattell's followers seems to start anew, each constructing a new test of some new personality entity.

One final problem with factor analysis deserves mention. Factor analysis was proposed as a solution to the problem of proliferation of abilities. But instead of solving the problem, it introduced a new one, the proliferation of factors.

THE PIAGETIAN REVOLUTION

Early in his career Piaget actually worked in Binet's laboratory at the Sorbonne (though Binet had by then been dead a few years). Looking at Binet's work from present day perspective, one can see in it a continuation of the idea of a kind of mental homunculus. That is, the only dimension of interest is how far the child has grown "up" mentally. Everything else is disregarded. Piaget, being a revolutionary, turned this around. When a child had grown up to adult status in some field, Piaget lost interest. His interest, one could say, was entirely in what kind of "mistakes" the child made. The revolutionary discovery was that those mistakes were not simply random error, not simply missing the target. Those mistakes had a form and content of their own; the child was aiming at a different target. These forms of intellectual structure of the child could have been discerned only by a genius, as one learns by rereading the early books of Piaget. Everyone had access to the basic data of Piaget's early studies, yet no one had discerned as clearly as he did the structure of childish thinking.

The topics that Piaget first investigated are concerned with periods of life when cognitive and affective development are not sharply differentiated. At any rate, many of his early studies concerning moral judgment, dreams, construction of the world of objects, can be termed cognitive-affective in nature. Probably partly for this reason, the paradigms of Piaget now are proving to be highly congenial to a growing school of new developmental psychologists. Piagetian or post-Piagetian developmental psychologists look at development as a succession of qualitative steps rather than purely quantitative accretion of knowledge or abilities. Each Piagetian stage represents a structure, even a frame of reference, within which the bits of knowledge studied for years by learning theorists and traditional developmentalists fit as small pieces.

In his later and purely cognitive studies, especially with Inhelder, Piaget (Tanner & Inhelder, 1956, 1960) sharpened the stage theory in ways now familiar. Kohlberg (1964) and his school, as well as many others—Sullivan, Grant, and Grant (1957) and Perry (1970), among others—have reimported into the field of personality measurement a more or less Piagetian model of stages.

SUBSTRUCTURES OF PERSONALITY

Now that the technique of creating or discerning Piagetian stage sequences is well known and widely practiced, psychology once again is facing the problem of the proliferation of sequences, much like the problem of proliferation of abilities that was addressed by factor analysis. Just as the plethora of abilities resulted in a halt to finding new ones and led to factor analysis, and the plethora of factors has put something of a brake on factorial studies, so the plethora of stages (Loevinger & Knoll, 1983) may threaten the continuation of this Piagetian approach to personality.

Undoubtedly the received opinion among well-trained, well-brought up psychologists will prescribe factor analysis for this ailment too. But factor analysis, on theoretical grounds, as I have indicated, is in several ways or from several points of view inappropriate. Moreover, the track record of factor analysis in solving problems to date has not been spectacular, nor have its solutions gained general assent.

To review: Personality traits do not, in general, grow montonically with age; the relations between different personality traits are not necessarily linear or even monotonic; one cannot assume a positive manifold, i.e., that all relations between personality traits are positive. Indeed, elsewhere (Loevinger, 1983) I have shown that even two different manifestations of the same underlying developmental sequence can have any correlation whatsoever, even a zero or a negative one.

Kohlberg and his colleagues (1981; Snarey, Kohlberg, & Noam, 1983) have proposed a new kind of solution to the problem of the proliferation of stage sequences. In their model there is a hierarchy of sequences such that a given stage in one sequence is necessary but not sufficient for achieving a corresponding stage in another sequence. Thus they propose that a given stage of cognitive development is necessary but not sufficient for achieving a corresponding stage in development of social cognition as measured by Selman (1980), and the latter is necessary but not sufficient for achieving a corresponding stage of moral judgment, as measured by Kohlberg's Moral Maturity Index.

In one version (Snarey, Kohlberg, & Noam, 1983), the overall domain is taken to be that of ego development. Within that broad domain they discern three types of environment, natural, social, and "ultimate", each subject to three types of "meaning-making", epistemological, moral, and metaphysical. Within that nine-cell matrix many or perhaps all of the structural stage theories can be located. The source of this matrix appears to be primarily philosophical or at least logical rather than psychological considerations. The case they make is that this fine-grain level of analysis is more useful than such global concepts as ego development, as my colleagues and I have used the concept.

We began our work on the Sentence Completion Test (Loevinger & Wessler, 1970) with four stages drawn from a paper by Sullivan, Grant, and Grant (1957), giving stages in the development of what they called "interpersonal integration". From that point on, every stage in our work has been guided by actual data. Every response in our scoring manual has come from an actual protocol of some subject, and most of them from more than one subject. Revisions of the stage title, description, or sequence have in every case been dictated by results from numerous subjects drawn from more than one sample, by methods that have been described in some detail elsewhere (Loevinger, 1979b; Loevinger & Wessler, 1970).

In consequence, the content of the scoring manual, containing actual responses, appears to and indeed does contain materials that are not easily classed as purely "structural," which Kohlberg claims his manual is restricted to. (However, that claim is tempered by the fact, as Colby, 1978, admits, that the structure-content distinction has been redrawn several times during the past few years of their work, and others, Locke, 1983, have questioned the distinction.)

Admittedly, for either Kohlberg's work or mine to draw assent outside our own small coteries (much smaller, indeed, in my case than in his), support must finally come in terms of empirical verification of theoretical deductions, or theoretical backing for empirical findings. In my opinion all of the post-Piagetian research into ego and moral development and related variables has far to go to approximate this ideal. Hauser (1976) and I (Loevinger, 1979a) have summarized some of the studies on the construct validity of the Sentence Completion Test.

While we are waiting for the ultimate convergence of theory and data, the two methods stand in opposition. For Kohlberg and his collaborators, colleagues, and followers the logical analysis is the court of last appeal in definition of stages. For me, the responses of subjects constitute the court of last appeal.

Perhaps an example will bring this topic alive. Kohlberg (1981) cites as a particularly heinous example of our empiricism the classification of "I steal" as a Self-Protective response in answer to the stem, "My conscience bothers me if—" (Loevinger, Wessler, & Redmore, 1970). Stealing, according to Kohlberg, is not an action that logically belongs with the intellectual structure implied by the Self-Protective character sketch in its other manifestations. But that is true only if one looks at stealing either as something those subjects actually do or as something that would in fact bother their conscience. We did not follow our subjects around to see who stole, much less monitor their physiological responses to see whose conscience might be troubled. All we did was to look at their responses to sentence completion tests. For us, "My conscience bothers me if— I steal" is in the first instance a test response, not a description of transgressions or even a description of response to transgression. Empirically, persons who give that response seem to be best classified at the Self-Protective level. We do draw inferences about potential behaviors and attitudes from the ensemble of responses at each level, but never from individual responses.

What is implied primarily by a given stage location, in this case the Self-Protective Stage, is a frame of reference, a way of viewing the world, and especially interpersonal relations. At the Self-Protective Stage, stealing is what is considered a weighty transgression. If that is not evident from the definition of the stage, so much the better for the method: It has yielded a small but not implausible discovery. The response is psychologically consistent with the Self-Protective world-view, even if it is not logically compelling.

Taking the responses at a given stage as a whole, we have done reasonably well at inferring expectable behavior patterns, as Blasi's (1976) study of social interaction of children of different ego levels showed. Nonetheless, the system is not undermined by the fact that single responses, out of context, are not indicative of particular behaviors. On the contrary, using the probabilistic logic on which our method is based, that is what is to be expected. Indeed, the most fundamental distinction between Kohlberg's reasoning and mine is that at heart I am a Brunswikian and a psychometrician, reasoning probabilistically (Loevinger, 1966), whereas at heart he is a clinician and a philosopher, engaged in a quest for certainty.

Suppose we agree with Kohlberg et al. that it is possible to subdivide the domain of ego development into several subdomains. Never mind that those subdomains follow the cleavages dictated by classical philosophy. Surely they are right in supposing that any kind of test or measurement addressed to a single one of those subdomains will display more unity than a test or measurement that cuts across many of them. However, experience with subdivision of factors suggests, unfortunately, that there is no limit to that process, that a suitable logical or empirical analysis also would reveal subdivisions within the subdomains explored by Kohlberg (1964), Selman (1980), Broughton (1980), Perry (1970), Damon (1979), and others.

That brings us back to the question Humphreys (1962) has addressed: What is then the most useful level of analysis? The smallest subdivision, as Snarey et al. (1983) seem to assume, and as the term *primary abilities* implies? Or the largest, most encompassing categories? When psychologists measuring abilities have to justify their work in the public forum, there is no question what they do. Scholastic aptitude tests, those used for college admission and for evaluating potential graduate students, generally measure verbal and mathematical abilities in general, not the far more complex hierarchy of primary abilities that workers such as Thurstone or Guilford (1956) have adumbrated.

In a longitudinal study of ego development in the college years (Loevinger et al., 1985), we found, surprisingly, that whereas men in a technical institute and in a liberal arts college showed a small, consistent gain in ego level over the college years, as did women in the technical institute, women in liberal arts showed a smaller but consistent decline. Separating the liberal arts students by major, the one group for which both men and women showed a decline was the business school group (Sargent, 1984). The two cases differ in one respect: On the whole, the women in liberal arts start out higher than the men and end up even with them, whereas the students in business school start out lower in ego level than other students and decline.

The size of the sample of students in individual majors is too small to justify any grand conclusions about what happens to students in our business schools and what implications that might have for American business. Let us look instead to the implications for Piagetian theory, more modest in social implications but more significant theoretically.

Any sizeable group of people, particularly when chosen on some basis other than their score on the Sentence Completion Test, must be presumed to include some people who will show at least a small gain in ego level during their college years. In principle, according to Kohlberg's version of Piagetian stage theory, no one should regress in college years except under the most extraordinary circumstances. The declines observed are not statistically significant in the case of any single class, but only when cumulated (via meta-analysis) over more than one cohort. Even if there were no real decline in the group of women as a whole but only an average staying the same, it still could be taken as evidence that, because some individuals can be assumed to rise, others must have shown a decline. No test is infallible, certainly not the Sentence Completion Test. Nonetheless, a significant decline of a group cannot be accounted for on the basis of random measurement error.

These results raise the question of whether Piagetian theory really requires that stages in this cognitive-affective universe of discourse be nondecreasing. Once the question has been raised, several reasons turn up why it should be taken seriously.

Witness A: Kohlberg himself (Kohlberg & Kramer, 1969), before he completed his final revision of his scoring manual, found some students regressing markedly when they got to college. Several investigators using earlier versions of Kohlberg's manual found more regression than his study did, and even with the present version, Erickson (1980) and Gilligan and Murphy (1979) find regression.

Witness B: Perry (1970), studying growth of intellectual-ethical development in the college years, made a special category in his system for students who retreated in the face of the challenge of growth.

Witness C: A study by Redmore (1976) of the fakability of ego level, found that some college women actually lowered their scores under instructions intended to test how far they could raise them. Evidently they construed as an advance what the test recorded as a regression. The number of cases was small, and the circumstances of that study were such that statistical regression was a possible alternative hypothesis.

Witness D: Piaget (1932) cannot be called as a witness for the defense, for he was at pains in his study of moral judgment, one of the most immediate sources of Kohlberg's work, to reiterate that the results cannot be interpreted as consistent with a strict stage sequence. Only on the basis of a strict stage theory can one infer that regression is an excluded possibility.

Moreover, even with respect to purely cognitive development, Piaget (1972) has warned that a person may regress or backslide with respect to formal operations outside his own field of specialization.

Indeed, comparing Piaget's treatment of the possibility of regression with Kohlberg's, one must conclude that Kohlberg is in this case subscribing to a stricter stage definition than Piaget did. It is worth considering whether Piaget's early work in fact resembles our empirical definition of stages more than it does the logical "philosophic" method of latter day Kohlbergians.

Kohlberg's group now finds that they have essentially no regression when scoring their old longitudinal cases by their new scoring manual (Colby, Kohlberg, Gibbs, & Lieberman, 1983). The problem is that the criterion on which their new scoring manual has been predicated is that a strict version of sequentiality would obtain. What price have they paid for satisfying that criterion? There is at least a possibility that what has happened, with the successive revisions of the Colby-Kohlberg manual toward ever more refined definition of "structural" as opposed to "content" scoring categories, is that the scoring has been increasingly tilted toward a purely intellectual-cognitive mode. If that is so, they would have to that extent lost the affective element that is precisely what is distinctive for this universe of discourse.

We began the longitudinal study of college students (Loevinger et al. 1985) with the hope of establishing the sequentiality of ego development in the college years. Instead I find myself ending with the question whether seeing development in this arena as a nondecreasing function is necessarily implied by the conception of stages. There are many questions which my coworkers have challenged me with, such as: What does it mean to regress? Or for that matter, what does it mean to be "in" a stage? Is the regression we have observed real or only apparent? Those are the questions that await clarification by all those working in the arena of cognitive-affective developmental theory not only with respect to ego development.

REFERENCES

Blasi, A. (1976). Personal responsibility and ego development. In R. deCharms, *Enhancing motivation: Change in the classroom* (pp. 177–199). New York: Irvington Press.

Broughton, J. (1980). Genetic metaphysics: The developmental psychology of mind/body concepts. In R. W. Rieber (Ed.) *Mind and body* (pp. 177–221). New York: Academic Press.

Cattell, R. B. (1965). *The scientific analysis of personality*. Baltimore: Penguin.

Colby, A. (1978). Evolution of a moral-developmental theory. *New Directions in Child Development, 2*, 89–104.

Colby, A., Kohlberg, L., Gibbs, J. C., & Lieberman, M. (1983). A longitudinal study of moral judgment. *Monographs, Society for Research in Child Development, 48*, serial no. 200.

Damon, W. (1979). *The social world of the child*. San Francisco: Jossey-Bass.

Erickson, V. L. (1980). The case study method in evaluation of developmental programs. In L. Kuhmerker, M. Mentkowski, & V. L. Erickson (Eds.)., *Evaluating moral development* (pp. 151–176). New York: Character Research Press.

Gilligan, C., & Murphy, J. M. (1979). Development from adolescence to adulthood: The philosopher and the dilemma of fact. In D. Kuhn (Ed.), *Intellectual development beyond childhood* (No. 5, pp. 85–99). San Francisco: Jossey-Bass.

Guilford, J. P. (1956). The structure of intellect. *Psychological Bulletin, 53*, 267–293.

Hauser, S. T. (1976). Loevinger's model and measure of ego development: A critical review. *Psychological Bulletin, 83*, 928–955.

Humphreys, L. (1962). The organization of human abilities. *American Psychologist, 17*, 475–483.

Kohlberg, L. (1964). The development of moral character and ideology. In M. L. & L. W. Hoffman (Eds.), *Review of Child Development Research* (Vol. 1). (pp. 383–431). New York: Russell Sage Fundation.

Kohlberg, L. (1981). *The meaning and measurement of moral development*. Worcester, MA.: Clark University Press.

Kohlberg, L., & Kramer, R. (1969). Continuities and discontinuities in childhood and adult moral development. *Human Development, 12*, 93–120.

Locke, D. (1983). Doing what comes morally: The relation between behavior and stages of moral reasoning. *Human Development, 26*, 11–25.

Loevinger, J. (1948). The technic of homogeneous tests compared with some aspects of "scale analysis" and factor analysis. *Psychological Bulletin, 45*, 507–529.

Loevinger, J. (1957). Objective tests as instruments of psychological theory. *Psychological Reports, 3*, 635–694.

Loevinger, J. (1966). Psychological tests in the conceptual framework of psychology. In K. R. Hammond (Ed.), *The psychology of Egon Brunswik* (pp. 107–148). New York: Holt, Rinehart & Winston.

Loevinger, J. (1979a). Construct validity of the sentence completion test of ego development. *Applied Psychological Measurement, 3*, 281–311.

Loevinger, J. (1979b). Theory and data in the measurement of ego development. In J. Loevinger, *Scientific ways in the study of ego development* (pp. 1–24). Worcester, MA: Clark University Press.

Loevinger, J. (1983). On the self and predicting behavior. In R. A. Zucker, J. Aronoff, & A. I. Rabin (Eds.), *Personality and the prediction of behavior* (pp. 43–68). New York: Academic.

Loevinger, J., Cohn, L. D., Redmore, C. D., Bonneville, L. P., Streich, D. D., & Sargent, M. (1985). Ego development in college. *Journal of Personality and Social Psychology, 48*, 947–962.

Loevinger, J., & Knoll, E. (1983). Personality: Stages, traits, and the self. *Annual Review of Psychology, 34*, 195–222.

Loevinger, J., & Wessler, R. (1970). *Measuring ego development 1. Construction and use of a sentence completion test.* San Francisco: Jossey-Bass.

Loevinger, J., Wessler, R., & Redmore, C. (1970). *Measuring ego development 2. Scoring manual for women and girls.* San Francisco: Jossey-Bass.

Perry, W. G., Jr. (1970). *Forms of intellectual and ethical development in the college years.* New York: Holt, Rinehart & Winston.

Piaget, J. (1932). *The moral judgment of the child.* New York: Free Press.

Piaget, J. (1972). Intellectual evolution from adolescence to adulthood. *Human Development, 15*, 1–12.

Redmore, C. (1976). Susceptibility to faking of a sentence completion test of ego development. *Journal of Personality Assessment, 40*, 607–616.

Sargent, M. (1984). *Ego development and choice of major in college.* Washington University, unpublished manuscript.

Selman, R. L. (1980). *The growth of interpersonal understanding.* New York: Academic Press.

Snarey, J., Kohlberg, L., & Noam, G. (1983). Ego development in perspective: Structural stage, functional phase, and cultural age-period models. *Developmental Review, 3*, 303–338.

Sullivan, C., Grant, M. Q., & Grant, J. D. (1957). The development of interpersonal maturity: Applications to delinquency. *Psychiatry, 20*, 373–385.

Tanner, J. M., & Inhelder, B. (Eds.) (1956). *Discussions on child development* (Vol. 1). New York: International Universities Press.

Tanner, J. M., & Inhelder, B. (Eds.) (1960). *Discussions on child development* (Vol. 4). New York: International Universities Press.

Thurstone, L. L. (1938). Primary mental abilities. *Psychometric Monographs*, No. 1. Chicago: University of Chicago Press.

6

Guiding the Study of Cognition to a Framework of Greater Complexity

Herbert Zimiles
Bank Street College of Education

In a recent examination of the field of cognition, Neisser (1976) begins with a harsh appraisal of the burgeoning research output in cognition. He notes that research in cognition has been disappointingly narrow, focusing inward on the analysis of specific experimental situations rather than outward toward the world beyond the laboratory. He calls for a cognitive psychology that is more attuned to "cognition as it occurs in the ordinary environment and in the context of natural purposeful activity" (p. 7) and " . . . to analyzing the environment that the mind has been shaped to meet . . ." (p. 8). His trenchant methodogical criticism continues with a sentence that alludes to a multiplicity of sins of contemporary research in cognition: "A satisfactory theory of human cognition can hardly be established by experiments that provide inexperienced subjects with brief opportunities to perform novel and meaningless tasks" (p. 8). Almost obscured in this tightly compressed sentence is a four-fold enumeration of methodological trends that impede progress: (a) most investigations of cognition are in the form of experiments, thereby restricting the study of phenomena to that which can be experimentally manipulated and which produces measurable effects; (b) most research uses inexperienced subjects who may not fully understand what is expected of them or who may not be adequately motivated to perform well, and may be distracted by the confrontion with a strange examiner whose presence interferes with the cognitive processes that are being studied; (c) the typical study of cognition provides only a brief opportunity to perform so that observations are made on the basis of a comparatively small sample of behavior; and (d) the tasks usually administered in cognition experiments are designed to be novel and meaningless in order to minimize the confounding impact of previous exposure to the phenomena. As a result, they are less likely to evoke

75

routinized and well-organized modes of behavior that reveal how the subject typically responds. In summation, the current study of cognition is distorted by its restriction to variables that can be studied experimentally. It is likely to be deficient because it is based on mere glimpses of behavior evoked under unusual and unnatural circumstances wherein subjects are asked to deal with novel and/ or meaningless problems that may not evoke customary modes of behavior. Neisser is neither the first nor the last to question the heavy emphasis of psychological research on experimental methods and to call for greater ecological validity of research. His comments are noted because they refer specifically to the field of cognition and because they come from an author whose wisdom in scanning the cognitive forest is widely acknowledged.

In seeking to deepen our understanding of the relation between cognition and affect, this chapter begins with the premise that progress in this area has been stifled by the widespread adoption of a set of methodological conventions. These conventions have become established ways of working and border on being inviolate methodological tenets. Neisser's critique has been recruited to keynote this call for a reassessment of methodological strategies that will provide greater access to the phenomena of cognitive-affective interaction. Following a methodological review that goes beyond the important points raised by Neisser, the chapter explores some issues pertaining to the relation between cognition and affect in the light of some old theoretical observations and some recent empirical findings.

OVERCOMING THE METHODOLOGICAL BARRIERS TO ASSESSMENT

At the core of current approaches to the study of cognition is a search for methods of measurement, methods that are not likely to be effective in probing the complexity that is inherent to the phenomena of cognitive-affective interaction. Toward this end, cognitive phenomena have been reduced to their simplest elements and voided of associations and contextual influences that detract from objectivity and precision of measurement. Nowhere in psychology has logical positivism been more assertive and dominant. Thus, intelligence, the first and for some still the only firmly established trait of intellectual functioning, still is cautiously defined in some quarters as that which the intelligence test measures. In attempting to identify the basic building blocks of cognition, an austere psychometric framework has taken hold that has given rise to contrasting elementaristic research perspectives. On the one hand, there is a struggle to arrive at an index of the common core of intellectual functioning, to measure its central axis. At the same time, there is a keen interest in capturing its multifaceted character, in identifying its full spectrum of elements. The tensions between these two poles and the efforts to reconcile them have distracted investigators from other agendas. In the meantime, the voluminous number of tests and experimental problem-solving tasks devised by members of these opposing camps, both wed to a psychometric orientation and to psychological testing as the main method for assessing and observing cognitive behavior, has led to such a proliferation of measures that they have become the reality rather than the vehicle for indexing reality. Thinking about thinking has come to mean examining a matrix of test scores; the errors of omission and distortion shared by all such measures are conveniently overlooked.

Even when alternative theoretical and methodological approaches are introduced in reaction to the prevailing psychometric approach, they are either distorted or simply appropriated (as in the case of the work of Piaget) to fit the psychometric mold. When a new construct surfaces, the law of parsimony is relentlessly invoked to determine whether it clarifies the phenomena under study. Is it really needed? Are we adding redundancy and error to an equation or improving its description of reality?

Just as football may be described as a game played in circumscribed space between the 50-yard line and the goal line, the measurement of cognition is a correlation/components-of-variance game played between the points of .00 and 1.00. In order for players to gain points by wedging new measures on to the board (a powerful way of winning but one that is so difficult to accomplish that it is seldom attempted), these measures must not correlate too highly with others or their degree of useful distinctiveness will be suspect, or so lowly that they will seem too alien to the phenomena they are expected to enhance but not duplicate. But the optimal magnitude of intermediate correlation is never really defined precisely, nor can any definition be fully justified. In this respect, Loevinger (1976) reminds us that even though the correlation between height and weight is very high, too high in many samples for us to regard such variables as really different from each other (if they were hypothetical constructs and their identity unknown to us), it would be a grievous error to abandon the use of either one because of their covariation with the other.

The fuzzy rules of the game also call for the exclusion of measures with low reliability coefficients, although here again the cut-off points are never made clear and the resourceful player may insist that there is enough new true variance being introduced to justify the error that accompanies a new measure. There also is the disquieting fact that many of the reliability coefficients and other coefficients of covariation are extremely sensitive to the conditions of measurement, including especially the variance of the sample, so that each new measure has to demonstrate its utility under new conditions. Over and above these complicated and ambiguous considerations is the fact that the main goal of the game, the one for which the most points are awarded—validity—is usually based on a criterion that is either trivial or controversial. Either an operational definition of a criterion is arbitrarily adopted (and just as easily rejected), or a theoretical construct is invoked whose meaningfulness is challenged.

Hemmed into playing a game whose rules are ambiguous and arbitrarily enforced (so that persistence, assertiveness, and accident become dominant determinants of the outcome) and at the same time confining, many players gravitate to a more reliable strategy for scoring points. The strategy often chosen is to simplify existing measures by shortening or changing them in other ways so that they require less time and/or less expert administration. According to this line of reasoning, because it is difficult within the existing framework to measure cognition better, we should at least strive to measure it more efficiently. Some tests are even subjected to radical change for the sake of efficiency, as in the case of Witkin's (Witkin, Dyk, Faterson, Goodenough, & Karp, 1962) shift to the Embedded Figures Test as a stand-in for the more cumbersome and time-consuming rod-and-frame test as a means of assessing cognitive style.

The psychometric approach, with its demand for multiple measures from large numbers of subjects, thereby limits measurement to brief assessments in an austere framework that preserves objectivity and comparability. It has as its main virtue a commitment to quantification, an ability to gauge the magnitude of sampling error and an appreciation for objective measurement. It leads, however, to an infinite regress to the common core of existing measures of cognitive functioning as the only defensible statement of reality. Once investigators move off this dime, their claims are disputed and tend to disappear in a cloud of controversy.

Despite the limitations of the psychometric perspective, alternative approaches are assimilated into this method of study and analysis. Thus, Piaget's work was welcomed by most researchers not as a new theoretical-philosophical approach to the study of cognition, but mainly as identifying new dimensions of cognitive functioning to be incorporated into the psychometric mode. His methods were gradually revised to fit into the framework of psychometric assessment, which then gave rise to a mass of conflicting data that have left Gelman and Baillargeon (1983) and Flavell (1982) to question some of the most basic elements of Piaget's approach. By the time a new set of ideas is run through the ringer of the psychometric/nomothetic machine, it is indistinguishable from all other data, and becomes equally suspect.

The body of research conducted within the psychometric framework has helped to document the nature of sizeable individual differences in overall levels of cognitive functioning, a differentiation not unlike, but more rigorous than, those made by teachers and other informal assessments of intellectual functioning. But one must seriously doubt whether this approach, in light of the great amount of uninformative data that it has generated, can go beyond providing an appraisal of gross differences in overall ability. In order to advance the study of cognitive functioning, including the manner in which affective factors interact with cognition, we need to introduce the following changes in method: (a) to shift from molecular to molar levels of analysis that will reveal the nature of integrative functioning; (b) to base our measures on more intensive forms of assessment that reflect enduring organizational patterns; and (c) to adopt an idiographic rather than nomothetic framework of assessment.

Integrative Functioning. Integrative functioning refers to a summative mode of thinking that embodies the organizational structure of the mind. It deals not with the individual elements of concept formation but with stock-taking, with how we sort and synthesize experience, the kinds of inferences that are drawn and how this ordering process brings about a selective sensitivity to environmental events. It operates both explicitly and implicitly, consciously and unconsciously, and it occurs in different degrees and with different points of emphasis.

Insofar as integrative functioning consists in large measure of reflective thinking, then it is Piaget who has been singularly attuned to this issue. His distinction between the stages of preoperational thought and concrete and formal operations offered a way of looking at aspects of integrative experience developmentally. Piaget's concern with reflective thinking revolved around the laws of logic, with the degree to which children have constructed abstract principles of logical relations—regarding transitivity, conservation, reversibility, seriation, and so forth. Because these categories of logical thinking appear to be universal, he succeeded in devising problem situations that reveal (not without error or inconsistency) levels of integrative functioning. This, in effect, is one of Piaget's greatest contributions, to gain access to levels of reflective thought and integrative functioning by means of fairly systematic and efficient means of assessment. But he was circumscribed in his concerns, confining himself to the sphere of logical reasoning.

Integrative thinking, although mediated by logical reasoning, refers to a world outlook that also includes assumptions and beliefs about motivations and social relationships and issues of morality and values. Moreover, in his study of integrative functioning, Piaget was not interested in assessing the distinctive features of individual children's thinking. Yet it is in the study of individual children that different integrative levels are revealed that reflect aspects of cognitive-affective interaction. To gain access to integrative functioning and the degree to which it is interfered with, distorted, or enhanced and strengthened by emotional factors, requires the lengthy observation and detailed background information that only intensive methods of study can provide.

Intensive Methods of Assessment   The use of intensive methods of assessment is advocated because of the untenability of the premise of most assessment research—that brief samples of behavior are as revealing as more sustained and intensive forms of assessment. Although in some respects a two-page outline of a novel may contain the same information as a *Readers Digest* condensation, which, in turn may contain the same information as the full text, there also are vast differences among these renditions. The capacity for brief samples to tap accurately what is apprehended in the course of sustained observation varies over a wide range; in some realms of psychological functioning there is only the barest connection between what a brief sample can reveal and what closer inspection uncovers. In the interests of making progress quickly and easily, the earliest studies of psychological processes were directed at those spheres where a small behavior sample is a reliable reflection of what is likely to be learned from long-term study. But the reasons for that initial strategy have somehow been lost. Instead psychologists have come to believe that if phenomena cannot be reliably assessed by means of brief samples of observation, then what is being studied is either illusory or seriously flawed in ways that detract from its theoretical importance. As a result, we have generated a great deal of misplaced effort toward streamlining and shortcutting existing instruments.

The call for more intensive measurement of cognitive functioning arouses resistance because it leads to the shedding of convenient assumptions and practices and it is risky. It requires giving up the myth that well-planned and crisply analyzed glimpses are all that are needed; it entails greater cost without guaranteeing correspondingly greater output. A more intensive approach to assessment of cognitive functioning would not only dig deeper and stay down longer (as some wag has tersely described psychoanalysis), it would turn to other spheres of functioning than those normally assessed. It would examine typical modes of behavior as well as the response to new situations. Perhaps most disturbing in terms of our current canons of measurement, it would use methods and conditions of observation that are not necessarily comparable from one person to the next and it would abandon nomothetic measurement for idiographic procedures.

Idiographic Assessment.   The idea that useful assessment requires applying the same yardstick to all is, on the one hand, fundamental to the logic of measurement and on the other, flies in the face of our awareness that different processes and content need to be investigated to capture the essential features of psychological functioning in different people. It is not only impractical to administer a number of measures large enough to include all those attributes that are needed to record the essential elements of cognitive functioning in each of a sample of individuals; the tedium and inconvenience of so extensive an assessment would undermine its quality. Further, because most of the components of so large a battery of measures would not be relevant to the preponderance of the members of the sample, the scores on such tasks should not be allowed to contribute to the outcome. Were we to assign weights to the subtest scores of a large battery according to their differential relevance, we would, in effect, shift to an idiographic mode of assessment.

Idiographic measurement, first proposed by Allport (1937) in his treatise on personality, has been resoundingly rejected by researchers in psychology. As a result, particular areas of knowledge have remained underdeveloped—the study of personality at all developmental stages and the study of cognitive, as well as emotional functioning among adults. Our gaps of knowledge in these areas are tacit evidence of the inappropriateness of the application of nomothetic forms of assessment to certain spheres of research. It may be argued further that the application of the same measures to all individuals does violence to most realms of assessment if we are willing to acknowledge that any important psychological attribute must be composed of a complex of life experience, cultivated skills and preferred modes of thinking that entails a configuration of traits that are differentially salient for different people. The study of cognitive-affective inter-action is especially dependent on idiographic assessment; the role of affective factors may be expected to differ from one individual to another and to interact with different aspects of cognitive functioning in different ways.

Illustrative Findings of an Intensive and Idiographic Study of Integrative Functioning

This discussion has emphasized how little time and appetite there is for the qualitative assessment of cognitive functioning. Psychologists and educators have become so steeped in microscopic dimensions and quantitative measures that they have come to believe that the main reality of cognitive functioning is revealed by their assessment procedures. There is a tendency to forget that these procedures were devised to provide crude (and efficient) indices of levels of functioning whose actual character is more complex. Thus, most research and educational evaluation have been pitched to function in accordance with a data base consisting of easily measurable and quantifiable skills. But, if we come upon an educational setting that is not overburdened by hoards of students and ask teachers to describe each student, we obtain descriptions of cognitive functioning that go far beyond what quantitative indices tell us. Such detailed descriptions, based on sustained observation of each individual student, seldom refer to the categories used by objective methods devised to obtain quantitative data. Instead, they deal with integrative levels of functioning and come forth with descriptions that involve a configuration of attributes and dynamics unique to each individual.

One published account of such descriptions was provided by Murphy and Ladd (1944). The study consisted largely of case study descriptions (made by the authors and also excerpted from teacher evaluations) of the college careers of a small number of women who had been attending a private college that provided extensive tutorial experience in order to facilitate individualized learning. In their report, Murphy and Ladd describe various facets of the development of these students that both affected and reflected the manner in which each absorbed and used what they were learning in college. The authors refer to different degrees and forms of sensitivity and modes of assimilation and different patterns of resistance to life's threats and of resourcefulness in meeting them. These distinctive patterns are expressed in the way in which each student digested her experience and coped with her problems. Students showed very different conceptions of the role of thinking and the life of the mind, as is revealed in the following passage (Murphy & Ladd, 1944).

> To Caroline, her mind has been trained to fit her into the demands of social life; to Patsy, using her mind may be a symbol of being grown up; for Rebecca, her mind is a tool with which she can get at the root of things: Carol uses her mind to learn the right rules and patterns. Salvation from banality is one student's hope, while the intelligence of another serves chiefly the function of protection against shock. A somewhat similar purpose is served by the mental development of still another who covers up her fear of being too spontaneous by exhibiting an intellectual facade. For still other students, their minds may be tools to solve problems, to gain power and to master life, or similarly to bolster a wavering ego. Shy or detached students may use their minds to gain access to people, as a tool for understanding and rapport. (p. 69)

Equally revealing and varied were descriptions of what might be termed cognitive styles by Murphy and Ladd (1944):

> One student was painstakingly thorough even when it wasn't necessary; another could be thorough when it was important; another was never thorough. Either the thorough or the never-thorough student may be creative, capable of fresh percep-tions, original insights. One girl could collect data systematically and tabulate them accurately but could not plan original projects of her own based on the data; one got lost in details so that she could find no hypothesis nor conclusion while another overlooked details in far-flung generalizations that were never adequately founded. One student learned through being told what to do, another through identification, still another through her own trial and error. (p. 70)

The comments culled from individual instructors' reports illustrate the range of teachers' concerns in this unusual institution. They include the following categories:

> a pigeon-hole viewpoint . . . limited imagination . . . lack of critical attitude . . . emotional attitudes which prevent analysis . . . failure to see relationships . . . rigid prejudices . . . material does not make a deep emotional impression . . . inability to observe . . . inability to put experience to work . . . inability to relate observations with reading . . . difficulties in concentration . . . tendency to give stereotyped answers . . . antagonistic to new ideas . . . inability to generalize . . . difficulty in writing . . . glib superficial acceptance of new ideas . . . inability to apply understanding . . . disorganized approach to work . . . pseudo-intellectualism . . . . (p. 72)

The range of attributes mentioned by teachers illustrates the diversity of char-acteristics used in idiographic descriptions of cognitive-affective growth. Were these college instructors asked to rate each student on all of these attributes, the task would have been prohibitive in time and would have led to stale and invalid descriptions in the preponderance of cases simply because most of these attributes usually were not relevant to the descriptions of each student. It is the differential salience of these characteristics that lends validity to their descriptions and makes them come alive. They help to remind us that cognitive functioning is organized around a different body of concerns and experiences for different people and serves distinctive modes of adaptation.

The Murphy and Ladd volume is cited extensively to demonstrate the extent to which cognitive and affective traits are blended in these authors' and teachers' descriptions of a sample of students' progress. The mingling of emotional and intellectual attributes does not merely represent the authors' unique conceptual framework; the concepts used to describe the students were drawn from diverse instructors' written comments about individual students. Although it may be argued that these descriptions represent an approach to education that is unique to the particular college and its faculty, the key distinctive feature was the intensity of the interaction between students and faculty and the frequency with which individual conferences and tutorial experiences marked the instructional process. It is the depth of interest in individual intellectual growth and the opportunity for close observation that makes possible a psychological analysis and description in terms of integrative functioning and cognitive-affective interaction. The cognitive dimensions found in most measures and tests are categories of description reserved for mass and impersonal processing of students.

The age of the Murphy and Ladd study points to the fact that the idea of merging the cognitive and the affective in order to better understand the workings of the mind is old, and antedates the renascence of cognitive research in the 1960s. It is not based on a new line of thinking that has barely had a chance to take hold. On the other hand, the need to use so old a reference points to the rarity of such writing in the psychological literature despite the fact that a great deal of informal and implicit student evaluation proceeds along just such lines. The elementaristic, dimensional orientation of cognitive assessment research procedures, reinforced by the demands for evidence of reliability and validity, preclude such idiographic descriptions. Were we to turn to other educational settings in which there is a low teacher/student ratio, whether they be well-run nursery schools or private elementary schools or colleges that deliberately restrict the size of their enrollments, the teachers' descriptions of students' progress are likely to include similar patterns of cognitive-affective content.

Up to this point, this chapter has dwelled on methodological impediments to the study of complex forms of cognition, including cognitive-affective interaction, and has offered an illustration of how more productive study can be achieved. The remainder is given over to a consideration of some of the intricacies of the relation between cognition and affect.

ON THE NATURE OF THE RELATION BETWEEN
COGNITION AND AFFECT

In an effort to demystify the connection between thought and emotion and thereby render the topic less remote, the following section assembles evidence for the interaction between these two abstractions, and examines the nature of their linkage. It explores some ramifications of the widely held belief that the fundamental relation between thought and feeling is that affect is an irritant to cognition, an inhibitor and disruptor of thought. Three themes are central to the ensuing discussion: (a) the idea that cognitive processes are more inherently flawed than we are usually willing to recognize; (b) the theory of ego defense formulated in psychoanalytic theory presents a powerful demonstration of the manner in which thought is interpenetrated with affective forces, and (c) affect-derived distortions of cognitive functioning cannot be attributed simply to psychopathology, cannot be relegated to marginal areas of psychological functioning, to the twilight zone between normal and abnormal behavior. The superordinate role of affect in governing cognition is not necessarily linked to disordered psychological functioning; the overarching influence of affect is intrinsic to the natural functioning of cognition. Thus, this section begins with a conventional view of the disruptive influence of affect on cognition, and then cites some clinical-theoretical observations and experimental evidence that calls for a revision in thinking about such phenomena.

The Disruptive Force of Affect and the Veridicality of Cognition.   In contemplating the nature of the linkage between thought and emotion, we are likely to regard thought as a purposeful and logical process that is undermined by the volatile and irrational processes of emotion. According to this widely held view, cognition is predominantly rational and efficent, limited in power by genetic endowment and in scope by social experience, but moving on the right track only to be derailed occasionally by disruptive emotions. Thus, we are likely to embrace the idea, and have amassed a modest substantiating research literature, that anxiety and conflict interfere with cognitive functioning. Extensive clinical observation by Rapaport, Gill, and Schafer, (1945/1976), has provided a framework for diagnosing emotional disturbance on the basis of impaired cognitive performance on standardized tests of intellectual aptitude.

It also has been hypothesized that, in addition to acute distress, enduring emotional conflicts, though stabilized and incorporated into the individual's framework of functioning, nevertheless may interefere with cognition. Thus, Zimiles and Konstadt (1962) obtained a modest degree of substantiation for their hypothesis that emotional conflicts revolving around adherence to the demands of authority interfere with learning rule-governed aspects of such intellectual functioning as the ability to spell correctly.

In examining the disruptive impact of affect on cognition, it generally is assumed that cognitive behavior normally functions correctly and efficiently, that conceptual functioning is logical, and that perception and memory tend to be veridical. Yet there have always been ample grounds to contest this mythic image of the flawlessness of cognition. Piaget, in his occasional writing about education (1970), reminds us that we rapidly forget most of the facts that we are taught in school. The efficiency quotient of school learning, however computed, is appallingly low. Yet we continue to engage in educational planning as if the child's cognitive apparatus is a perfectly functioning unit, and the principal challenge to the educator is to find more efficient means for presenting the greatest amount of material to be learned.

The idea of veridical cognition also is difficult to reconcile with the unreliability and inconsistency of findings widely reported in the research literature if we view such flawed behavior not as resulting from error of method but as intrinsic to human performance. The research literature based on the application of Piagetian methods is replete with inconsistencies and incongruences. Whereas many of the differences in outcome found among investigators purporting to study the same phenomena may be attributable to differences in samples, procedures and examiners (see Miller, 1976, for an analysis of such differences), a sizeable portion of this variation, when one considers the substantial magnitude of intraindividual variation from the scant evidence available, appears to be intrinsic to children. There is a substantial amount of instability and lack of coherence that stems from characteristics of the subject rather than from the conditions of measurement (Zimiles, 1966). Furthermore, observations of the role of contextual factors in cognition, as cited by Zimiles (1965), Glick (1975), and Zimmerman (1983) provide additional evidence of inconsistency and instability even though these variations in performance may be demonstrated to be lawfully related to particular contextual factors.[1]

The most recently assembled body of evidence bearing on the fallibility of human cognition comes from the series of experiments conducted by Loftus (1981). In a series of studies of the accuracy of testimony, she has shown substantial declines in memory for explicit details. In a review of their own work as well as of others, Loftus and Loftus (1980) concluded that forgetting entails not merely failure to retrieve but the loss of substantial stored information. The circumstances that produce such loss, including affective factors, have yet to be identified.

---

[1]The fact that children engage in different forms of logical reasoning according to the manner in which a problem is presented to them or that they have a tendency to invoke a logical principle under one set of circumstances and not another raises new questions that bear on the dynamics of such phenomena. To what extent do affective factors define contextual differences in performance? The study of the role of contextual factors may identify new mechanisms of cognitive-affective interaction.

Cognitive-Affective Interaction in Ego Functioning. In searching for evidence of the fallibility of cognitive functioning, such phenomena are perhaps nowhere more clearly delineated than in the mechanisms of defense employed in ego functioning, a sphere of behavior that also is closely connected with the idea of integrative functioning. In the defense mechanisms, cognition is being used to conceal and subvert the instinctual life. Whereas academic psychology, with its elementaristic and positivistic outlook, has barely approached the issue of cognitive-affective interaction, focusing instead on the need to solidify the conceptual and knowledge base of cognition and affect as separate entities prior to examining their interaction, psychoanalysis has from the start been concerned with the connection between feeling and thought.

In describing the strategies used by the ego to reconcile the forbidden and therefore dangerous instinctual strivings of the id with the strict internalized forbidding values of the conscience, Anna Freud (1946/1936) delineates an array of mechanisms of defense previously cited in the psychoanalytic literature. The defenses of the ego are concerned not only with warding off instinctual impulses but with the affects associated with them. Thus the ego attempts to master these impulses by transforming such affects as love, longing, jealousy, mortification, pain, and mourning associated with sexual wishes; and hatred, anger, and rage associated with aggression. Included in this roster are the by-now familiar concepts of repression, regression, introjection, identification, projection, sublimation, reaction formation, isolation, undoing, projection, and denial. They are described by Anna Freud (1981) as entailing an impairment of ego function. Repression destroys the intactness of memory; it produces gaps and deletions that interfere with accurate and coherent recall. Rationalization deceives the individual about his motive and thereby contributes a distortion of the perception of reality. Denial obscures the facts dictated by reason and logic. Isolation estranges one aspect of one's personality or experience thereby disrupting the coherence of one's personality and appearance of reality. Projection ascribes to environmental figures attributes that reside in the perceiver rather than the external environment. In undoing the individual resorts to magical forms of reversing regretted or disturbing acts in order to diminish the guilt and anxiety associated with them. In order to disguise one's true feelings, reaction formation leads to the adoption of a sentiment or viewpoint that is diametrically opposite to the impulse or sentiment actually harbored by the individual.

What is to be said about such phenomena? Are they not prime examples of the interaction between thought and emotion, and is not Anna Freud's analysis of the mechanisms of defense a treatise on the nature of cognitive-affective interaction? Many of the terms used to denote these patterns of ego defense have been assimilated into our everyday language, but there are scant references to them among rigorous efforts to explore the domain of cognitive-affective interaction. They seem to be regarded by serious investigators of cognition as aberrations either of the clinicians who report observing them or of the pathological individuals who emit them. After all, rigorous researchers argue, these phenomena are observed in the course of clinical work, a field of inexact application of psychological science that is difficult to validate. On the one hand, the phenomena of defense mechanisms may be rejected as offering useful examples of the interaction between thought and emotion because they are marginal and deviant. On the other, the very intractability of neurotic behavior to treatment demonstrates how deeply rooted and difficult to modify are these patterns of defense observed by clinicians. The tenacity and vigor of such behavior leads to the inference that they are merely more rigid and maladaptive forms of ego defense that pervade psychological functioning. Reich (1933/1949) has described how defenses may become disassociated from their original stimulus and develop into character traits. If the latter is true, then the defense mechanisms of the ego deserve to be at the center of the study of the linkage between thought and emotion. It has been customary to portray defensive behavior as the cognitive loss associated with emotional frailty, as the price in distortion of reality one pays for emotional conflict, but it seems more appropriate to regard such phenomena as fundamental to the psychological fabric of humans.

Another View of Affective Distortion of Cognition.   Geleerd (1965) offered an elaboration and extension of thinking about the functioning of defense mechanisms without questioning their central role as vehicles of thought that help the ego to deal with neurotic anxiety and guilt. She concurs that much of psychoanalytic treatment consists of analyzing defenses, of clarifying and interpreting such thought patterns in order to reduce the distortion of reality they bring about. Noting how easily they are assimilated by children, she speculates that children adopt these mechanisms of repression, denial, and reaction formation as a way of gaining access to their parents' world, as an act of solidarity and as a way of forestalling the loss of their parents' love. They take on their parents' neurotic ways of thinking as a means of joining the human community, as a way of communicating with others and avoiding feelings of isolation. In effect, children readily learn their parents' faulty ways of dealing with conflicts, and the pattern of distortion in cognitive functioning spreads.

Of greater relevance to this discussion, Geleerd (1965), in reviewing her understanding of ego defenses, is prompted to observe that denial is a mechanism of thought that also is necessary for normal functioning. She notes that many of the worries and fears of potential disaster voiced by depressed and phobic patients in many ways constitute a more realistic appraisal of life than the hope and optimism exhibited by those unafflicted by psychopathology. Pointing to the magical actions, taboos, and religious ceremonies that are used to help cope with the tragedies of life, she concludes that a certain degree of denial and illusion is essential to allow people to live and function with tranquility. Thus, it is not uncommon to find profound denial of severe illness either in themselves or those close to them among otherwise level-headed individuals. Geleerd labels this benign mode "denial in the service of the need to survive" and describes it as a universal defense mechanism that wards off anxiety caused by external, painful reality. "Its operation is guided by the pleasure principle and therefore contradicts the reality principle" (p. 123). She emphasizes the need to differentiate between denials and reaction formations that interfere with human relationships and those whose roots are in warded-off and unresolved unconscious conflicts and those that are part of the wish to live. However, she offers only a post hoc distinction between denial stemming from infantile dependencies and that which derives from maturation.

That denial is found not only in pathological thought is more sweepingly stated by Becker (1973) in his analysis of how the psyche copes with the idea of human mortality. According to Becker, the overriding fact of life is its transitory nature; man is preoccupied with inevitability of his demise. His major psychological resources are invested in warding off this dreaded fact, with somehow coming to terms with it. The question is not whether we deny but how we deny. For Becker, denial is not seen as a primary mechanism of defense that permeates maladaptive behavior, or from the dualistic viewpoint of Geleerd, but as the fundamental preoccupation and mechanism that enables all of us to cope with the bitter knowledge of the inescapability of death. Denial, then, according to Becker, occupies a central place in our way of dealing with grim reality and is a universally and relentlessly practiced psychological activity. These observations regarding denial by Geleerd and Becker, among others, force us to reassess the assumed alignment of normal and effective psychological functioning with veridicality of cognition.

Additional evidence on this issue comes from a quite different source. Geleerd's clinical observation that depressed patients may actually have a more realistic appraisal of the conditions of life than normals presaged a series of research findings obtained during the past decade that have been concerned with the nature of depression and its manifestations in cognition. Originally designed from the standpoint of the construct of learned helplessness to assess the way in which depressives distort reality, the research has yielded results that suggest that the opposite is true—that depressives are less likely to use cognitive biases and illusions in their assessment of events and self-appraisals. Depressed individuals, as described in a survey of the growing literature by Abramson and Alloy (1981), make relatively evenhanded assessments of positive and negative events, whereas nondepressed individuals are more likely to attribute success to themselves and to deny responsibility for negative outcomes. The nondepressed persons are the ones who are likely to distort reality in accounting for the occurrence of particular events; it is they who, from the viewpoint of attribution theory, will show a "self-serving attributional bias" (Miller & Ross, 1975). Whereas it had been predicted that depressives would exhibit a "self-derogating attributional bias" (Abramson, Seligman, & Teasdale, 1978) by denying responsibility for successes and viewing themselves as the cause of failures, Alloy (1982) indicates that the differences found between depressed and nondepressed individuals are best explained in terms of the self-serving bias of nondepressed individuals. It is the depressed individuals rather than the nondepressed subjects who show a more accurate appraisal of the cause of events. Depressives show no attributional bias, whereas nondepressed subjects give signs of "attributional egotism". Similarly, after being subjected to an experimental situation, depressed students judged accurately that they had exerted little control over the noncontingent outcome regardless of whether it was associated with winning or losing; nondepressed students overestimated their control over a noncontingent event when it was associated with success. The nondepressed students harbored an "illusion of control." Further, nondepressed psychiatric patients and normal controls rated their own social competence more positively than did objective observers, whereas depressed psychiatric patients' self-ratings were in agreement with observers' ratings (Lewinsohn, Mischel, Chaplain, & Barton, 1980). In a study of selective feedback, Nelson and Craighead (1977) found that nondepressed students underestimated the frequency of negative feedback they received, whereas depressed students did not.

Thus, the basic assumptions underlying this program of research—that nondepressed subjects are rational and accurate information processors, are more likely to engage in logical inferential thinking, and are less likely to make biased judgments about the self—were shown to be false. Instead, depressives were found to be much freer from distortion in their self-evaluations and their assessment of events. In her literature review, Alloy (1982) notes that depressed individuals' perceptions and inferences appear to be more accurate and realistic than those of the nondepressed. Alloy adds that a principal difference between those who are depressed and those who are not is that nondepressed people are motivated to maintain or protect their self-esteem, whereas depressives are not. The absence of such biases among depressed subjects is interpreted as indicating that they have experienced a breakdown either in the self-esteem protective mechanism or in the mechanism for maintaining others' approval and esteem. This leads to the conclusion that the dysfunctional aspects of depressive behavior appear to stem not from their distortion of reality but from their failure to engage in self-protective behaviors and to adopt information-processing biases. The data, then, suggest that denial and distortion of reality are adaptive patterns that are widely practiced by nonpathological subjects and that indeed, in this realm at least, pathology is associated more with accurate information processing and failure to adopt such distorting mechanisms of perception and judgment.

The aforementioned observations and findings suggest the need to revise our model of the nature of cognitive functioning. We had come to think of cognitive equipment as a camera/computer-like apparatus that has the capacity to apprehend and record reality with great fidelity according to the limits of its intrinsic capacity, a fidelity-capacity that varies according to the power and refinement of its lens system and computer. We had also grown comfortable with the idea that the efficacy and fidelity of the system is affected by the steadiness of the hand holding the camera or operating the computer, as well as by other "human factors" that induce malfunctioning, including aberrations that sometimes lead to the reversal of the image of what is rather than a mere blurring or distortion. However, it seems from the foregoing discussion that it is more useful and accurate to think in terms of a central overarching cognitive-affective system (that we might well call ego-functioning), which contains within it a camera/computer-like processing unit and memory function whose operating characteristics are more flawed and less autonomous than previously supposed. The cognitive subsystem needs to be seen as operating in the service of a larger framework that is concerned with psychological adaptation. This overarching orbit not only monitors the functional cognitive habits and skills of daily living, but also devises protective ways of presenting the self, and of warding off painful and disturbing aspects of reality. The constellation of dangers and terrors and barriers with which all of us must content are partly universal and partly determined by specific characteristics of our social-emotional and physical environments. What is noteworthy about this revised perspective is that it leads to a view of cognition not as an independent and error-free system that is intruded upon by affective factors and that must be coordinated with other systems of the psyche, but as a subsidiary unit, imperfect in functioning, which operates within a larger framework that is dominated by issues of organismic survival and adaptation.

REFERENCES

Abramson, L. Y., & Alloy, L. B. (1981). Depression, nondepression, and cognitive illusions: A reply to Schwartz. *Journal of Experimental Psychology: General, 110*, 436–447.

Abramson, L. Y., Seligman, M. E. P., & Teasdale, J. (1978). Learned helplessness in humans: Critique and reformulation. *Journal of Abnormal Psychology, 87*, 49–74.

Alloy, L. B. (1981). *Depression: On the absence of self-serving cognitive biases*. Paper presented at the Annual Meeting of the American Psychological Association, Washington, DC.

Allport, G. W. (1937). *Personality: A psychological interpretation*. New York: Holt.

Becker, E. (1973). *The denial of death*. New York: Free Press.

Flavell, J. H. (1982) . Structures, stages and sequences in cognitive development. In W. A. Collins (Ed.), *The concept of development. Minnesota Symposia on Child Development*. (Vol. 15, pp. 1–28). Hillsdale, NJ: Lawrence Erlbaum Associates.

Freud, A. (1946). *The ego and the mechanism of defence*. New York: International Universities Press. (Originally published in 1936).

Freud, A. (1981). Insight and normal development. *The psychoanalytic study of the child. Vol. 36*. New Haven: Yale University Press.

Geleerd, E. R. (1965). Two kinds of denial: Neurotic denial and denial in the service of the need to survive. In M. Schur (Ed.), *Drives, affects, behavior* (Vol. 2, pp. 118–127). New York: International Universities Press.

Gelman, R., & Baillargeon, R. (1983). A review of some Piagetian concepts. In J. H. Flavell, & E. M. Markman (Eds.), *Cognitive development* (Vol. III, pp. 169–230) of P. Mussen (Ed.), *Handbook of child psychology* (4th ed.). New York: Wiley.

Glick, J. A. (1975). Cognitive development in cross-cultural perspective. In F. D. Horowitz et al. (Eds.), *Review of child development research* (pp. 595–654). Chicago: University of Chicago Press.

Lewinsohn, P. M., Mischel, W., Chaplain, W., & Barton, R. (1980). Social competence and depression: The role of illusory self-perceptions? *Journal of Abnormal Psychology, 89,* 203–212.

Loftus, E.F. (1981). Mentalmorphosis: Alterations in memory produced by the mental bonding of new information to old. In J. Long & A. Baddeley (Eds.), *Attention and performance, IX* (pp. 417–434). Hillsdale, NJ: Lawrence Erlbaum Associates.

Loftus, E. F. & Loftus G. R. (1980). On the permanence of stored information in the human brain. *American Psychologist, 35,* 409–420.

Miller, D. T., & Ross, M. (1975). Self-serving biases in the attribution of causality: Fact or fiction? *Psychological Bulletin, 82,* 213–225.

Miller, S. A. (1976). Nonverbal assessment of Piagetian concepts. *Psychological Bulletin, 83,* 405–430.

Murphy, L. B., & Ladd, H. (1944). *Emotional factors in learning.* New York: Columbia University Press.

Neisser, U. (1976). *Cognition and reality: principles and implications of cognitive psychology.* San Francisco: Freeman.

Nelson, R. E., & Craighead, W. E. (1977). Selective recall of positive and negative feedback, self-control behaviors, and depression. *Journal of Abnormal Psychology, 86,* 379–388.

Piaget, J. (1970). *Science of education and the psychology of the child.* New York: Orion.

Rapaport, D., Gill, M. M., & Schafer, R. (1976). *Diagnostic psychological testing* (rev. ed.) (Edited by R. R. Holt) New York: International Universities Press. (Originally published 1945).

Reich, W. (1948). *Character Analysis.* New York: Farrar, Straus, & Giroux. (Originally published 1933).

Witkin, H. A., Dyk, R. B., Faterson, H. F., Goodenough, D. R., & Karp, S. A. (1962). *Psychological differentiation: Studies of development.* New York: Wiley.

Zimiles, H. (1965). *The development of differentiation and conservation of number* (U.S. Office of Education Cooperative Research Project No. 2270). New York: Bank Street College of Education.

Zimiles, H. (1966). The development of conservation and differentiation of number. *Monographs of the Society of Research in Child Development, 31* (6, Serial No. 108).

Zimiles, H., & Konstadt, N. (1962). Orthography and authority: A study of cognitive-affective interaction. *Psychological Reports, 10,* 623–626.

Zimmerman, B. J. (1983). Social learning in theory: A contextualist account of cognitive functioning. In C. J. Brainerd (Ed.), *Recent advances in cognitive-developmental theory.* (pp. 1–50). New York: Springer Verlag.

7

Putting Thoughts and Feelings into Perspective: A Developmental View on How Children Deal with Interpersonal Disequilibrium.

Robert L. Selman
Harvard University

Amy P. Demorest
Duke University

INTRODUCTION

The focus of this chapter is on the joint roles of emotional and cognitive functioning in the child's social development. In particular it deals with the development of the child's ways of coping with the experience of disequilibrium generated by situations of interpersonal conflict with peers. We suggest that in interpersonal situations, disequilibrium may be experienced both internally and interpersonally in feeling and cognition. We also suggest that developmental maturity involves the ability to differentiate and coordinate the disequilibrium in feeling and cognition, both within the self and between the self and the other.

Starting with a case example of the two children involved in a stressful social interaction, we consider issues and alternative views for studying how children growing up deal with emotion and cognition in interpersonal conduct. Then we provide a brief synopsis of the kind of theoretical and empirical analysis our own research group has adopted to look at the development of the interaction between emotional and cognitive components in conduct in one type of social interaction situation. This involves the use of strategies to deal with situations of interpersonal disequilibrium. Based on our earlier analysis of levels in the child's understanding of the coordination of social perspectives, as well as formal and informal observation of troubled and normal children and adults, we propose a way to classify interpersonal negotiation strategies simultaneously according to both hierarchical levels and interpersonal orientation.

Our first thesis is that in order to understand the developmental meaning of a particular negotiation strategy, (or a sequence of strategies) we must attend to the developmental quality of the cognitive, emotional, and motivational components that make up a strategy. Specifically, we identify these components as the way self and other are construed (the cognitive component), the way emotional disequilibrium is perceived and controlled (the emotional component), and the primary purpose being pursued (the motivational component); we identify their change with development as involving increasing differentiation and coordination. Our second thesis is that at each level action may be oriented toward changing the self or changing other; with development these initially polar orientations also become integrated. We illustrate this *two-factor* developmental model with vignettes and analyses of strategies from each orientation and developmental level. Finally, we consider the implications of the model for the further study of emotional and cognitive development, and for broader developmental issues raised in studying the role of cognition, emotion, and motivation in social conduct.

While reading this chapter the reader may note that there is a paucity of theoretical and empirical references. We do not mean to deny the significant influence of past psychological theories on the model presented, nor to deny the value and necessity of empirical approaches to the problem at hand. Our work arises out of a context built by many past theoretical frameworks. Theoretical perspectives such as those of Bateson (1979), Habermas (1975), Hinde (1976), Kohlberg (1981), Loevinger (1976), Mead (1934), Piaget (1970, 1981) and particularly Werner (1948, 1957) have provided formulations critical to the nature of the model to be proposed. Likewise it has arisen from and been subjected to empirical method (Selman & Demorest, 1984; Selman, Schorin, Stone, & Phelps, 1983).

However, this chapter is intended more as a descriptive piece on our curent thinking and on the clinical element of our approach to the issues here considered. Here we use the term *clinical* to convey a focus on methods of case study and naturalistic observation of children dealing with difficult social interactions. In this phase of our enterprise, our goal is the analytic dissection of "scripts" of social action. It is an "inside job," trying to describe the nature of the elements that together made up a social phenomenon: an interpersonal negotiation strategy. The chapter focuses on an hermeneutic description of the inner clockwork of the model, the workings of thought and emotion in conduct. It leaves as a separate task, for another chapter, the hypothetico-deductive or explanatory study of factors that may cause certain strategies to be implemented, or the correlates between strategy use and other aspects of the individual's personality or social context.

DEALING WITH FEELINGS: A CASE EXAMPLE OF THE INTERACTION OF EMOTIONAL AND COGNITIVE ASPECTS OF SOCIAL BEHAVIOR

The setting is a school yard during recess period. Eight children ranging in age from 8 to 10 are playing kickball under the guidance of a well-seasoned physical education teacher. There are two teams, each comprised of four players: a pitcher and three infielders, roughly approximating the positions of first, second, and third base. Some of the children are well-coordinated; some clumsy. Being second to fourth graders, all of them have a pretty good working understanding of the specific rules of the game. They vary more widely, however, in their working sense of the strategic aspects that are involved in the game. For instance, some understand better than others that it is wise to be cautious when running from second to third base with only one out, particularly if the ball is popped up in the air. If it is caught, there is some chance that you may get "doubled up," (i.e. the ball may be thrown to the base of departure by the fielder who caught it before you can get back, and therefore, you are out). Of course, at this age (if not at all ages), it often is the case that even knowing both the rules and the strategies does not provide the control necessary to help some people manage their impulse to "run on the pitch."

Essentially, this is the situation as we report the following incident. The score is tied 2 to 2, with a runner on second and only one out. The ball is rolled toward the kicker and kicked sharply on a linedrive to the third baseman, a boy not known for his athletic prowess or physical agility. The third baseman catches it on the fly, his eyes wide with astonishment. Meanwhile, at the time of the kick, the runner on second has charged off for third base with a rush of adrenalin and excitement. At this point, the second baseman appears to be beside himself, (itself an interesting conception), for he realizes his opportunity to be an important part of the first double play ever implemented in this school yard. He calls frantically for the third baseman to throw him the ball in order to make the double play. Momentarily dazzled by his own skill on making the initial catch, the third baseman registers the second baseman's frantic call at about the same time as does the runner, respectively each reacts to the call. The runner turns to scamper back to second and the third baseman, in his haste to heed the call of his teammate, throws the ball both somewhat errantly, and perhaps a bit too hard, toward second. Rather than being caught by him, the ball catches the second baseman on the side of the head. The ball bounces aimlessly toward the batter's box, and the runner returns safely to second, eliminating the chance to complete this seminal double play. The second baseman's eyes darken, and with a reddening face and an increasingly angry tone, he begins to heap abuse and accusation on the third baseman. "What's wrong with you, you jerk? Don't you know how to play? Why did you throw that ball at my head? Are you trying to kill me?" Instead of returning the abuse and violence to the second baseman in equal or escalated share, or clarifying his actions to justify himself, the third baseman appears to absorb the tirade. Turning to the adult and shrugging his shoulders somewhat plaintively, he responds with a somewhat dejected and despondent, almost self-blaming expression, "I didn't mean it. Sorry."

This brief incident serves to raise a number of critical issues with respect to viewing emotional and cognitive aspects of behavior from a developmental framework. For example, let us look at the third baseman's behavior on catching the fly kick. His eyes are widened in astonishment at his uncharacteristic success. Somewhat stunned, he appears to be unable initially to decenter from a focus on this event and to hear the second baseman's call, to see the whole field and the runner dashing back to second, to anticipate the consequences of this action and his own inaction. Yet how literally should this be taken? Does he actually not hear the call or see the field? If in some respects the auditory and visual input is not being registered, what is causing this to happen? Should we take the view that his emotional arousal is blocking his perception? And once the third baseman throws the ball, he does so wildly. Is the arousal now interfering with his physical competence—his ability to judge distance and to control his arm's throw with a certain speed and direction?

These questions raise consideration of the role of emotional arousal in the implementation of cognitive and physical abilities in social action. When we say in an every day vernacular that the third baseman "lost it," we probably picture a kind of separate emotional force that is aroused and prevents the individual from performing up to his cognitive and physical abilities. Emotions viewed in this way, as separate from cognition and from behavior, are seen as playing the role of *interference factors*.

An alternative way of thinking about the emotional and cognitive aspects of behavior is to consider emotional and cognitive functioning in the self to be interrelated components of any behavior. For example, there is cognitive perceiving and interpreting involved in the course of experiencing emotions: The third baseman felt emotionally aroused, in part because he viewed the act of catching the ball as an unusual and wonderful success. The feelings about an event will influence the cognitive interpretation of it: The second basemen interpreted the other's intent to be to kill him with the ball in part because he felt very frustrated. With this view of emotion and cognition as interrelated aspects of conduct, we look at the role of cognition and emotion in situations such as that above as involving inner and interpersonal disequilibrium in a context of social interaction. Inner and interpersonal disequilibrium is experienced both emotionally and cognitively. The task for the individual is to deal with this disequilibrium in conduct; socially mature conduct can be seen to involve putting emotions and cognitions in perspective.

Let us look at the second baseman's behavior to explore the nature of this task of putting disequilibrated cognitions and emotions into perspective. After being hit by the ball, and unable to complete the double play, the second baseman yells angrily at his teammate and accuses him of being more interested in decapitating him than in completing the double play. Does he really think the third baseman meant to throw the ball to hurt him? Is he not able to detect that the third baseman, in the panic and impulsivity of the moment, unintentionally threw the ball too hard? We raise the question here whether his construal of the other's intent resulted from a specific misperception in this context, or from a general lack of understanding capacity for discriminating intent. These are two very different errors, the first being inaccurate attribution but an adequate understanding of the distinction between intentional and unintentional acts; the second being a lack of comprehension of this distinction. Thus, whereas the second error results from a limited capacity in understanding, the first involves an unsuccessful implementation of this understanding capacity in the actual world of social conduct. We propose that in his cognitive construal of the moment, the second baseman does not accurately discriminate and coordinate the influence of the third baseman's motives, emotions, and perceptions on his action of hurling the ball.

Further, we propose that the second baseman has some difficulty, in this situation, differentiating and coordinating the various emotions within himself, as well as between his feelings and those of the third baseman. We suspect that he confuses his psychological feelings of disappointment and frustration (at not completing the play successfully) and his physical feelings of pain and irritation (at being physically hurt by the ball). Further, his angry verbal attack on the third baseman may well be a deflection of his negative feelings about himself (disappointment with himself at not completing the play) toward another (anger directed at the third baseman); in this way he does not have to own bad feelings toward himself but only toward another. We also propose that, in accusing the third baseman of trying to take off his head, the second baseman may be projecting or externalizing his own feelings of anger onto the third baseman, attributing to the other feelings of anger that he himself experiences internally. Therefore, we find that the second baseman is neither differentiating clearly among the various feelings going on within himself nor differentiating the feelings that are his own from those that are another's. The tasks to be handled for mature social conduct in this case are to differentiate accurately and coordinate the feelings within the self and between self and other, and to act with this perspective on the feelings.

It is likely that this boy, at 10 years of age, has the capacity to discriminate intentional from unintentional acts; and he likely has the capacity to distinguish among various types of feelings (e.g. disappointment vs. frustration), and feelings owned by one individual as distinct from another. However, the issue here is that when he is involved in a situation of inner and interpersonal disequilibrium, he does not demonstrate a use of these cognitive and emotional perspective-coordination capacities in his conduct of the moment.

There are many factors that may have caused this situation to be particularly disequilibrating for him, preventing him from acting up to his optimal capacity level. For instance, considering interpersonal dynamics, it could be that past relationships with significant people in his life have "created a chip on his shoulder," such that he is especially sensitive to situations of potential attack or mistreatment by others. Or perhaps he is particularly sensitive to situations where a group of peers is focused on and potentially judgmental of him; or he may simply be in a bad mood that day.

The point is that, in actual conduct, there are many factors besides optimal capacity that can influence the way an actor thinks, feels, and carries out his purpose in a strategic or expressive interpersonal action. We may look at acts taken under conditions of high disequilibrium as more vulnerable to inadequate perception and dealing with the construal, purposes, and feelings of self and other. Thus, when an individual deals immaturely in such situations, we may say that he has lost perspective or could not deal with his feelings. Functionally, these statements may be equivalent. We do not see emotions as interfering with cognition. Rather, we look upon interpersonal situations as involving disequilibrium that is experienced and dealt with both emotionally and cognitively. When there is great arousal of affective disequilibrium there will likewise probably be arousal of cognitive disequilibrium; such arousal can lead either to regression or to progress in conduct, as in the case of an individual who is more able to problem solve when aroused by anxiety.

There are other issues that we might consider from this example regarding the relations of emotional and cognitive aspects of behavior. For example, where do we locate the emotional and cognitive aspects of behavior: Are they in the person, the interaction, or both? Gaining a sense of perspective in an interpersonal interaction may not simply be a sense of knowing what is going on in the self or, alternatively, knowing what is going on in the other, but instead may be a truly interpersonal activity, at least at more advanced developmental levels. With modest exceptions, developmental psychologists, with their primary interest in ontogeny, have not tended to look beyond the individual to examine the locus of affective and cognitive processes. Feelings strike us as being very interactive, perhaps even transactive, phenomena. They may travel easily from one to another person and then back again. Others have to deal with our feelings. This generates feelings in others that we, in turn, have to deal with. For instance, the third baseman has to deal with the second baseman's anger as well as his own feelings. Although the experience of emotional and cognitive disequilibrium may be internal, the cause and nature of this disequilibrium likely is interpersonal.

Another issue raised by the preceding example is the extent to which inadequate dealing can be seen to result from insufficiencies in cognitive or emotional capacities versus the implementation of these capacities. Who is the prime villain (or scapegoat) in the second baseman's losing perspective cognitively? Is it inadequate conceptual understanding or poor perception? Or is it that the existing higher level conceptual-emotional structures are not well enough established to overcome the naturally occurring regressive, stress-related pulls toward distortion and misperception?

This introductory example and analysis is meant to raise a number of issues relevant to the study of emotion and cognition in conduct. In particular, it is used to suggest that one useful way of looking at the developmental relation between interpersonally generated feelings and cognitions is to consider these elements as differential components of a common process that can be directly observed: social interaction. In the following pages we describe our study of one type of social interaction, interpersonal negotiation, through which we have begun to look at how emotional and cognitive aspects of behavior interact developmentally. Our work has resulted in a preliminary model for understanding how, as they grow older, children develop a repertoire of strategies to deal with disequilibrium both within the self and between the self and others involved in interpersonal negotiation.

A DEVELOPMENTAL MODEL OF
INTERPERSONAL NEGOTIATION STRATEGIES:
AN ORTHOGENETIC APPROACH

We have pointed to the utility of the distinction between the *capacity* to coordinate perspectives of thought or emotion (competence), and the *use* of perspective coordination in actual conduct (performance). In the past, structural-developmental social-cognitive theorists, orienting to Piaget (1970), have predominantly examined the ontogenetic development of particular social-cognitive capacities of the growing child. However, as one turns from the study of social-cognitive competence to the study of actual social conduct, the ontogenetic model appears insufficient, for it focuses on the acquisition of levels of understanding which, once attained, are not easy prey to regressive forces. The developmental study of interpersonal conduct needs to allow the influence of external or internal factors of the moment on the level of conduct exhibited. What is needed is a way to study the developmental nature of social conduct, not primarily in terms of acquired epistemological growth with age, but in terms of changes in organizational structure. For this we feel it useful to turn to the orthogenetic approach outlined by Werner (1948, 1957).

Werner's model of organization provides a way by which developmental aspects of structural reorganization may be used as a core for the analysis of various associated phenomena. As defined by Werner, orthogenesis is a principle whereby development proceeds from a state of relative globality and lack of differentiation to a state of differentiation and hierarchic integration. Thus the orthogenetic approach provides for a developmental or hierarchical analysis of a number of different organismic processes that hold some potential telos or forward direction. This includes what might be called longitudinal processes such as the ontogenetic acquisition of social understanding over time, but also includes the analyses of processes such as pathogenesis, comparing the degree to which types of mental disorders are pathological within or across individuals, or of microgenesis, the degree to which instances of mental functioning are developmentally advanced in one individual from moment to moment. Our study of interpersonal negotiations in conduct can be seen to include the analysis of each of these types of developmental processes. The initial acquisition of new types of negotiation strategies occurs ontogenetically, whereas the use of strategies, once acquired, is comparable by means of other orthogenetic analyses.

The core for our application of the orthogenetic approach to the study of interpersonal conduct is this view of interpersonal development as involving increasing differentiation and integration. As this is applied in the social realm, we use as our basis for analysis the theoretical tool of developing levels in the ability to coordinate social perspectives (Selman, 1980). In our past work we have studied the ontogenetic development of the capacity for social understanding in terms of the ability to differentiate and coordinate the perspectives of self and others. We feel that this developmental model can be seen not only as articulating developmental forms of understanding but also as a structural framework with direct implications for the way other kinds of social functions are organized. Specifically, we feel it can be used to organize the developmental analysis of interpersonal negotiation strategies.

The developmental model of social perspective coordination posits that the extent to which a child understands the coordination of multiple social perspectives, both within the self and between self and others, reflects an underlying structure of social thought identifiable as one of a hierarchical sequence of levels. Each level is a uniquely shaped conceptual lens through which the child views and understands the self in relation to the social world. With respect to the interpersonal component of perspective-coordination, according to this model, during the toddler and early preschool years the child's interpersonal understanding is at an initial level where, reflectively, there is no clear differentiation between the social perspective of self and others (level 0). At subsequent levels of understanding, the child comprehends that another person's subjective thoughts, feelings, and intentions are distinct from the self's (early childhood: level 1); that the other person can reflect upon and consider as distinct the self's subjective attitudes, feelings, and motives (middle childhood: level 2); that self and other can view self's and other's psychological points of view mutually and simultaneously (early adolescence; level 3); and that there is a general integrated social viewpoint that transcends individual perspective and involves a mutual understanding of deeper psychic processes within and between persons (later adolescence and adulthood: level 4).

In the following discussion we lay out a developmental model of interpersonal negotiation strategies, and illustrate its relation to these social perspective coordination levels. We confine our focus to strategies at levels 0 through 3, and leave a complete analysis, which would include strategies related to level 4, to some future discussion. Most of our empirical work, formal and informal, has been with children and early adolescents. We are most familiar with data and observation of individuals in this age range and have only clinical or anecdotal evidence for strategies used by older individuals at the uppermost level in our current sequence.

As we define interpersonal negotiation strategies, they are the methods for dealing with both self and other to pursue goals in an interpersonal context. We identify two conditions that define a situation in which an interpersonal negotiation strategy can occur. First, it occurs in a context where at least one person in the interaction is in an initial state of disequilibrium with respect to a self-perceived goal. This disequilibrium may be felt because the individual has a wish that may not be satisfied by the other, or it may be because the individual is reluctant to meet the other's wishes. This can be called the condition of *internal disequilibrium*.

Second, an interpersonal negotiation occurs in a context in which the attempt of one or both individuals to return to a state of inner balance has an impact on the other, whether or not the individual(s) involved perceive or acknowledge this effect. Thus at issue is not only inner disequilibrium but also *interpersonal disequilibrium*. From the observer's perspective, the psychological impact of the interpersonal negotiation for each individual involved has a reverberatory effect between parties.

Interpersonal negotiation strategies represent the ways that individuals deal in conduct with this inner and interpersonal disequilibrium in their attempt to return to a balanced state. We identify two aspects of negotiation strategies, one involving their developmental level, and one involving interpersonal orientation. We adopt the framework of levels in the coordination of social perspectives in order to describe the developmental aspect of negotiation strategies. The coordination of perspectives appears to be useful to the process of dealing with disequilibrium, inner as well as interpersonal.

The three components of the developmental aspect of interpersonal negotiation strategies are the construal of self and other, the perception and control of emotional disequilibrium, and the primary interpersonal purpose. The *self-other construal* component involves the conception of self and other that operates at the moment in the particular interactive context. Development in this component moves from the lowest level where self and other are construed as non-psychological objects, with inadequate differentiation between self and other, and between persons and their actions, to an increasing appreciation and valuation of the thoughts, feelings, and wishes of both self and other at higher levels. For example, if a child impulsively grabs a ball away from his peer because he wants to be pitcher, he is most likely acting with a construal of the other as merely a physical challenge to his wants, his acts, and himself (a low level construal). If, on the other hand, attempts to persuade the other to let him pitch by offering to let her play with his new computer game in return, his strategy most likely represents a construal of the other as having distinct wants that can be manipulated to be in line with the self's wants (a somewhat higher level construal, psychologically speaking).

The emotional component of a negotiation strategy involves the way the individual perceives and controls emotional disequilibrium arising in an interpersonal context. The development of this component results in increasing differentiation and integration in both the perception and control of feelings. At the lowest developmental level, emotional disequilibrium is experienced as diffuse, all-encompassing, and uncontrollable. At higher levels of development, specific feelings within self and between self and other are differentiated in perception, and the self's inner disequilibrium is controlled by putting these various feelings into the perspective of a larger social context. For example, at a low developmental level a child may impulsively drop the kickball and run away when another requests it from her, overwhelmed by the unreflective distress of confused conflicting wants. At a higher level she may differentiate between her feelings of wanting the ball for herself at the moment and her more long-term wish to get along with this peer, choose to prioritize the long-term goal above the immediate, and offer to let the other pitch if she can pitch the next time they play.

The primary interpersonal purpose component of a strategy is the dominant conscious motivation of the behavior. At the lowest developmental level the strategy's purpose is the simple and direct pursuit of solely the self's own immediate wants; usually these are construed in physical terms. Moving to the higher levels, the purpose of both self and other becomes discriminated and coordinated with increasing valuations of each, such that at the higher levels the purpose involves a differentiated focus on the relational process of the interaction toward pursuit of mutually satisfying needs. For example, the purpose of a low level strategy would be to physically hold and pitch the ball, whereas at a higher level the primary purpose would be to change the other's wishes to be in line with self's in pursuit of a general activity, such as pitching in the game.

Working in relation to the developmental factor is the action-orientation factor. The interpersonal orientation factor refers to upon whom the actor predominantly acts in his attempts to deal with disequilibrium between self and other. In the other-transforming mode the individual primarily attempts to change the thoughts, feelings, and act of the other; whereas in the self-transforming mode he predominantly works on changing his own thoughts, feelings, or acts. For example, if two children each want to pitch a game, the one who grabs the ball or tries to persuade the other to give it to him is acting in either case in an other-transforming orientation. A child who obediently yields the ball, or spontaneously offers to give the ball to the other, is acting in each instance in a self-transforming mode. At higher developmental levels of interpersonal negotiation, the individual's actions are increasingly integrated between the two orientations, both distinguishing and giving more credit to the thoughts, feelings, and acts of both self and other. Therefore, development in interpersonal negotiation strategies incorporates movement from rigid, isolated use of one or the other orientation at lower levels to a differentiated and integrated interplay between orientations at higher levels.

Our working hypothesis is that both developmental and interpersonal-orientation factors need to be considered simultaneously in the assessment of a strategy. A detailed description of each component at levels of 0 to 3 is provided in Table 7.1. The three components of the developmental factor—self-other construal, perception and control of emotional disequilibrium, and primary purpose—work together to determine a strategy's developmental level (0-3), whereas the interpersonal orientation factor identifies a strategy's orientation (self-transforming or other-transforming). Thus the model allows for consideration of observed behavior along both developmental and personality-like social action dimensions, and it stresses that development occurs in two ways: both upward in terms of level and integratively in terms of orientation.

Figure 7.1 depicts these types of development in strategies for interpersonal negotiation. Movement occurs from the use of unreflective, impulsive strategies to pursue material and self-focused goals at one or another distinct orientation; to the use of self- and shared-reflection to pursue mutual or relational goals with a balance between changing self and other. This figure also illustrates the way

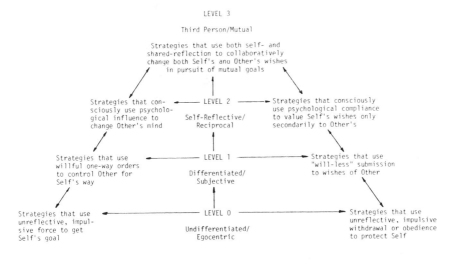

FIG. 7.1

Table 7.1

Overview of Developmental Levels and Orientations in Interpersonal Negotiation Strategies

	Level 0. *Negotiation for Concrete* *Goals by Unreflective,* *Impulsive, Physical Force or* *Flight*	*Level 1.* *Negotiation for Control by* *One-Way "Will"—Driven* *Implicit Power*	*Level 2.* *Negotiation for Influence by* *Conscious Psychological* *Persuasion*	*Level 3.* *Negotiation for Collaborative,* *Mutually Satisfactory Ends by* *Reflective Communication of* *Feelings*
Developmental Components				
Construal of *Self and Other*	Each (self and other) is viewed as a non-psychological object, a means to, or barrier to, the goal-impulses of self or other. Feelings, wishes, goal-impulses of self and other are not recognized as distinct from goals or from the actions toward these goals. Further, the wishes of self (if self-transforming) or other (if other-transforming) are not *valued* in their own right in negotiation.	Each (self and other) is accorded the capacity for independent will, where will is the capacity to recognize and regulate impulses, affects, needs, etc.; i.e., the capacity to separate actions from impulse without outside help. Interpersonally, one will is expected to obey, at its own expense, the wishes of the other will. Negotiations are thus viewed as confrontations where one wins and one loses. The individual feelings, wishes, etc. of self and other are differentiated, but no value is given to the feelings or wishes of the "loser" or "less powerful" negotiator, only to those of the "winner."	Each (self and other) is regarded as capable of action based on reflection on and choice among multiple impulses. The possibility of one actor's changing another's mind, wishes, and will through discourse is recognized. The feelings and wishes of both self and other are recognized to exist independently, but those of one individual are accorded value only to the extent that they can be aligned with those of the other.	Each (self and other) is seen as introspective, i.e., can reflect on self as actor and subjective object, and is recognized to have a capacity to reflect simultaneously on the self, the other, and the mutuality of effect in the dyad. Each is seen as separate yet related, capable of mutuality and commitment. The feelings, wishes, needs of both self and other are respected in their own right and as they are interrelated.

The self's emotional state is experienced as diffuse and undifferentiated in nature. Feelings of the moment are experienced as all-encompassing; there is no discernible awareness of or reflection on feelings as distinct entities, nor is there integration of immediate feelings into a broader context of feelings existing over time. The experience of inner disequilibrium is directly expressed in impulsive action. There is no conscious attempt to control disequilibrium through planned action. Feelings appear to control (propel) the self, rather than the self, as the agent of actions, dealing with the feelings.

The self's own emotional state is recognized as distinct from action taken in its service. However, it is perceived as an objective reality ("I have this feeling because I don't have that toy and I will have it until I get the toy") rather than a subject reaction ("I *could* feel better by forgetting the toy and doing something else"). Although emotional disequilibrium is perceived to be transitory and time limited, feelings of the moment are not integrated within a longer-term context. Although emotional disequilibrium is now seen as separate from the actions it affects, the cause of disequilibrium is still seen to rest in events and actions external to and acting on the self. Thus, inner disequilibrium is confused with interpersonal disequilibrium, and equilibrium is sought only by taking action on events external to the emotional state rather than by acting directly on the feelings, as well.

Different or conflicting concerns are recognized to occur within the self in a given context, and inner disequilibrium is seen to result at times from the conflict between the self's personal and interpersonal needs. Yet the self's interpersonal concern is also seen as possibly caused by a conflict with the wishes of other. Disequilibrium is now dealt with directly by self's actions on feeling, rather than only on actions or events. Interpersonally, this is accomplished by (unilaterally) arranging and ordering (prioritizing) the feelings of self and other. Internally, this is achieved by using will to control the conflicting feelings, such as by pushing one of them "out of mind." This is done with immediacy rather than as a slow and progressive "working through" of feelings.

Inner disequilibrium is seen to result from conflicting feelings within the self that arise out of either different internal concerns and levels of concern, or differences between self and other. Immediate feelings arising in the present context are distinguished from, and understood in relation to, a more stable underlying field of feelings related to the self-in-general. Thus, the self deals with inner disequilibrium by acting, through reflection, to integrate the perception of present feelings into the larger context of the self's affective structure, for example, by realizing that the self is over-reacting to a criticism because of a general sensitivity to a particular issue. Interpersonal disequilibrium is dealt with by communication (*shared reflection*) with others involved in the self's affective arousal. Current feelings of disequilibrium are slowly and reciprocally integrated into a larger internal and interpersonal context by this process of internal and interpersonal reflection.

Table 7.1 (*continued*)

Overview of Developmental Levels and Orientations in Interpersonal Negotiation Strategies

	Level 0. *Negotiation for Concrete* *Goals by Unreflective,* *Impulsive, Physical Force or* *Flight*	*Level 1.* *Negotiation for Control by* *One-Way "Will"—Driven* *Implicit Power*	*Level 2.* *Negotiation for Influence by* *Conscious Psychological* *Persuasion*	*Level 3.* *Negotiation for Collaborative,* *Mutually Satisfactory Ends by* *Reflective Communication of* *Feelings*
Developmental Components				
Primary *Interpersonal Purposes*	The individual is motivated *solely* towards the one person's immediate "goods-oriented" goals, without reflection on the goals themselves; how they relate to the actions taken in their pursuit, how these actions will have future effect on self, other, or the relationship, nor how these goals relate to the other's goals and wishes. There is no conscious consideration of purpose—self's or other's—in the negotiations.	The primary purpose is to establish one person's goals at the expense of, and distinct from, the other's; fulfillment of wishes is seen as an either-or-issue. Intent is to establish the locus of self in a stronger-weaker relation. Other's intent is likewise read to be the establishment of control. Establishing control is usually expressed in the form of who has the power to divide short-term goods, physical or personal., i.e., who makes the choice of decision.	One person's "good-oriented" goals are acquired by making use of, influencing, or playing up to the thoughts and wishes of the other. Goals do not need immediate expression, as individuals can postpone goal attainment in bargaining with the other. The process of reciprocity is recognized, but it is the outcome for the one person whose goal is pursued that is of primary importance, rather than the outcome for both or the process of reciprocity itself.	The individual is motivated toward a communicative process and an end that is mutually satisfactory to self and other. The mutuality of the outcome and the communication in its pursuit are at least as important as the particular outcome (initial goal) itself. The primary intent is to establish open paths for building mutual understanding and satisfaction and caring in the long-term relationship.

Interpersonal Orientation in Interaction

Other-transforming mode	Individual is entirely demanding of other regarding self's needs, or rejecting of other's needs. Other is transformed as if a tool to meet the self's ends.	Individual is commanding/bullying over other, using threat of force to change other for the sake of attaining the self's ends.	Individual uses influential/persuasive actions to change other's wishes or views, so that they match with, and thus allow, the self's wishes.	Individual uses both self- and other-transforming modes in mutual and simultaneous balance or is able to alternate in their use as the context calls for. Individual is explicitly self-reflective, communicative, and sharing in working to accommodate and find accommodation from the other in pursuing a communicative process and mutually satisfactory end.
Self-transforming mode	Individual totally discounts self's needs and is unreflectively obedient to wishes of other, or unreflectively withdraws the self totally from the field of interaction, when confronted with wishes of other.	Individual is submissive to other or reflectively withdraws self's will from the field of conflict to meet the needs of other or self.	Individual uses compliant actions to meet other's wishes and allows the self to be convinced to change its views and feelings to meet with those of other.	

the developmental levels in social perspective coordination are logically related to levels of development in interpersonal negotiation. Negotiation (a form of conduct) and perspective coordination (a form of understanding) both involve increasing differentiation and integration. The directions of the vertical arrows are meant to signify the distinction between social-cognitive and social-behavioral development. In the ontogenetic capacity for coordination of social perspectives, movement is only unidirectional, toward higher levels. We see the initial development of the capacity to use strategies at different levels to be parallel to and logically, but not temporally or causally, based on this social perspective coordination capacity, occurring only from lower to higher levels. However, once the capacity for their use is in the individual's repertoire, strategies are variable and subject to various forms of regression as well as progression.

Theoretically, the use of any strategy at a given developmental level *logically* requires that the child have achieved the corresponding level of social conceptual competence (of social perspective coordination) that underlies the strategy. However, in actual temporal development action at a particular level may indeed precede understanding at that level; most likely the relation is reciprocal. Further, regarding orientation there is no structural requirement that a child use strategies of both orientations, use one before the other, or employ a prescribed range of strategies of either orientation within a given level.

The three components that determine a strategy's developmental level (cognitive, emotional, and motivational) play an important role in distinguishing strategies that on the surface may appear morphologically similar yet that may reflect different underlying developmental levels. For example, consider a child who wants a toy that a peer is using; when the peer refuses to let her use it, the child exits the room saying "I'm leaving." This gross behavior and correspondent verbal statement can mean different things and can be assigned to different developmental levels in this system depending on the child's construal, perception and control of disequilibrium, and primary purpose. The strategy may represent a thoughtless, impulsive and frantic bolt from the room with the only purpose being to physically avoid the disturbing interpersonal context (level 0). On the other hand, it may reflect a self-other conscious, controlled and manipulative attempt to influence the peer to feel badly so she will let her use the toy (level 2).

The orientation factor identifies that strategies may appear quite different because of their different interpersonal action-orientations, yet be at the same developmental level of organization. This is the case with the following two strategies: pushing a peer away from a water fountain when the self wants a drink, or immediately backing away oneself when another wants a drink. Both are level 0 strategies, if they are both undertaken without regard to other's or self's wishes (the construal component), with unreflective impulsivity (the perception and control of disequilibrium component), and with immediate purpose only to get or give up physical possession (the primary purpose component).

ANALYSIS OF CASE STRATEGIES

In Table 7.2 a sampling of some prototypical self- and other-transforming strategies at each of levels 0-3 and in each orientation are provided. In the following pages, we present analyses of the first strategies in this table for each level and orientation to illustrate how each of the component factors operates in conduct. A description of the strategy in the course of interpersonal interaction is given, with the name italicized of the child whose strategy is being studied. We then analyze the three developmental components of the strategy and discuss why the strategy fits at this level as distinct from the level preceding or following. The interpersonal orientation factor also is elaborated with reference to how it would differ if the strategy involved the other orientation or another level of integration. This section is an attempt to concretize the formal model of Table 7.1 and to breathe life into the abstract definition of components.

Examples are chosen from age-typical groups, i.e., children who are acting with age-appropriate strategies, strategies that typically are newly constructed and implemented during that age period. Because the function of these examples is to make the formal characteristics of strategies at varying levels of development

Table 7.2
Some Prototypical Interpersonal Strategies Coded at Developmental
Levels 0–3 in Each Orientation

Other-Transforming Orientation	*Self-Transforming Orientation*
Level 0	
A. Forcefully blots out other's expressed wish	A. Takes impulsive flight
B. Unprovoked impulsive grabbing	B. Uses automatic affective withdrawal
C. Absolute repulsion of other	C. Responds with robot-like obedience
Level 1	
A. Uses one-way threats to achieve self's goals	A. Makes weak initiatives with ready withdrawal
B. Makes threats of force	B. Acts victimized
C. Criticizes other's skill as a rationale for self's activity	C. Appeals to source of perceived power from a position of helplessness
Level 2	
A. Uses "friendly" persuasion.	A. Asserts self's feelings and thoughts as valuable but secondary.
B. Seeks allies for support of self's ideas	B. Follows but offers input into other's lead
C. Goal-seeking through impressing others with self's talents, knowledge, etc.	C. Uses self's feelings of inadequacies as a tool for interpersonal negotiation
Level 3	
A. Anticipates and integrates possible feelings of others about self's negotiation	
B. Balances focus on relations with focus on self's concrete goal	

and orientations more meaningful through the introduction of content, the description of the interactions is relatively circumscribed and de-contexualized. For instance, although the stream of real life interactions involves sequences of strategies, perhaps at varying levels and orientations, the following examples are limited to an analysis of one strategy used by one individual. Furthermore, the examples do not give information of the short- and long-term history of the interpersonal relationship between the parties involved, nor of each individual's interpersonal functioning with other partners in other contexts.

The purpose of the following presentation of observed examples is to demonstrate how a particular means of interpersonal negotiation corresponds to a particular level of self-other construal, perception and control of disequilibrium, primary interpersonal purpose, and to a particular action-orientation. However, if the major objective was instead to score most accurately a given strategy under examination, then the information provided in these examples would be insufficient. This would require richer data, such as information on the relational context, the immediate negotiation context of which the particular strategy is a part, and cues toward purpose and feeling such as facial expression, tone of voice, speed of movement, etc. Such data would help minimize the inferential activity that necessarily enters into a developmental coding process which hopes to account for construal, feeling, and purpose. In the following examples, however, we simply provide the information that is necessary to illustrate the developmental and orientational aspects of the strategy.

Level 0: Other-Transforming Orientation Protypical Strategy: Forcefully Blots Out Other's Expressed Wish

This kind of strategy reflects pursuit of the self's goal by direct sensory drowning out the expression of the other's conflicting wishes. "What I don't know (perceive) won't hurt me" is taken literally, so that if the other person's wishes cannot be heard or seen, then, for all intents and purposes, they do not exist.

Specific Example

Carol, age 6, and Alice, age 5, are playing at Carol's house with a record player. Carol wants to play a song, Old MacDonald, but Alice wants to hear a different song. As Alice starts to say why she should have her turn to choose, Carol yells, "Quiet!" Alice puts her hands on her hips and starts once more to argue for her choice, but *Carol* yells more loudly and frantically. "Shut up!" As Alice tries to continue speaking, Carol's volume escalates and she screams repeatedly, "Shut up! Shut up! *Shut up!*" until finally she stands, red faced, yelling into Alice's face, drowning out Alice's words. As she does this she puts on her record and begins to listen to it, without apparent concern for Alice, as if the issue were settled.

Analysis

Characteristic of level 0 stategies in general, Carol's conduct acts to completely cut off the possibility of further negotiations. She screams loudly, using vocal force to blot out the expression of Alice's wishes, prohibiting Alice from communicating her claim as if this would be equivalent to Alice having no claim. To the extent that Alice's wishes conflict with her own, Carol appears to construe Alice and Alice's wishes as one and indistinct, and as a barrier to her own wishes. Emotionally Carol appeared to be overwhelmed by distress from facing conflicting wants that she cannot differentiate; this distress is directly and impulsively expressed in action. Her act demonstrates an immediate pursuit of her own goal, without any reflective consideration of her own or Alice's purposes or of the effect of her goal-pursuit on herself, Alice, or their relationship. This strategy is other-transforming because it seeks to change the other: to remove Alice and her conflicting wishes by silencing them.

This "out of sight-out of mind" type of strategy can be distinguished from a similar-appearing level 1 strategy in which the child attempts to "shout down" another in a competitive way. In that case the shouting has a combative purpose and reflects an awareness of the distinctness of that other's needs, and thus a wish to overcome them. In distinction, the screams in the present example appear to be a kind of physical expression where the self's needs are asserted and the other's needs are just denied and therefore are not actually competed with.

Level 0: Self-Transforming Orientation
Prototypical Strategy: Takes Impulse Flight

With this strategy the child reacts to the disequilibrium of conflicting wants by taking impulsive, uncontrolled flight away from the field of interaction. By leaving the conflict behind, it no longer exists.

Specific Example

Four-year-old Mike is playing with a playmate Terry, from down the street. Mike says, "Terry, let's play hockey." Terry says, "No, let's play soccer" and begins to kick the soccer ball. *Mike* impulsively grabs his hockey stick and runs out of the yard. He does not look for Terry to follow; in fact he does not seem aware of Terry at all once he starts to leave.

Analysis

In this example, Mike demonstrates an impulsive, physical response to interpersonal disequilibrium; he leaves the physical space when conflict occurs as if the conflict can be solved if it literally disappears. Thus, Mike construes the conflict and solution in physical terms; he does not differentiate himself, Terry, and their respective wants from the physical act of conflict or conflict removal.

Emotionally Mike seems to be ruled by a diffuse undifferentiated feeling of frustration, and he directly expresses this feeling in the physical act of leaving. When his immediate goal to play hockey is blocked, he does not consider how or why his and Terry's wishes are distinct and may be aligned. Instead he immediately pursues the goal of avoiding disequilibrium by exiting, without considering the possible effects of this act. This is a self-transforming strategy because Mike is removing himself from the field, as opposed to changing the field as in the previous example.

This strategy is distinct from a level 1 form of running away, such as when a child forcibly stamps away in anger, threatening that the other better follow and play with him else they won't be friends. In the present case the leaving is impulsive and without consideration of its effect on the other, rather than the level 1 case where the strategy is intended to affect and control the other.

Level 1: Other-Transforming Orientation Prototypical Strategy: Uses One-Way Threats to Achieve Self's Goals

The individual using this strategy tries to bully the other in order to get her own way. Often what is most important is getting the self's own way at the expense of the other's rather than acquiring the particular good or goal under negotiation.

Specific Example

Liz and Cindy, two 8-year-olds, walk over to a table with drawing materials on it. As Liz starts to sit down, Cindy fairly arbitrarily picks up a purple pen from the table. *Liz* dives up from her chair and leans forward to glare at Cindy, saying firmly, "That's my pen. You better give it to me or else!" With a shrug Cindy drops the pen onto the table. "I don't care," she says, "you can use the dumb old pen." Liz responds: "Well, I don't want it anyway," and she knocks the pen off onto the floor.

Analysis

This example illustrates the level 1 manifestation of a "battle of wills"; when Liz rejects the pen at the end it is quite apparent that she is more interested in "winning" the battle for the pen than in having the pen itself. Although getting the pen, she appears angry to have not won a victory over Cindy, for Cindy chose not to fight. Thus, Liz negotiates with a view of herself and Cindy as having distinct wills. Her purpose is to force Cindy's will to succumb to her own will and wishes. Liz sees her own emotional disequilibrium as a function of Cindy's not doing what she wants, rather than as an internally-generated need to control the interaction. Thus, she deals with this disequilibrium externally, by attempting to force Cindy to succumb. This attempt to change Cindy reflects an other-transforming orientation.

A level 0 strategy would not embody the same awareness of and control of the feelings or acts of other as distinct from self. For example, at level 0 Liz would simply grab the pen away without an immediate awareness of the impact of this act. However, this strategy is not level 2 because, although it acknowledges that Cindy has a will of her own, it does not give any credit to that will. The strategy is "one-way"—Liz will dictate what Cindy will do—whereas level 2 negotiations embody some reciprocity in considering the other's wishes, although still pursuing the self's. At level 2, Liz would try to convince Cindy to change her mind to be in line with Liz's own, rather than to overpower her.

Level 1: Self-Transforming Orientation Prototypical Strategy: Makes Weak Initiatives with Ready Withdrawal

Here the individual tentatively takes the initiative to make a suggestion but is ready to give in quickly if this suggestion is perceived as rejected. The immediate rejection of the suggestion is not well-differentiated from an overall rejection of the self.

Specific Example

Ted, age 7, is working on an airplane model as he sits on the floor. *Peter*, also 7, shuffles slowly toward where Ted is working and he leans his body down slightly to ask in a quiet voice, "Ted, please may you have a checkers game with me?" Ted is still bent over his model as he responds, matter-of-factly, "I'm doing a model right now. You can just watch me doing it." Ted continues working with his head down, not looking at Peter, and Peter stands for a moment staring at Ted with a blank expression. Peter then slowly drops to sit next to Ted, his head and gaze bent towards the floor, and the corners of his mouth turned down into a frown. He says quietly, out loud, "Okay, if you don't want to play with me I'll just watch."

Analysis

We can see by the words "Please may you" that Peter's initiation of a request already is quite weak. He appears to anticipate a strong willful directive by Ted, and his total compliance by sitting and watching reinforces this view. Thus, although the "will" of both self and other are clearly acknowledged as distinct by Peter, he perceives their relation to rest upon the power of one will over another, rather than equal credit to and coordination of each. His purpose in dealing with the disequilibrium is to establish a stable level of control through one "will" having all the force. Peter appreciates the distinction of inner wishes and external acts, yet he appears to see the cause and source for dealing with his inner disequilibrium to be an external function of Ted. That is, the issue is not to deal with his feelings internally but rather to deal through external action by submitting to Ted's power. Peter is self-transforming here by readily giving in to Ted's desires. However, note that there is some advance toward more balance in orientation than at level 0, for Peter does initially put forth his own wants.

At level 0 a self-oriented strategy would be to not attempt any initiative at all, because the self's wants and acts would be totally determined by the acts of the other. This strategy also is distinct from a level 2 strategy, however, for at level 2 there would be more credit given to Peter's own wishes. Resolution of the disequilibrium raised by differing wants would not exist in only one person having his way. Peter might suggest a trade to Ted, such as "If you spend the next 10 minutes finishing your model, then let's spend 10 minutes playing checkers, okay?"

Level 2: Other-Transforming Orientation Prototypical Strategy: Uses "Friendly" Persuasion

This strategy involves the use of psychological persuasion in an attempt to change the other's feelings or thoughts so that the other's will corresponds with the self's wants. Thus, although the underlying purpose still is primarily self-oriented, the purposes and wishes of the other now are acknowledged as valid.

Specific Example

Eddie, age 10, wants to go sledding and he asks Jim, also 10, to go with him. Jim is wearing a new pair of pants that he does not want to get wet, and he is not sure whether he wants to go sledding. *Eddie* smiles endearingly and says, "Come on, Jim, you're such a good sledder and it's so much fun to go with you. You're so good at sledding you won't even get your pants wet." Actually, however, Eddie knows that Jim is not a very good sledder at all.

Analysis

Here we can see that Eddie pursues his goal to go sledding with Jim by trying to manipulate Jim's feelings so that he will want to go sledding, too. He recognizes that Jim's feelings, thoughts, or motives can be changed through flattery or manipulation. Thus, this strategy suggests a construal of self and other as each capable of decisions based on reflection, where multiple desires within self and other are in play. He deals with his emotional or inner disequilibrium by controlling his immediate wishes to postpone gratification until he can arrange a coordination of the other's wishes in line with his own; he works on the interpersonal disequilibrium by manipulating the other's wishes to be in line. His primary purpose is to effect change in the other's goals to be congruent with his own so that his own may eventually be met. The strategy is other-transforming because Eddie is trying to change Jim's wants. Note, however, that there is a greater sense of the opposite orientation than at lower levels reflected in the openness of his communication to feedback and exchange.

Whereas at level 1 the individual attempts to get the other to just "*do* things my way," level 2 strategies represent an attempt to get the other to "*see* things my way." This orientation toward convincing makes the aforementioned strategy level 2 unlike a level 1 threat of force. However, this strategy is not yet at level 3 because it still seeks to achieve a self-oriented goal rather than a goal that represents an integration of desires of both self and other. Eddie does not really respect Jim's worry of getting his pants wet. He merely seeks to overcome that concern with a stronger one, the need to feel skillful, so that they will go sledding.

Level 2: Self-Transforming Orientation Prototypical Strategy: Asserts Self's Feelings and Thoughts as Valuable but Secondary

With this strategy the individual asserts the credibility and value of his own wants or thoughts although still placing them in a secondary position to the other's. The individual still attempts to protect equilibrium by appeasing the other, but there is a building trust in the self's capacity to tolerate inner disequilibrium and in the other's capacity (or potential) to act equitably to resolve interpersonal disequilibrium.

Specific Example

Joey and Mark, both 9, are sharing a soda from a can. Joey says that he wants to drink the first half, and then Mark can finish the second. After a moment of apparent thought, Mark nods. When Joey has finished his half, he drops the soda can onto the table, saying "Here, Mark," and leaves to work on his drawing. Mark picks up the can and steadily downs the rest of the soda. Soon after, Joey returns to the table, picks up the can, and peers inside. Finding no soda left, he begins to berate Mark: "What do you think you're doing pigging all the soda? I told you to save me some!" Mark appears taken aback, and he only slowly fumbles out, "But you said you were done!" Joey denies it and continues forcefully, "You owe me another soda now." *Mark* shakes his head slowly and says with quiet firmness, "You gave it to me, Joey. Next time I'll make sure you're really done before I start it."

Analysis

In this example Mark shows a willingness to stand up for his own views when he perceives himself as being unfairly treated. This indicates a trust that, although self and other may have differing thoughts, feelings, or motives, each is potentially capable of reflection, self-restraint, and compromise. Mark seems able to recognize that his experienced disequilibrium results from a conflict between personal and interpersonal wants. He does not want to be controlled, yet he does not want to offend Joey; he wants his views to be respected, yet he wants to keep Joey's acceptance. He deals with this disequilibrium by prioritizing feelings internally (putting his desire for respect above his fear of rejection) and ordering the feelings of self and other by external action (saying that he will abide by a deal where his wants follow after Joey's). Mark's purpose in this case is to use self-reflection and self-control to establish equilibration through fairness rather than through controlling force. On the whole, this strategy is self-transforming: Mark is more willing to comply than to influence. However, he shows relatively less changing of himself in the face of Joey's accusations and orders than would be evident at lower levels.

At level 1 a self-transforming strategy in this case would be to submit to Joey's construal of the situation, agreeing that he should have saved Joey some soda. If Mark were acting at level 3, however, there would be a more equilibrated balance between the wants and thoughts of self and other. Mark would be able to articulate that he feels Joey is making an unjust claim—perhaps to say that he understands that Joey may really want more soda but Mark does not owe it to Joey, because he fulfilled their original arrangement.

Level 3: Integration of Other- and Self-Transforming Orientations Prototypical Strategy: Anticipates and Integrates Possible Feelings of Other About Self's Negotiation

Level 3 strategies deal as much with reflections on the self's and other's feelings about the particular relationship or negotiation as with acts toward overt goals. In employing this particular strategy, the individual anticipates the possible feelings of the other to the self's intended negotiation, and so she articulates her sensitivity to these feelings and, if necessary, modifies her negotiation in consideration of them.

Specific Example

Two 12-year-olds, Kathy and Sally, are making their own props for a puppet show. Kathy is in charge of making the puppets, and Sally is building the show box. Kathy makes the puppets out of scraps of cloth, and she becomes increasingly frustrated as she tries to glue the first puppet's arms closed at the seams. The glue keeps smearing and will not hold. *Sally* sees Kathy's frustration and she watches for awhile in silence. Finally she offers, in a careful voice, "Kathy, I've never made puppets before, so you may want to decide whether you think this idea would work any better or not, but maybe you could try stapling the cloth together instead of using glue."

Analysis

In this example Sally appears to express her own ideas and feelings while also being aware of and respecting Kathy's feelings and possible reactions to her input. She conveys with her tone and words a sensitivity to Kathy's frustration and a wish to help out, not to stand above and criticize. Thus, Sally employs in this strategy an understanding of and respect for the separate and related feelings of self and other. She appreciates the emotional disequilibrium in Kathy, experienced as frustration, and the potential effect of her own acts upon this inner disequilibrium, and upon their interpersonal disequilibrium, such as by fostering resentment. This disequilibrium is dealt with by shared reflection and articulation of feelings, and sensitivity to their place in the larger relationship. Her purpose is primarily to use communication to promote a process for mutual satisfaction toward collaborative ends: that they together will feel good as their puppet show works well. Note that there is relatively equilibrated use of other- and self-transforming orientations: Sally initiates a suggestion that could lead to a change in Kathy's behavior, and also implicitly leaves herself open to change by allowing that Kathy may decide against this idea, and they may together rework the ideas to arrive at a wholly different solution.

A comparative level 2 strategy in this situation would not place such a value on the feelings of other and on the open process of communication for mutual influence, leading to a solution which fulfills the needs of both parties. Rather, Sally would try to persuade Kathy to accept her idea, such as by saying, "You know, I've made puppets before and I can tell you it'll be a lot easier for you if you staple the cloth."

SUMMARY OF THE MODEL AND ITS IMPLICATION FOR DEVELOPMENTAL ISSUES

The development of each component of a negotiation strategy (in Table 7.1) and the relation of this development to that of the ability to coordinate social perspectives (in Fig. 7.1) have been articulated. A logical relation among the components in their organization across development is asserted. Yet we see as open to empirical study the validity of a psychological relation of the components, such as is illustrated by the case examples of strategies by level and orientation. Let us consider in turn the logical and psychological relations among the components.

At level 0 an individual demonstrates in conduct a construal that lacks appreciation of the distinctiveness of internal states and their expression in action, as well as of the internal states of self versus other. It is logical that at the same time one has this type of construal, one also would be unable to distinguish feelings from their influence on the self, or to recognize a variety of feelings operating at once in one's experience of disequilibrium. Without these abilities, one will be unable to effect any control over this diffuse disequilibrium, and feelings will be immediately and impulsively translated into action. This should logically result in direct pursuit of one individual's immediate physical goals: *direct pursuit* because goals are not discriminated from acts; *one individual's immediate physical goals* because the goals of only one individual are valued, and long term or psychological ends are not appreciated. Thus, the individual can be expected to be entirely other-transforming with no flexibility to change at all, wholly overwhelming the other physically; or to be completely self-transforming and physically overwhelmed by the other as if self is a tool for other.

In level 1 negotiation there is a construal of both self and other as having separate wills and purposes, which are distinct from acts. However, in interpersonal negotiations each individual's motives and wills are seen in "either-or," "mine versus yours" terms, rather than a variety of motives within and between self and other being recognized. Likewise at this level feelings are now seen as separate from their expression in action, but as only pure, transitory, and not part of a larger context. The possibility of internally coordinating a variety of feelings cannot be recognized; disequilibrium is seen to result from "me versus you." Thus it is acted on externally rather than internally. Relatedly, the primary purpose is to secure control by establishing the weaker "will" at the beck and call of the stronger "will." In action orientation, there is one-way bullying to change only the other to abide by the self's will, (other-transforming) or will-less submission to change self for the other's wishes (self-transforming).

A greater capacity for differentiation, and now for coordination, emerges at level 2. Self and other each are seen as capable of taking action based on reflection and choice among multiple motives or ideas. At the same level, inner and interpersonal disequilibrium is recognized as possibly resulting from conflicting feelings within the self and between self and other. Thus, emotional disequilibrium is controlled by ordering and prioritizing feelings, within self or between self and other. The primary interpersonal purpose at level 2 is to use manipulation to establish one's goals as more primary, to de-emphasize the goals of the other. At this level we would expect the orientations in action to be distinct but more open to flexibility: a primarily other-transforming orientation demonstrates persuasive tactics, whereas a primarily self-transforming orientation is manifest in thoughtful compliance to another's influence.

At level 3 an individual accords both self and other the capacity to reflect on the self, other, and relationship, and to appreciate the needs of all three. It follows logically that at the same level a variety of feelings arising within the present context in self and other could be discriminated and viewed for their place in the broader contexts of the self's and relationship's history. With this perception, control of emotional disequilibrium is carried out by integrating feelings through self- and shared-reflection. Logically this would result in the primary interpersonal purpose to use self- and shared-reflection to coordinate the appreciated needs of self, other, and the relationship to pursue mutual goals. This implies that the needs of both self and other, because mutually valued, will be made equally open to change in action. The individual acts at level 3 with open communication, balanced in orientation between a readiness to change and to be changed.[1]

If this logical relation of the components across levels also resulted in their psychological synchrony, we would find "pure" strategies at each level: at level 0, strategies with unreflective, impulsive force to get self's goal or with unreflective, impulsive withdrawal or following to protect the self; at level 1, strategies using willful orders to control the other or using will-less submission to the other; at level 2, strategies of conscious psychological influence to change the other's mind or of compliance in changing the self's mind in the face of influence; and the use of self- and shared-reflection to coordinate feelings and wishes in a relational context at level 3.

Thus far our study of the synchrony of the components across levels has been only theoretical or informally empirical. We analyze the level of each component based on an underlying ability level for social perspective coordination, and we work with the assumption that all components function at the same developmental level in conduct, in a particular negotiation strategy. Thus, our confidence in the validity of the developmental diagnosis of a particular strategy is increased as we make a developmental assessment of all of the components of a strategy, and find them mutually confirming. For example, when in the first example we

---

[1] It is important to elaborate, at least in passing, on one of the heuristic attributes of the model as it is here proposed. Figure 7.1 suggests that at level 3 there is a coming together of orientations such that there is no possibility of distinctiveness between orientations at this level. That is, the impression is given that strategies at level 3 are fully balanced, or equilibrated, with respect to whether actions are directed toward the self's or toward other's perspective and concern. But earlier in this chapter, and elsewhere, we noted that at least one higher level in the coordination of social perspective (level 4) has been defined and delineated and that there are a set of negotiation strategies associated with this level as well. Of course, it follows that these strategies are more advanced, i.e., more differentiated and integrated, than those strategies classified at level three or below. Thus, should it not be that complete integration is achieved at level 4, and that at level 3 the orientations do not yet come together fully?

We believe that this is quite probably the case; that with the delineation of strategies at the fourth level, those that appeared balanced and equilibrated at level 3 will be found not to be so, in ways not heretofore considered. For example, it can be seen from the case example of Sally's level 3 strategy that the balanced transformation of self and other involves mutual transformation in the sense that each is considered to have the capacity to change and involves simultaneous transformation *within* Sally's construction of the situation as she considers both Kathy and herself. However, it may be that at level 4, when the issue of negotiation is interpersonal intimacy, equilibrated transformation of self and other involves mutual and simultaneous change in shared thoughts or feelings. That is, transformation is simultaneously and mutually carried out on the conduct of individuals negotiating together, rather than being carried out within one person's consideration before implementing a negotiation strategy.

saw Carol's negotiation strategy toward Alice around playing a record, we could initially assess her act at level 0 by the clue of how she was perceiving and dealing with feelings: she reacted impulsively as if overwhelmed by neediness. If we looked also at the cognitive component, we would have further evidence of the validity of a level 0 assessment, for she construes the problem as solved once Alice has been physically silenced. Thus far in our experiences diagnosing the developmental level of strategies, we have mostly found such concurrence among components.[2]

However, if we were to find a discrepancy in developmental level between two or more components of a particular negotiation strategy, two distinct conclusions could be indicated. It may be that our assessment of one or more of the components was inaccurate. Alternatively, it may be that components are not necessarily synchronous in a negotiation strategy, as we have assumed. We think it possible that the level of differentiation and coordination of perspectives may not be applied and used evenly at all times in all realms of conduct— cognitive, emotional, or motivational. We propose that the extent, nature, and constraints on the synchronicity of these aspects of conduct in this system is a valuable area for further empirical and theoretical work.

Some points should be made explicit about the theoretical nature of the emotional and cognitive components and their relation in this model. The emotional component considers the way emotional disequilibrium is perceived and controlled. It does not attend to the content of the disequilibrium, e.g. whether fear or delight or anger, but focuses on the form of disequilibrium instead. This is because we do not find the content of feeling to be different at different developmental levels of conduct, thus content is not essential to a strategy's developmental nature. For example, the model does not suggest that certain emotions, such as rage, are automatically low level. Although recognizing that factors that engender a feeling (like rage) change with age-related experiences and maturity, the model asserts that how one deals with the (rageful) feelings has a strong developmental factor that is essential to an individual's conduct. If a young child gets enraged at a parent for reneging on a trip to the lake because it is raining, we note the child's inability to distinguish feelings of sadness and disappointment differentially from feelings of frustration and rage. Most adults in the same situation, with a broader perspective, could both differentiate the feelings and differentially control them, and they would likely neither experience nor express rage. On the other hand, a broader perspective enables adults to feel enraged over certain acts of social injustice that a young child, with a limited perspective, would not be expected to understand in a way to allow rage. Thus,

---

[2]These examples have been drawn from a coding manual constructed on the basis of observations in a number of contexts; every day observation, clinical research (Selman & Demorest, 1984) and quasi-naturalistic research (Selman, et al, 1983). The manual is available by request from the first author at the Judge Baker Guidance Center, 295 Longwood Avenue, Boston, MA 02115.

social experience and perception engender changes in the generation of emotional disequilibrium, yet emotional disequilibrium is experienced at all levels. It is how this disequilibrium is perceived and dealt with to which we apply our developmental analysis. Furthermore, we may note that this development of perception and control of disequilibrium can rest on perspective coordination levels, and embodies both cognitive and conative views of emotional disequilibrium. The cognitive aspect rests in the perception of disequilibrium (its locus and cause); the conative aspect, in its control.

This view is elaborated in Table 7.3. Here is provided a specific theoretical formulation and description of the "affective" component of the interpersonal negotiation strategies model at each level. This table breaks down the perceptual aspect of emotional disequilibrium into two subcategories, the *locus*, meaning where in time and psychological space the feelings of imbalance are experienced by the developing child; and the *cause*, meaning how the disequilibration has been perceived to come about. Table 7.3 also specifies in developmental terms the primary ways in which the self, at each level, controls or deals with the experience of disequilibrated feelings.

In effect, this table provides a more directed and precise look at one of the components specified in Table 7.1—as if one had taken a microscope and focused its lens solely on this component for a more thoroughgoing examination. Table 7.3 puts forth a proposal of the developmental structuring of specific elements of the affective component, a proposal that emerges theory-based or theory-driven from the broader framework of social-perspective coordination. This type of endeavor is useful for at least the following two reasons. First, it demands greater descriptive specificity of a process that is an important part of psychological development. It suggests that affective development can be concretely described, given the appropriate theoretical and heuristic tools and language. Second, and perhaps more pertinent here, it generates these descriptions at a level precise enough for empirical operationalization and hence for research. There are many ways in which the descriptions in Table 7.3 can be studied, and hence tested or validated. Interviews on how children growing up perceive and deal with feelings, observations of actual feelings and dealings, are two that strike up as potentially fruitful.

Regarding the working nature of the interpersonal negotiation strategies model, we would stress that any strategy, regardless of its developmental level or orientation, represents an attempt to exercise some kind of control over disequilibrium. The *way* that control is asserted varies with orientation, whereas the *nature* of control sought differs with developmental level. A self-transforming strategy is a way of controlling in which the medium through which control is achieved is the self—disequilibrium is abated by changing the self. Conversely other-transforming strategies seek to restore equilibrium by changing the other. And with level the type of control changes: At level 0 there is no self-control over inner or interpersonal disequilibrium, rather the disequilibrium controls the

Table 7.3

A Proposed Analysis of the Perception (Locus and Cause) and Control of Emotional Disequilibrium for Each Developmental Level

	Level 0	Level 1	Level 2	Level 3
Identifying the locus of emotional disequilibrium in a spatio-temporal frame	Emotional disequilibrium is experienced as diffuse, unbounded, undifferentiated, and all-encompassing. The feelings of the specific moment are experienced as timeless. There is no conscious placement of the immediate disequilibrium within a larger or superordinate context of a "stream of feeling states." There is no "chunking" or categorizing/demarcation between an emotional state and a reaction.	Emotional disequilibrium is recognized as limited or bounded in time and space, but present states of disequilibrium are not related to prior or future states. Emotional disequilibrium is still viewed in dichotomous terms, e.g., all or none, good or bad, there or not there; there are no gradations. Emotional disequilibrium is viewed as an objective reality (something that happens to the self) rather than as a subjective experience.	Specific emotional disequilibrium of the moment conceptually is located in the larger context of previous and future states but is still experienced as more powerful than the past and future context. The present "mood" is seen to dominate the self's general temperament. Feelings are now located within the self and not of the self. The self becomes a receptacle to hold feelings or to be emptied of them.	Emotional disequilibrium begins to be located in the space and time between people as well as within person, i.e., it becomes identified as intersubjective as well as subjective. Similarly, temporally, feelings are viewed as part of an ongoing time-oriented network with associations to both present and past events and future expectations.
Differentiating the causes of emotional disequilibrium in an interpersonal frame	Causes of emotional disequilibrium within the self are equated with the perceived surface actions of other persons as differentiated from the self. Personal equilibrium is not seen as directly related to the subjective actions of the self, or of the subjective interpretation of actions by the self.	The identified emotional disequilibrium of the moment is seen as distinct from its cause and from its effects. However, the proximal causes of interpersonal disequilibrium are still seen to reside in events and/or the actions of others. Feelings arise because of what others do to the self, or because they don't do what the self wants. The feelings of	Subjective mediation of external actions and internal reactions is now recognized as a cause of emotional disequilibrium. The self can act on the self in ways that are disequilibrating. Thus, emotional disequilibrium is now understood to be due partly to inner conflict, not just conflict between self and other, even if another is involved.	Causes of emotional disequilibrium are recognized to be possible conflicts solely within the self, but also as an interaction of conflicts within the self and conflicts between self and other. That is, it is understood that interpersonal conflicts may feed inner conflicts and vice versa.

one person are not directly linked to the feelings of the other, but to the other's actions.

| Dealing with emotional disequilibrium in a developmental frame | Emotional disequilibrium propels the self, rather than being channelled by the self in a planful action-oriented way. Controls for self's reactions to disequilibrium are largely external, from without rather than from within, i.e., through parents, caretakers, or peers with greater power or force. The self is at the mercy of feelings as a boat is at the mercy of the motor that is running without an active agent at the controls. Distraction or deflection is a major source of change in "motion" and hence of dealing with feelings. | Attempts to restore emotional equilibrium are made by the self's taking action on events or persons perceived as the cause of the disequilibrium, rather than dealing directly with the subjective feelings so engendered. Feelings of disequilibrium are viewed as impediments or intrusions, and attempts are made to extirpate them, kick them out, push them away. | Attempts to restore emotional equilibrium now include attempts to deal directly with the subjective experience as well as with the external or objective situation. Conflicts are dealt with by pushing one component of the conflict away, rather than by working with both or all components. Attempts are made to quickly disperse the disequilibrium rather than integrate it. | Attempts to restore emotional equilibrium are made through two types of processes: self-reflection and shared reflection. Feelings are seen as processes rather than objects and therefore are dealt with as such, not by ostracism but by integration. They are viewed as signals of distress and an indication that psychological work needs to be done on them. Emotional disequilibrium is viewed as an over-heated motor that needs to be cooled slowly (worked through) rather than dunked in ice water. |

individuals and their acts; at level 1, control rests in enforcing a source of power by one individual controlling the other's acts; at level 2 control includes ordering thoughts and feelings as well as acts; by level 3 control of disequilibrium rests on understanding its sources and nature and mutually integrating it into the relational context.

However, too sharp a line must not be drawn between control as it changes across levels versus control as it changes between orientations. These types of change in control are interrelated, just as orientation is not independent of developmental level. At level 0 only the one individual's disequilibrium is experienced, with no perspective on the role of the other or of complex feelings on the disequilibrium. Thus, an other-transforming strategy is totally independent of and sharply distinct from a self-transforming strategy, and vice versa. Yet as the various perspectives of both self and other are acknowledged and various feelings and motives are seen to rest in and between individuals, other- and self-transforming orientations begin to converge to a point where, at level 3, no distinction is made in the model as herein proposed. Acting at this level, the individual simultaneously reflects on his own and the other's perspective so that the notion of one party transforming self independently of other, or vice versa, is incongruous.

In other words, the polarity of self- versus other-transforming strategies decreases with developmental maturity because the perspectives of self and other are themselves brought into conjunction in the management of control at higher levels of developmental maturity. In Piagetian terms, to the extent that other-transforming strategies represent an assimilation of something external to self and self-transforming strategies can be considered accommodative to something external to self, higher level strategies strive for equilibrium, in which the assimilative and accommodative forces are better balanced.

As a second point on the working nature of this model, we note from our observations that it should not be expected, nor by the model should it be predicted, that an individual will negotiate consistently across all relationships or contexts at any one level or in any one action-orientation. The interpersonal orientations and interpersonal negotiation levels are essentially cartographic descriptions of negotiation behaviors in the context of dyadic or group interaction. Context is a factor in the level and orientation of strategy used. Thus, although individuals may have a disposition to function within a particular orientation and/or at a particular level, only an interactive context can allow assessment of the actual level or orientation observed. For example, we are not surprised when the level 1 "scape-goat" (self-transforming) becomes the level 1 "bully" (other-transforming) in the presence of a new other whose interactions are more accommodative. This suggests that the model also can be used to examine the factors that elicit conduct at any particular orientation or level.

Earlier in this chapter, we speculated on the transactional nature of the quality of emotions an individual feels and expresses in an interpersonal context. A similar case can be made for negotiation strategies, at least up to a point. Whether to use (or choose) a high or low level strategy may not always be the isolated choice of each individual participant. Instead, it is very likely that the level and orientation of the strategy used by one participant in a context for negotiation has a strong influence upon the level and orientation of the strategy utilized by the other. One individual can bring another down to his or her level; conversely one individual can raise another (within ontogenetic limits). Because the model is not focused solely on ontogenesis, it is capable of being utilized to look not only at individual social behavior occurring across age spans, as has been the thrust of this paper, but also at the sequences of strategies, both within and between persons, that occur during specified social interactions or within social relations.

It is important to recognize that one individual's strategies may be variable across contexts, and the model provides a way to categorize these strategies, not the individual himself. Furthermore, although it may be tempting to characterize as aggressive people who use predominantly other-transforming strategies, and to characterize as submissive those who use many self-transforming strategies, this equation of an orientation-use with a personality type is dangerous. First, many of the distinctive features of strategies within any given developmental level hold true for both orientations—e.g. at level 0 both other- and self-transforming strategies are impulsive. Furthermore, the strategies within a single developmental level and the same orientation may be different enough behaviorally to connote different character styles. For example, at level 1, the individual who uses threats of force (an other-transforming strategy) is likely to be seen as bossy or hostile; whereas the person who critizes the other's skills to pursue the self's activity (also other-transforming) is likely to be viewed as arrogant, conceited, and critical. Both strategies reflect the same orientation and level, yet they can both be assigned distinct *personality styles*. Thus, before one thinks of personality dimensions, an individual should be observed in various contexts. Depending on an individual's variability in levels, orientations, and strategy types (and the degree of variability may itself reflect individual differences), it may be necessary to examine a large number of the person's strategies before acquiring the sense of consistency connoted by the term *personality characteristic*.

It should be stressed, as illustrated by the symmetry in Fig. 7.1, that it is no more or less adaptive per se to use an other-transforming or a self-transforming orientation. Likewise, low level strategies are not by definition immature or pathological. For young children they are expected and appropriate. The descriptions of strategies at lower developmental levels are not intended pejoratively. Although these strategies include threats, grabbing, and automatic obeying, all of which may connote undesirable behavior from the adult's standpoint, it is important to remember that they reflect structures that are part of normal development and are therefore age-appropriate for young children.

Furthermore, even for older individuals, low level strategies may in fact be appropriate in certain contexts of negotiation. Whereas in the domain of reflective understanding higher levels are preferable, in that they signify greater conceptual competence, in the domain of negotiation strategies it is not always the case that higher is better. Various levels and orientations of negotiation strategies may be *optimal* or *adaptive* in various contexts. In a context of mutuality the higher level strategies are most preferable because they show a consideration of the feelings and cares of both self and other and of the growth of the relationship itself. However, in a context where the prevalent issues are urgent, short-term goals, higher level strategies are less appropriate than those of lower levels, which attend to immediate goals. The qualities that characterize lower level strategies, such as immediate reactivity to a situation, make them the strategy of choice in such contexts regardless of the conceptual maturity of the user. Thus, if two firemen have to decide who will climb the ladder to the roof of a burning building, the optimal strategy may be a lower-level direct order that speaks to short-term urgency, rather than a higher-level reflection on feelings, which does not.

We distinguish such context-appropriate usage of a low level strategy by an older individual from a context-inappropriate, regressive use of a low level strategy. In the former case, the individual may be credited with the act of finding from a repertoire of strategies the one that is most in line with the requirements of the interpersonal situation. In the latter case, the individual is not credited with such choosing but rather can be seen as a victim of regressive forces. Thus, although these two types of strategies may be at the same level, they have different significance in the context of the individual's and relationship's history.

We also may ask whether the regressive employment of a low level strategy by an individual capable of using developmentally mature conduct is the same as the use of the same strategy by a developmentally unsophisticated individual. For example, consider the age-appropriate behavior of a 5-year-old who impulsively runs out of room when confronted with conflict. The use of this strategy is one possible direct and predictable outgrowth of the limitations of the child's level of interpersonal understanding and repertoire of interpersonal negotiation strategies. On the other hand, consider a wife who runs out of the house in the midst of an unpleasant interaction with her husband. It appears that this strategy represents a reversion to less mature interpersonal conduct due to situational influences; under stress a higher level strategy was harder to employ.

First, as we have pointed out by the model, these two strategies, although similar on the surface, may be structurally (developmentally) distinct. The 5-year-old may be impulsively exiting in order to physically avoid (and so end) the conflict; the wife may be exiting to demonstrate purposefully to her husband the force and importance of her feelings so that he will consider them more strongly. However, it also is possible that the adult could use the strategy of running out the door with the same state of construal, perception and control of emotional disequilibrium, and purpose *at that moment* as the child's. That is, she may at the moment impulsively remove herself from the area of conflict to remove the conflict, with no thought of the effects of this act on her husband. This strategy, then, would be codable at the same developmental level as that of the child. Again, however, it would have significantly different meaning in the context of the individual's and relationship's history.

In form and structure the strategies are the same, and their immediate function may be the same—to cut off the other from dealing with the self. However, in the context of the individual's interpersonal competence, the strategies are different. The adult has achieved a level of competence in social perspective coordination that would enable her to use higher level strategies. Thus, she is a different organism using a low level strategy than is the child: an organism still with the higher social competence that is not being put to use because of uncharacteristic stress, as opposed to an organism acting at her modal, but still low level capacity of social perspective coordination. The difference between the two is like that between an individual paddling a simple raft and an individual who rides on a sea plane that has temporarily broken down and so is paddling it across the water.

Furthermore, the adult's strategy will have a different relational impact and will be dealt with in the future by both the wife and husband in a different way than it would be if exhibited by a child. Both wife and husband will later be able to reflect on the strategy as an impulsive reaction to stress, indicating feelings that are very strong but not functional in resolving the conflict. The wife, unlike the child, has the ability to consider the long-term continuity of the relationship and to integrate her strategy into this larger context.

Thus peripheral dimensions surrounding the use of a strategy—its immediate interpersonal context as with the firemen, and its broader personal context of capabilities and longer term relational context as with the wife—determine the ways in which strategies that are viewed as structurally similar in developmental level can nonetheless have significantly different meaning in their personal and interpersonal context. It is essential to appreciate that the levels by orientations model should not be seen as a template for automatic and direct mapping of the true meaning of conduct; it should always be used with consideration of the conduct's context.

Still, this model does make partial claims about the universality or homogeneity of what we consider interpersonally mature conduct. It implies that certain social interactions and competencies are shared by individuals functioning at the higher levels. For a strategy to be coded at higher levels requires evidence of an observing self; the capacity to tolerate feelings of anxiety, pain, fear, and sadness; the ability to give and take; the capacity to perceive and understand with compassion the complexity of other's feelings and, equally important, to perceive and understand the nature of feelings within the self; and to synthesize these conceptions and perceptions in action.

CONCLUSION

In this chapter we have tried to illustrate that to identify the developmental nature of one form of social conduct, interpersonal negotiation strategies, we must attend to what we infer to be the developmental nature of its underlying cognitive, emotional and motivational components. We have suggested that the study of these components as they interact in conduct that attempts to deal with disequilibrium is a useful way of understanding their form and function in human development. It should be stressed that assigning kinds of strategies to levels or orientations by the model presented is a theoretical heuristic. The strategy types exist whether organized developmentally or not. They describe methods of negotiation and repertoires of strategies that can be related to such validating criteria as age, degree of pathology, or social maturity. Assessing the observed strategy at any one level or orientation is an inferential process based on a particular developmental perspective and on a view toward particular underlying components. Whether these components are equally essential to defining the nature of any given strategy and whether they function at concurrent levels of differentiation and coordination as they interact in conduct are questions yet to be addressed. The real work now is operational and empirical: developing reliable methods to test the extent of the model's validity.

REFERENCES

Bateson, G. (1979). *Mind and nature: A necessary unity*. New York: Dutton.

Habermas, J. (1975). Moral development and ego identity. *Telos, 24*, 41–56.

Hinde, R. (1976). On describing relationships. *Journal of Child Psychology and Psychiatry, 17*, 1–19.

Kohlberg, L. (1981) *The philosophy of moral development*. (Vol. 1) San Francisco: Harper & Row.

Loevinger, T. (1976). *Ego development*. San Francisco: Jossey-Bass.

Mead G. H. (1934). *Mind, self, and society*. Chicago: University of Chicago Press.

Piaget, J. (1970). *Structuralism*. New York: Basic Books.

Piaget, J. (1981). *Intelligence and affectivity: Their relationship during child development*. Palo Alto: Annual Reviews.

Selman, R. L. (1980). *The growth of interpersonal understanding*. New York: Academic Press.

Selman, R. L. & Demorest, A. P. (1984). Observing troubled children's interpersonal negotiation strategies: Implications of and for a developmental model. *Child Development, 55*, 288–304.

Selman, R. L., Schorin, M. Z., Stone, C., & Phelps, E. (1983). A naturalistic study of children's social understanding. *Developmental Psychology, 19*(1), 83–102.

Werner, H. (1948). *Comparative psychology of mental development*. (Rev. Ed.) Chicago: Follett.

Werner, H. (1957) The concept of development from a comparative and organismic point of view. In D. B. Harris (ed.), *The concept of development: An issue in the study of human behavior* (pp. 125–149). Minneapolis: University of Minnesota Press.

8 Transactional Cognition in Context: New Models of Social Understanding

David J. Bearison
The Graduate School and University Center
of the City University of New York

Recently there has been growing discontent among many developmental psychologists who have studied social cognition using structural developmental models. These models, for the most part, have been derived from children's responses to hypothetical social situations in decontextualized settings that were relatively unencumbered by affective and motivational considerations. Empirical tests of these models rested on semistructured interviews with children in which the presentation of others as social agents was generally in the form of hypothetical individuals interacting in hypothetical social contexts that lacked compelling subjective meaning for the knower. Consequently, our knowledge of children's reflective social cognition did not correspond to how children socially interact in naturally occurring, spontaneous, real-life situations in which the struggle to achieve and maintain interpersonal relations entails considerably more than the cognitive mastery of concepts about the self and others. Those of us who work with children, as therapists or educators, have found that structural or formal models of cognitive competence have had limited practical application. There seems to be a growing theoretical gap between reflective social cognition and cognition in conduct (i.e., between form and experience).

There have been several interesting approaches to formulating theoretical models that are sensitive to the *transactional* features of social cognition as a means of bridging this gap between reflective and practical social knowledge. In a transaction, at least two people are interacting in such a manner that the intentions and actions of one individual will reciprocally affect the intentions and reactions of the other(s) (Bruner, 1984). The cognitive challenge in transactional conduct is the ability to interpersonally negotiate the satisfaction of one's own intentions as they relate to the intentions of others. Much of what we regard

129

as the process of social cognitive development is the formation of mutually intentional relations with others. Such relationships are established and maintained through a variety of dialogical symbol systems, including language, gestures, vocal intonations, and body postures. These symbol systems allow for infinite variations on intentional themes and behavioral narratives within culturally bound transactional systems. They are derived from and applied to ongoing series of transactions in which we learn to share perspectives and coordinate interpersonal negotiations.

This "new look" at social cognition sees it as both the process of social development and the acquisition of social knowledge. It has its roots in two complementary yet epistemologically distinct theories of cognitive development—Vygotsky's and Piaget's. According to Vygotsky (1981), there is a temporal and logical priority to the social matrix from which individual knowledge is constructed. Vygotsky (1981) said that cognitive development "first appears between people as an interpsychological category and then within the child as an intrapsychological category" (p. 163). In other words, "what the child can do in cooperation today, he can do alone tomorrow" (Vygotsky, 1962, p. 104). Whereas Vygotsky stressed the function of language as a symbolic dialogical social system that structures thinking, Piaget conceptualized thinking in terms of interiorized and reversible coordinations of actions (i.e., operations). According to Piaget (1971), these coordinations are both individually and socially structured; " . . . individual operations of the intelligence and operations making for exchanges in cognitive cooperation are one and the same thing, the 'general coordination of actions' to which we have continually referred being an interindividual as well as an intraindividual coordination . . ." (p. 360). Although empirical studies of Piaget's theory historically have focused on the organismic-environmental interactions of individuals thinking alone instead of engaging in collective dialogical endeavors, the theory has more of a social transactional perspective than even Piaget fully explored. However, Piaget (1950) recognized that "it is precisely by a constant interchange of thought with others that we are able to decentralize ourselves . . . to coordinate internal relations deriving from different view points" (p. 64). To varying and relative extents, all of the new approaches to social cognition have benefited from these two theories of cognitive development. Other prominent developmental theorists whose work has contributed to transactional approaches to social cognition include Mead (1934), Baldwin (1897), Dewey (1949), Werner (1948), and Sullivan (1953).

Although the primary purpose of this chapter is to comment on the particular approach espoused by Selman and Demorest (this volume), it would be helpful to consider it in regard to other theoretical approaches that attempt to capture the transactional features of social cognition. These include psycholinguistic models, script models, socio-cognitive conflict models, and adult-child interaction models. These models share a common assumption that cognitive development is fostered by appropriate social conditions.

PSYCHOLINGUISTIC MODELS

In the field of developmental psycholinguistics, recent models of how children acquire natural languages (syntax, semantics, pragmatics, etc.) assume that language is not acquired for its own sake but in order to serve the speaker/listener in fulfilling his or her intentions. Thus, the mastery of language is motivated by and is instrumental in achieving adaptive social transactions with others (peers and superiors) who engage the learner in systems of social exchanges (i.e., transactions). Language acquisition begins long before a child's first utterance of words. According to Bruner (1983) it ". . . begins when mother and infant create a predictable format of interaction that can serve as a microcosm for communicating and for constituting a shared reality" (p. 18). Language becomes a process by which the behavior of others is understood and regulated. Studies of children's discourse have shown how the development of linguistic and paralinguistic systems emerge in social contexts in which children reciprocally coordinate their actions with others (e.g., Bernstein, 1971; Dore, 1974; Shatz & Gelman, 1973).

SCRIPT MODELS

Another approach that has become popular within several different fields of psychology—learning, developmental, information processing and computer simulation, and social psychology—is concerned with the schematic nature of cognitive representations of naturally occurring, familiar, socially organized interpersonal transactions. According to this approach, knowledge of social transaction is highly context specific and is both constructed and enacted in the form of scripts. A script is a type of cognitive schema in which the generalized aspects of temporally organized sequences of social transactions and their causal connectives are presented (Abelson, 1981; Schank & Abelson, 1977). Scripts are organized around a central goal (i.e., intention) and specify actors, roles, and props, together with temporal and causal sequences by which one interaction enables the next interaction to occur. Scripts constitute the generalized sequence of social transactions appropriate to particular social contexts. They not only structure the representation and recall of social knowledge, but they determine in part how individuals interact with one another by specifying an organized set of interpersonal expectations in relevant social contexts. Scripts are "derived from and applied to social contexts" (Nelson, 1981, p. 101).

Empirical evidence supporting the hypothesized properties of scripts is impressive. Studies with adults have shown that scripts enable them to predict a probable sequence of events in ways that guide their social decision making (Abelson, 1976; Bower, 1978; Bower, Black, & Turner, 1979). Scripts usually are obtained by asking subjects "What happens when . . ." types of questions. For example, among children, scripts have been obtained about what happens when you go to a restaurant (Nelson, 1981), to a birthday party (Gruendel, 1980), to school, and to bed (McCartney & Nelson, 1981). These studies have found that children as young as 3 years old derive scripts from familiar social experiences and organize their knowledge of them in temporal and causal sequences of activities (Nelson, 1978; Nelson, Fivush, Hudson, & Lucariello, 1983). With age, children's scripts become more complex, differentiated and hierarchically organized (Gruendel, 1980).

Scripts also have been shown to structure our representation and knowledge of affect states. Descriptions of the emotional states of actors and their emotional reactions to the social transactions they encounter occur with frequency in script narratives. This has led Dyer (1983) to formulate a model of affect processing in script form in which emotional reactions are initiated by script narratives, and the intentional significance of an actor's emotions are known in the context of such narratives. In this model, the satisfaction of intentions in transactions mediates a range of states and expressions of positive affect arousal, whereas the frustration of intentions mediates negative affect arousal within the context of the script narrative.

Memory studies also have shown that the recall of social interactions is largely script based and that scripts facilitate event recollection (Mandler, 1978; Stein & Glenn, 1979). According to Nelson et al. (1983), ". . . scripts for familiar events are a powerful form of general knowledge organization and . . . specific or episodic memory is influenced by script structures through transformations of the input to fit canonical structures . . ." (p. 118). For example, scripts that were presented to subjects in a misordered form that violated the canonical order of events were recalled in the direction of the canonical script (Bower, Black & Turner, 1979; Mandler & DeForest, 1979). Scripts also organize recall by allowing the memory of frequent transactions to become fused with their general scripts (Nelson et al., 1983). As people familiarize themselves with initially novel transactions, their scripts for these events are transformed from episodic to increasingly more generic representations. For example, as the retention interval increases between an event and its recall, the memory of atypical activities that are not script based is forgotten at a faster rate than script-based activities (Graesser, Woll, Kowalski & Smith, 1980). This is similar to the normalizing processes in adult memory first reported by Bartlett (1932). It also has been found to occur in children as young as 4 years (Slackman & Nelson, 1984).

Scripts account for much of the habituated aspects of social transactions; they mediate the satisfaction of interpersonal goals and intentions in social contexts. Consider, for instance, the enactment of a restaurant script. It provides for efficient and effective transactions between the one who is dining and the restaurant personnel with minimal cognitive effort. The restaurant personnel, for their part, enact their respective scripts as waiters, bartenders, bus boys, and so on. The reciprocal intentions and activities of actors in a restaurant script are expected and the range of behavioral variations in satisfying these intentions are clearly specified (see Nelson, 1981 for illustrations of children's "restaurant scripts"). However, the cognitive efficiency of script knowledge in carrying out social transactions becomes apparent when there is a script violation. For example, suppose the waiter spills a cup of coffee in my lap. I would immediately edit my restaurant script to try to understand what this violation meant (i.e., the waiter's intentions) and how I should react: Was it an accident, or did the waiter do it on purpose? If it was an accident, should I simply forget it or seek compensation of some sort? If it wasn't an accident, then is this waiter out to get me? Should I fear this person? Am I being paranoid? Unless having waiters spill coffee in my lap is a familiar occurrence, I will not have a script that would enable me to proceed with this transaction in an habituated manner. Instead, I would experience internal conceptual conflict and would seek more information about this transaction in context in order to coordinate intentions between myself and others.

As a form of social cognition, script knowledge is significant because it accounts for the vast majority of our daily and routine transactions. Thus, within the structural framework of the restaurant script, we can monitor and appropriately accommodate our social behavior, whether we are in a pretentious restaurant where waiters interact with us with an air of subservient superiority, or in a cheap coffee shop where we are grateful if they interact with us at all. In either place, script knowledge is an efficient mediator in formulating social transactions that carry us through temporally organized sequence of events that enables us to satisfy our intention of having dinner. Probably there are some people who violate script narratives more than others and do so for reasons other than a lack of adequate script knowledge. For example, script violations can be used as a way of asserting control and manipulating others in social contexts. Also, young children probably violate script narratives as a method of testing the limits of their knowledge of social interaction and interpersonal relations.

ADULT-CHILD TRANSACTION MODELS

Another transactive approach to cognitive development is derivative of Vygotsky's (1978) concept of the "zone of proximal development," which explains transactions between novices and experts or children and adults in problem solving situations. The zone of proximal development is ". . . the distance between the actual developmental level as determined by independent problem solving and the level of potential development as determined through problem solving under adult guidance or in collaboration with more capable peers" (p. 86). What is new to this approach, compared to traditional pedagogical models whereby a teacher attempts to transfer knowledge to a learner, is that the transaction between teacher and learner is neither teacher directed nor learner determined, but is an emergent and self-organizing property of the dyadic relationship (Renninger & Winegar, 1984). This is consistent with Vygotsky's position that knowledge emerges on the social plane before it becomes individualized through speech in transactive contexts.

A serious methodological problem that has limited earlier attempts to test critical aspects of Vygotsky's theory was how to operationalize the zone of proximal development so as to capture the fluid boundaries between "actual" and "potential" levels of development as they emerge in collaborative problem solving activities. Vygotsky never provided an operational definition of the zone of proximal development (Werstch, 1984). However, the resurgence of interest in transactional systems in social cognition has led to some innovative attempts to determine how mothers regulate their children's learning within the zone of proximal development and how children participate in the transaction at different levels in the transition from other to self-regulation.

Wertsch (1979) has determined four sequential levels in the transition from other-regulation to self-regulation derived from observations of mothers guiding their children in a puzzle-making task. At the first level, the child begins to develop a definition of the task situation that is similar enough to the mother's so that he or she will be able to participate in the transactive context with mother. The child begins to recognize that the mother's utterances are task related in several critical ways. For example, the mother might define the task situation as involving the selection and placement of copy pieces relative to a model, whereas the child, on his or her own, might fail to see any connection between the copy pieces and the model. Thus, the same task setting can be defined in different ways by the mother and the child, and a common definition must be negotiated between them before a cognitive transaction can occur. Wertsch (1984) refers to this process as establishing a "negotiated inter-subjective situation definition" (p. 13). At the second level, the mother helps the child to attend to critical task attributes through the use of explicit linguistic directives. Once the child is fully capable of interpreting the mother's directives, he or she begins to assume strategies necessary to solve the task, often using egocentric speech to regulate the self's activities (level 3). At this level, egocentric speech is similar in form to the speech used earlier by the mother in regulating the child's activities (other-regulation). At the fourth and final level, the transition of problem-solving activities from the interpsychological to the intrapsychological plane of functioning is complete. The child is capable of mastering the task without assistance from the mother by means of the self-regulating function of egocentric speech that has become increasingly more abbreviated and internalized.

In the course of the transaction, both the child and the mother come to adopt ways of interpsychologically understanding the task situation differently from how they initially understood it intrapsychologically. The mother accommodates her understanding of the task situation to the cognitive needs of the child, and the child comes to understand the task in terms of correspondences between the mother's speech and his or her task-related activities. The child's continuing effort to establish and maintian coherence between the mother's other-regulated speech acts and his or her self-regulated behavioral acts (semiotic mediation) constitutes the motive for the transition from one level to the next through the zone of proximal development. The developmentally progressive direction of cognitive change in the child is assured by the mother's use of directives to the child that require an understanding of the task situation that is just beyond his or her level of mastery. Thus, the problem is initially understood by the child in terms of the adult's definition of the task situation and other-regulated directives, but, by carrying out the directives specified by the adult, the child eventually understands the problem in terms of his or her self-regulated directives. This process completes the cycle by which the child constructs knowledge interpsychologically and then intrapsychologically.

Because the zone of proximal development is constituted within the transactional context between adult and child (expert and novice), it cannot be measured in terms of the child's individual abilities. Instead, it is necessary to capture the ways in which the adult and child reciprocally organize and pace their transaction as they jointly manage the transfer of responsibility for task mastery from adult to child. There have been several studies seeking to determine the mechanisms that enable adult/child transactions to proceed in a smooth and progressive manner through the zone of proximal development. Most of them have focused on mothers attempting to teach their preschool children how to construct a copy-object in accordance with a model-object (Saxe, Gearhart, & Guberman, 1984; Werstch, McNamee, McLane, & Budwig, 1980; Wood, Bruner, & Ross, 1976; Wood, Wood, & Middleton, 1978). A central theme of these studies is the process by which adults are able to adjust their directives to children either progressively or regressively as a function of the children's successes or failures in carrying out the adults' previous directives. These studies have been able to capture the transactional features of adult/child relations by devising task analyses that developmentally order sequentially more progressive steps toward task mastery and, using such analyses, to determine at what level mothers intervene in the task situation relative to their children's ability level. Under ideal conditions, if the child responds appropriately to the mother's directive, the mother will shift subsequent directives toward the next mastery level. If the child responds inappropriately, the mother will shift toward the next lower mastery level. In this way, the adult, using feedback from the child regarding his or her intrapsychological comprehension of the situation, creates different transactive levels of intersubjective reasoning. By continually monitoring the child's level of functioning, the adult is able to alter the goal structure of a task. For example, Saxe, Gearhart, and Guberman (1984) found that mothers introduced and defined a number reproduction task for their preschool children according to their children's initial ability levels. Mothers of high-ability children gave less direct task assistance than mothers of low-ability children. As more difficult tasks were introduced, mothers shifted down their directives to more subordinate levels. Also, mothers tended to shift their directives to the previous task level after their children made an inappropriate response to a directive and to the next higher level after an appropriate response. In this fashion, mothers segmented the task into manageable subgoals for their children, so that the children were continually being challenged to participate in the transaction at levels that were slightly beyond their actual level of task proficiency toward their potential level.

According to Saxe et al. (1984), studies of children's progress through the zone of proximal development requires ". . . coordinated analyses of three aspects of the social context of children's developing conceptual understanding: an analysis of children's developing operations within a knowledge domain, a functional analysis of the cultural task context in which these operations are deployed, and an analysis of the way in which other people can bridge and adapt the cultural definition of the task to the child's developing operations" (p. 28).

SOCIO-COGNITIVE CONFLICT MODEL

Another approach to bridging the gap between reflective cognition and practical social interaction has been to observe children working collectively with peers, instead of adults, to solve problems and resolve mutual differences. In some ways that are similar to the previous models, transitions in children's social cognitive development are studied as they occur in an uninterrupted stream of social discourse. According to some investigators, peer transactions have the potential to reveal cognitive conflicts and resistances that are not apparent in individual problem solving activities (e.g., Bearison, 1982; Damon, 1983; Kuhn, 1972).

In studies of children solving problems in peer groups, conflicts can arise between a subject's initial perspective or understanding of a problem and the perspective of one or several others. Thus, a subject is pressed not only to satisfy him or herself regarding the best solution, but to satisfy others as well. This need to verify one's own perspective in coordination with other perspectives structures the process of interpersonal negotiations in ways that can promote cognitive growth. According to Piaget (1932), "contact with . . . others produces doubt and the desire to prove. . . . The social need to share the thoughts of others and to communicate one's own with success is at the root of our need for verification" (p. 204).

Compared to other transactional models of social cognition, this one is most clearly derivative of Piaget's theory, particularly his conceptions of cognitive conflict (i.e., disequilibration) as a primary motivating force in development. Extending earlier theoretical findings showing that intraindividual conflicts of centration can account for cognitive development (e.g., Bearison, 1969; Inhelder,

Sinclair, & Bovet, 1974; Murray, 1968; Smedslund, 1961), Doise and his colleagues in Geneva have shown that children working in dyads solve problems at a more advanced level than do children working individually on the same problems. Children initially were pretested to determine their basal levels of performance on a target problem and then were randomly assigned to individual or collective problem-solving conditions. Subjects later were individually posttested on the target and sometimes on related problems. Different studies used different cognitive tasks as the focus of social interaction, including the conservation of length (Mugny, Giroud, & Doise, 1979), number and liquid conservation (Perret-Clermont, 1980), and the coordination of spatial perspectives (Doise, Mugny, & Perret-Clermont, 1975; Mugny & Doise, 1978). In these studies it was found that it was not necessary to pair subjects with more advanced partners for the subjects to show individual improvement on the posttests, and generally subjects who were paired with less advanced partners did not regress (Mugny & Doise, 1978). The most successful dyadic combinations were those in which subjects who functioned at intermediate levels of mastery worked together (Mugny & Doise, 1978). In such conditions, both the less and the more advanced partners progressed. Also, a substantial number of subjects in collective conditions who progressed on conservation tasks used logical arguments on the posttests that were different from those used in the pretests and to which they were not exposed during the course of collective problem solving (thereby advancing the case for the occurrence of cognitive restructuring). Weinstein and Bearison (1984) found that having control subjects individually observe the social interaction of dyads who progressed on conservation tasks was not sufficient to promote cognitive gains. Thus, the progress shown by interacting subjects appears not to have been a simple function of the amount of task-relevant information that was yielded during the course of interaction, but of the reciprocal and dyadic coordination of such information. According to Perret-Clermont (1980):

> The cause of the cognitive development observed is to be found in the conflict of centrations which the subject experiences during the interaction. The interaction obliges the subject to coordinate his or her actions with those of others, and this brings about a centration in the encounter with other points of view which can only be assimilated if cognitive restructuring takes place. (p. 148)

According to this explanation, it should not be necessary for subjects, in the course of social interaction, to be exposed to a "correct" solution but only to a "conflict of centrations." In several studies, cognitive progress was evidenced by exposing subjects to preoperatory centrations on conservation problems that were contrary to their own preoperatory centrations (Ames & Murray, 1982; Mugny, Doise, & Perret-Clermont, 1975–1976).

A socio-cognitive conflict model of social cognitive development can be contrasted with explanations of social transaction and cognitive growth produced by imitating a model. Social learning theorists (e.g., Bandura, 1977; Zimmerman & Rosenthal, 1974) have shown that children evidence cognitive gains by observing a model who consistently demonstrates the correct solution. However, social learning models could not account for how subjects who interacted with less advanced partners had as much cognitive gains as subjects who interacted with more advanced partners. Modeling effects, thus, might be better understood as a particular instance of the general effects of socio-cognitive conflict. Where modeling appears to be effective, it is not a result of imitating the model but of the cognitive discrepancy generated between the subjects' cognitive expectations and the model's behavior.

According to the socio-cognitive conflict model, effective social interactions will generate perturbations (i.e., disequilibrations) in subjects' existing knowledge schemes that can be resolved through operational coordinations (interpersonal and intrapersonal) that yield cognitively more advanced levels of understanding (Kuhn, 1972; Moessinger, 1978; Piaget, 1977). For Piaget, equilibration and development are practically synonymous. Development proceeds in ontogenesis because each and every perturbation to an equilibrated cognitive system gives rise to a higher form of equilibration (Piaget, 1977). In social transactions, the context of confronting and coordinating conflicting or contradictory centrations promotes cognitive restructuring. Thus, transactions in which task-relevant disagreements, contradictions and contrary solutions are expressed among dyads theoretically should be more effective in enhancing cognitive gains through the process of disequilibration and reequilibration than should dyadic interactions that lack these kinds of cognitive disconfirmations.

Despite theoretical arguments and empirical evidence for the facilitating effects of social discourse on cognitive development, there have been very few attempts so far to observe directly and measure the process of children's social transaction in order to determine (a) specific, theoretically relevant patterns of peer transaction that provoke developmental changes and (b) why they are sustained by some groups of children more than others. Damon and Killen (1982) studied the effects of peer interaction on children's (kindergarten, first, and second graders) concepts of distributive justice. They found that a rejecting and conflicting style of discourse was inversely associated with progressive changes. Such a finding seems more congruent with a Sullivanian model of collaborative co-construction than a socio-cognitive conflict model. Berkowitz and Gibbs (1983) analyzed the verbal discourse of college-age peer dyads who engaged in a series of moral discussions and found that dyads who had significant pre- to post-intervention gains in their levels of moral reasoning differed from dyads that didn't produce changes in terms of their engagement in a type of transactional dialogue in which "one's own reasoning confronts the other's antithetical reasoning in an ongoing dialogic dynamic" (p. 402). Ames and Murray (1982) and Miller and Brownell (1975) found limited support for socio-cognitive conflicts. They found that statements expressing contrary assertions between dyads attempting to solve conservation problems were one of several discourse categories associated with cognitive gains.

Bearison, Magzamen, and Filardo (1984) studied children's dyadic transactions while they worked collaboratively on spatial perspective problems. Consistent with a socio-cognitive conflict model, they measured the range and extent of task relevant contradictions and disconfirmations expressed between partners. They found a curvilinear relationship between the expression of dyadic conflict and cognitive growth. Neither too few nor too many conflicts were associated with significant positive change scores. They also found that partners who disagreed with each other in a relatively balanced pattern had significantly greater cognitive gains than dyads in which one partner dominated the other in terms of the expression of conflict. It appeared that when partners expressed a balanced pattern of conflicts, they were better able to enact mutually coordinated roles in attempting task solutions. Bearison et al. (1984) concluded that socio-cognitive conflicts optimally occur in a cooperative social context in which each partner is able to contribute equally to the social dialectic that structures the coordination of interindividual perspectives.

Continued systematic observations of children's collaborative negotiations in problem-solving situations will provide a rich data base for defining and testing theoretically meaningful units of transactional analyses. The test of what kinds of transactional features provoke cognitive development can be functionally determined according to pre- to post-intervention changes in children's operational competence as well as comparisons between the cognitive gains of children working collaboratively and individually on the same sets of problems. This particular research design allows for the control of a variety of interesting variables that may influence the cognitive effectiveness of children's transactions. For example, some studies in progress by students at the Graduate Center involve transactional differences between close friends and acquaintances, partners with similar and dissimilar ability levels, same sex and opposite sex partners, and those with different levels of operational reasoning.

SELMAN AND DEMOREST'S MODEL

The model that Selman and Demorest present (this volume) is similar in many respects to the previous models we have discussed. It seeks to bridge the theoretical gap between reflective cognition and cognition in conduct, and it is committed to the primacy of social transaction in cognitive development. Like the other models, it offers an alternative to those methods of studying social cognition that are based on children's responses to hypothetical social situations in decontextualized settings that lack emotional and motivational considerations. It seeks instead to explain social cognitive development as it naturally evolves in the stream of children's peer transactions. Like the other models, this one considers developmental processes that are applicable to both microgenesis and ontogenesis. Selman and Demorest's model has its closest affinities with socio-cognitive conflict models, in that development is motivated by disequilibrium generated by situations of interpersonal conflicts with peers. The transactional features of peer interaction are captured in a developmental taxonomy of inter-personal negotiation strategies that children use to deal with situations of inter-personal disequilibrium. These strategies reflect cognitive, emotional, and motivational components which, in synchrony, define levels of transactional competence.

Despite features that Selman and Demorest's model have in common with other models of transactional cognition, particularly socio-cognitive conflict models, it differs from them in several critical ways. In models based on chil-dren's collaborative problem-solving activities, either with adults or peers, the developmental parameters of social transaction rest on the direction and mag-nitude of task mastery as it reflects some underlying level of children's operational competence. The ways in which children resolve the task permit the investigator to determine, in part, which attributes or patterns of social transaction provoke development and which are developmentally maladaptive. In contrast, the model proposed by Selman and Demorest does not define the social context in terms of the mastery of cognitive tasks. The social context consists of naturally occur-ring social conflicts that children create for themselves. Instead of assessing development in terms of levels of task mastery, it is assessed according to the kinds of interpersonal negotiations children use to resolve their differences. Selman and Demorest have formulated a structural-developmental model of inter-personal conduct that corresponds in many respects to structural-developmental levels of reflective cognition in terms of increasingly more complex levels of coordination between self/other perspectives, although more highly developed negotiation strategies are not necessarily more socially adaptive than earlier strategies given the diversity of socio-emotional constraints on interpersonal conduct. In effect, they are proposing formal correspondences between two cognitive structural systems—reflective cognition and transactional cognition. However, there are critical differences between these two systems, differences that reflect the nature of structural forms of rational thought and practical expe-rience. Structures function according to principles of logical necessity, they are universal (i.e., acultural), increasingly transcendental in regard to content, con-sistently progressive in development, and concerned with issues regarding cog-nitive competencies. Experience, on the other hand, is contextual, not necessarily rational, subject to both progressive and regressive forces in development, and concerned with issues regarding practical performance (Glick, in press). In the dynamic interaction between form and experience, each is derivative of the other. The challenge in the Selman and Demorest model is to achieve a reconciliation between these two developmental systems in providing an explanation of the organization of social cognitive development without conflating their distinctive properties.

According to Selman and Demorest, formal models of cognitive competence, like Piaget's, provide developmental analyses of the emergence of new capacities for interpersonal negotiations; however, they are insufficient for developmental analyses of children's real-life conduct in interpersonal negotiations once those capacities have been developed. Competency-based models neglect the affective and motivational features of development. Also, they don't allow for oscillations between the behavioral expression of more and less advanced strategy levels. For example, there is more to within and between subject variations in interpersonal conduct than differences in logical-operational structures. However, a structural-developmental model of social cognition based on a progressive and sequential series of logical coordinations between self/other perspectives is used as a "core analytic tool" or standard by which Selman and Demorest are able to order both progressive and regressive variations in children's transactional strategies. The coordination of perspectives is a way to understand the hierarchical relationships among the different components of an interpersonal negotiation strategy at different developmental levels such that "the developmental levels in social perspective coordination are logically related to levels of development in interpersonal negotiation." Perspective coordination provides the conceptual bridge between reflective, competency-based cognition and interactive, practical cognition. Equilibration remains the core motivating force in this model of transactional cognition. In reflective cognition, it is intraindividual conflicts and perturbations represented on the symbolic plane that yield to increasingly more inclusive forms of equilibration, whereas, in social interaction, interindividual as well as intraindividual conflicts and perturbations are presented on the plane of practical action. There is an "internal disequilibrium" with respect to "a self perceived need" and an interpersonal disequilibrium with respect to the other as being capable of fulfilling "a self perceived need." Interpersonal equilibrium occurs between the "wants and claims of self and other," whereas intrapersonal equilibrium occurs between conflicting intentions within the self. According to Selman and Demorest, both intrapersonal and interpersonal disequilibrium need to be present for assigning an interpersonal negotiation strategy a developmental level. This constitutes the formal or structural relationship between reflective cognition and social transaction.

The functional relationship between these two systems is not isomorphic. There is not a one-to-one correspondence between developmental changes in reflective cognition and interpersonal conduct. Explanations of conduct must consider components that are essentially absent in reflective cognition and that would explain the greater contextual variability within and between subjects in social transaction than in reflective knowledge. What are these components that conjointly define developmental levels of interpersonal conduct? According to

Selman and Demorest, there are four of them: a cognitive component, a motivational component, an affective component, and a behavioral component. These four components must be considered simultaneously in the assessment of a strategy level; however, they are functionally organized in relative synchrony with one another at every developmental stage, so that there are not levels composed of all of the potential combinations of components by stages. Each component functions in coordination with the others to provide a complete developmental perspective of the derivation and application of an interpersonal negotiation strategy. In addition to the synchronous constellation of these components, there is a self-transforming and an other-transforming orientation at each strategy level. Together, the model provides an exceedingly rich description of cognitive transactions.

However, there appear to be some formidable problems in empirically validating the model, problems that have to do with reliably assigning developmental levels to children's negotiation strategies. Differential decisions regarding the assignment of interaction strategies to stage levels often rest on the investigator's ability to read consistently and unbiasedly the underlying intent "in the mind" of the strategy user. This is a problem because the same observed interaction strategy can reflect different underlying intentions and, similar intentions can yield different observed interactions. Furthermore, the stage criteria at each successive developmental level place increasingly greater reliance on the inference of underlying intentions, as more complex forms of transactional conduct reflect more complex and recursive levels of interpersonal understanding. In addition, assignments of observed interaction strategies to stage levels at times requires prior knowledge of the history of the interpersonal relations of partners in similar situations. Thus, the assignment of developmental levels among phenotypically similar negotiation strategies used by the same individual at different times under different affective and motivational conditions can be a problem.

In addition to the formal, functional, and methodological features of the Selman and Demorest model, the transactional context in which they have observed children's interactions in order to formulate and test attributes of their model should be considered. Their data were derived primarily from observations of children's psychotherapy sessions in which the children participated in "friendship pairs therapy" (Selman, 1980; Selman & Demorest, 1984). The children had serious emotional problems that were reflected in their inability to establish and maintain stable and mutually fulfilling interpersonal relationships. Observations of these children interacting in a therapeutic context allowed for the expression of a broader range of negotiation strategies within and between subjects than would be expected among adjusted children outside psychotherapy. Thus, the subject by context condition maximized the expression of both the progressive and regressive features of social transaction. Observations of troubled children in pair therapy, guided by a theoretical model with which to understand the developmental implications of their interpersonal negotiation strategies, have the potential to inform us about the etiology, symptomology, and treatment of emotional disturbances.

Finally, there are questions that could be asked of the Selman and Demorest model that may pose some interesting directions for future research. Does an individual's reflective knowledge of social understanding constitute a level of competence beyond which interpersonal negotiations cannot exceed, or can the negotiations reflect levels of cognitive competence beyond those revealed in reflective abstractions? Are interpersonal negotiation strategies more appropriate to interpreting peer interactions that generally are characterized by relations of cooperation than to adult-child interactions that generally are characterized by relations of constraint? What happens when, in the stream of interpersonal negotiations, a given strategy fails to satisfy the self's perceived need? Under such conditions, what will determine the use of alternative strategies (or the termination of negotiations)? Will alternative strategies vary consistently from the frustrated strategy previously used in terms of being developmentally more primitive or more advanced? In other words, what conditions account for the occurrence of progressive and regressive variations in strategy usage? Are certain systematic theoretical biases imposed on the interpretation of children's transactions because negotiation strategies are assigned individually rather than dyadically? Are self-transforming and other-transforming orientations within levels of strategy enactments relatively stable across contexts constituting a type of cognitive-style variable between individuals? Is there generally greater developmental consistency in strategy enactments and synchronicity among strategy components among emotionally adjusted children compared with children who have difficulties establishing and maintaining interpersonal relations? If less consistency in interpersonal relations is associated with emotional impairment in children, is it a cause or a sympton of impairment?

CONCLUSION

The model of children's interpersonal negotiation strategies formulated by Selman and Demorest is part of a larger approach to social cognition that recognizes the primacy of the transactional features of cognitive development and the need to study cognition in the ongoing stream of social discourse. This approach represents a significant departure from earlier models of cognitive development that were relatively incognizant of the affective and contextual features of transactions and that consequently provided a perspective of cognitive development that was predominantly universal, transcendental, logically necessary, and reflective. The perspective of cognitive development that is evolving from these new approaches is considerably different. Whereas each of the models that I have discussed focuses on a different aspect of the problem of how to reconcile universal forms of reflective cognition with the cultural, affective, and inter-personal constraints that give meaning and purpose to human behavior, each, I believe, will continue to benefit from comparative analyses of the others because they share a common conceptual object—social transaction.

REFERENCES

Abelson, R. P. (1976). Script processing in attitude formation and decision making. In J. S. Carroll and J. W. Payne (Eds.), *Cognition and social behavior* (pp. 33–45). Hillsdale, NJ: Lawrence Erlbaum Associates.

Abelson, R. P. (1981). Psychological status of the script concept. *American Psychologist, 36*, 715–729.

Ames, G., & Murray, F. B. (1982). When two wrongs make a right: Promoting cognitive change by social conflict. *Developmental Psychology, 18*, 894–897.

Baldwin, J. M. (1897). *Mental development in the child and the race.* New York: MacMillan.

Bandura, A. (1977). *Social learning theory.* Englewood Cliffs, NJ: Prentice-Hall.

Bartlett, F. C. (1932). *Remembering: A study in experimental and social psychology.* Cambridge: Cambridge University Press.

Bearison, D. J. (1969). The role of measurement operations in the acquisition of conservation. *Developmental Psychology, 1*, 653–660.

Bearison, D. J. (1982). New directions in studies of social interaction and cognitive growth. In F. Serafica (Ed.), *Social-cognitive development in context* (pp. 199–221). New York: Guilford.

Bearison, D. J., Magzamen, S., & Filardo, E. (1984). *Socio-cognitive conflict and cognitive growth in young children.* Manuscript submitted for publication.

Berkowitz, M. W., & Fibbs, J. C. (1983). Measuring the developmental features of moral discussion. *Merrill-Palmer Quarterly, 29*, 399–410.

Bernstein, B. (1971). *Class, codes, and control* (Vol. 1). London: Routledge & Kegan Paul.

Bower, G. (1978). Experiments on story comprehension and recall. *Discourse Processes, 1*, 211–231.

Bower, G., Black, J. B., & Turner, T. (1979). Scripts in memory for text. *Cognitive Psychology, 11*, 177–220.

Bruner, J. (1983). *Child's talk: Learning to use language.* New York: Norton.

Bruner, J. (1984). Interaction, communication, and self. *Journal of the American Academy of Child Psychiatry, 23*, 1–7.

Damon, W. (1983). The nature of social-cognitive change in the developing child. In W. Overton (Ed.), *The relationship between social and cognitive development* (pp. 103–142). Hillsdale, NJ: Lawrence Erlbaum Associates.

Damon, W., & Killen, M. (1982). Peer interaction and the process of change in children's moral reasoning. *Merrill-Palmer Quarterly, 28*, 347–367.

Dewey, J. (1949). *Knowing and the known.* Boston: Beacon Hill.

Doise, W., Mugny, G., & Perret-Clermont, A. N. (1975). Social interaction and the development of cognitive operations. *European Journal of Social Psychology, 5*, 367–383.

Dore, J. (1974). A pragmatic description of early language development. *Journal of Psycholinguistic Research, 3*, 343–350.

Dyer, M. G. (1983). The role of affect in narratives. *Cognitive Science 7*, 211–242.

Glick, J. (in press). Piaget, Vygotsky, and Werner. In S. Wapner and B. Kaplan (Eds.), *Toward a holistic developmental psychology* (pp. 35–52). Hillsdale, NJ: Lawrence Erlbaum Associates.

Graesser, A. C., Woll, S. G., Kowalski, D. J., & Smith, D. A. (1980). Memory for typical and atypical actions in scripted activities. *Journal of Experimental Psychology: Human Learning and Memory, 6,* 503–515.

Gruendel, J. (1980). *Scripts and stories: A study of children's event narratives.* Unpublished doctoral dissertation, Yale University.

Inhelder, B., Sinclair, H., & Bovet, M. (1974). *Learning and the development of cognition.* Cambridge: Harvard University Press.

Kuhn, D. (1972). Mechanisms of change in the development of cognitive structures. *Child Development, 43,* 833–844.

Mandler, J. (1978). A code in the node. *Discourse Processes, 1,* 14–325.

Mandler, J., & DeForest, M. (1979). Is there more than one way to recall a story? *Child Development, 50,* 886–889.

McCartney, K., & Nelson, K. (1981). Children's use of scripts in story recall. *Discourse Provesses, 4,* 59–70.

Mead, G. H. (1934). *Mind, self, and society.* Chicago: University of Chicago Press.

Miller, S., & Brownell, C. (1975). Peers, persuasion and Piaget: Dyadic interaction between conservers and non-conservers. *Child Development, 46,* 992–997.

Moessinger, P. (1978). Piaget on equilibration. *Human Development, 21,* 255–267.

Mugny, G., & Doise, W. (1978). Socio-cognitive conflict and structure of individual and collective performances. *European Journal of Social Psychology, 8,* 181–192.

Mugny, G., Doise, W., & Perret-Clermont, A. N. (1975–1976). Conflit de centrations et progrès cognitif *Bulletin de Psychologie, 29,* 199–204.

Mugny, G., Giroud, J. C., & Doise, W. (1979). Conflit de centrations et progrès cognitif, II: Nouvelle illustrations expérimentales *Bulletin de Psychologie, 32,* 979–985.

Murray, F. B. (1968). Cognitive conflict and reversibility training in the acquisition of length conservation. *Journal of Educational Psychology, 59,* 82–87.

Nelson, K. (1978). How young children represent knowledge of their world in and out of language. In R. S. Siegler (Ed.), *Children's thinking: What develops?* (pp. 255–273). Hillsdale, NJ: Lawrence Erlbaum Associates.

Nelson, K. (1981). Social cognition in a script framework. In J. Flavell & L. Ross (Eds.), *The development of social cognition in childhood* (pp. 97–118). New York: Cambridge University Press.

Nelson, K., Fivush, R., Hudson, J., & Lucariello, J. (1983). Scripts and the development of memory. In M. T. H. Chi (Ed.), *What is memory development the development of?* (pp. 97–126. J. A. Meacham (Ed.), Contributions to Human Development Monograph Series. Basel, Switzerland: Karger.

Perret-Clermont, A. N. (1980). Social interaction and cognitive development in children. *European Monographs in Social Psychology, 19.* London: Academic Press.

Piaget, J. (1932). *The moral judgment of the child.* London: Routledge & Kegan Paul.

Piaget, J. (1950). *The psychology of intelligence.* London: Routledge & Kegan Paul.

Piaget, J. (1971). *Biology and knowledge.* Chicago: University of Chicago Press.

Piaget, J. (1977). *The development of thought: Equilibration of cognitive structures.* New York: Viking Press.

Renninger, E. A., & Winegar, L. T. (1984). *Expert-novice systems in knowledge acquisition.* Manuscript submitted for publication.

Saxe, G. B., Gearhart, M., & Guberman, S. R. (1984). The social organization of early number development. In J. V. Wertsch & B. Rogoff (Eds.), *Children's learning in the "zone of proximal development," New Directions for child development,* (Vol. 23 pp. 19–30). San Francisco: Jossey-Bass.

Schank, R. C., & Abelson, R. R. (1977). *Scripts, plans, goals and understanding.* Hillsdale, NJ: Lawrence Erlbaum Associates.

Selman, R. L. (1980). *The growth of interpersonal understanding.* New York: Academic Press.

Selman, R. L., & Demorest, A. P. (1984). Observing troubled children's interpersonal negotiation strategies: Implications of and for a developmental model. *Child Development 55,* 288–304.

Shatz, M., & Gelman, R. (1973). The development of communication skills: Modifications in the speech of young children as a function of listener. *Monographs of the Society for Research in Child Development, 38.*

Slackman, E., & Nelson, K. (1984). Acquisition of an unfamiliar script in story form by young children. *Child Development, 55,* 329–340.

Smedslund, J. (1961). The acquisition of conservation of substance and weight in children. V. Practice in conflict situations without external reinforcement. *Scandanavian Journal of Psychology, 12,* 151–160.

Stein, N. A., & Glenn, C. (1979). An analysis of story comprehension. In R. O. Freedle (Ed.), *New directions in discourse processing* (Vol. 2, pp. 53–120). Norwood, NJ: Ablex.

Sullivan, H. S. (1953). *The interpersonal theory of psychology.* New York: Norton.

Vygotsky, L. (1962). *Thought and language.* Cambridge: M.I.T. Press.

Vygotsky, L. S. (1978). *Mind in society: The development of higher psychological processes.* Cambridge: Harvard University Press.

Vygotsky, L. (1981). The genesis of higher mental functions. In J. V. Wertsch (Ed.), *The concept of activity in Soviet psychology* (pp. 144–187). White Plains, NY: Sharpe.

Weinstein, B., & Bearison, D. J. (1984). *Social interaction, social observation, and cognitive development in young children.* Manuscript submitted for publication.

Werner, H. (1948). *The comparative psychology of mental development.* Chicago: Follett.

Wertsch, J. V. (1979). From social interaction to higher psychological processes: A clarification and application of Vygotsky's theory. *Human Development, 22,* 1–22.

Wertsch, J. V. (1984). The zone of proximal development: Some conceptual ideas. In J. V. Wertsch and B. Rogoff (Eds.), *New Directions for Child Development: Vol. 23. Children's learning in the "zone of proximal development"* (pp. 7–18). San Francisco: Jossey-Bass.

Wertsch, J. V., McNamee, G. C., McLane, J. B., & Budwig, N. (1980). The adult-child dyad as a problem-solving system. *Child Development, 51,* 1215–1221.

Wood, D., Bruner, J., & Ross, G. (1976). The role of tutoring in problem solving. *Journal of Child Psychology and Psychiatry, 17,* 89–100.

Wood, D., Wood, D., & MIddleton, D. (1978). An experimental evaluation of four face-to-face teaching strategies. *International Journal of Behavioral Development, 1,* 131–147.

Zimmerman, B., & Rosenthal, T. L. (1974). Conserving and retaining equalities and inequalities through observation and correction. *Developmental Psychology, 10,* 260–268.

9 Emotions and Cognitions in Self-Inconsistency

Augusto Blasi
Robert J. Oresick
University of Massachusetts - Boston

A long-standing ambition within the cognitive-developmental approach has been to extend the theory and transform it into a general theory of psychological functioning or, at least, into a general developmental theory. Thus, the principles formulated by Baldwin, Piaget, Werner, and other pioneers about the development of logic and of symbolic conceptual competencies have been applied to social understanding, including understanding of defense mechanisms, moral reasoning, the development of self-concepts and of the self. In this attempt, a persistent and almost intractable obstacle was represented by the emotional and motivational components of human functioning. The most successful extensions always concerned understanding, concepts, and reasoning. At times, affective processes seemed to be quite close, almost within our reach, but, in the end, they regularly eluded our grasp.

In discussing our topic, we felt that it may be wiser to restrain our ambition and to limit our scope to one set of emotions or to one category of affectively charged experiences rather than to attempt a broad formulation. In doing so, it is crucial to select the type of emotions that one considers paradigmatic. It makes a difference whether one chooses relatively simple emotions, such as fear or anger, or relatively complex ones, such as jealousy or respect. Quite possibly, one source of the difficulty that cognitive-developmental theory is encountering in dealing with affect is that psychology as a whole has somehow acquired the belief, never clearly verbalized, that certain emotions and feelings (e.g., desire, anger, and anxiety) are real, honest-to-god, emotions, whereas others (e.g., serenity and curiosity) are of a mixed, watered-down kind.

147

Our strategy in this chapter is to focus on the experience of *self-inconsistency*, in its affective and cognitive aspects. We then use this type of experience to discuss the relevance, and the adequacy, of a cognitive approach such as Piaget's to understanding certain kinds of self-emotions, and, more generally, the development of the self. One advantage of selecting self-consistency and self-inconsistency is that these processes, at least at first glance, seem to be related to the Piagetian concepts of equilibration and disequilibration. Not only are these concepts at the center of Piaget's theory, but they represent the only motivational and affective ideas that are *intrinsic* to the cognitive-developmental conceptual system. A comparison between disequilibration and self-inconsistency should allow us to grasp more precisely the potential of at least one cognitive theory to be extended into the domain of personality in its complex nature.

In the following, occasional reference is made to empirical data; the thrust of our discussion, however, does not rely on research findings. We feel that one could go a long way by simply reflecting on our shared understanding of what self-inconsistency is and what should be involved in its experience. In this respect, literary descriptions, fictional and nonfictional, seem to offer important advantages: By necessity, they must represent the meanings that are embedded in our language and in our shared categories and must speak to them, even when their goal is to renew and revitalize our perception; moreover, in their dramatic style, they frequently sharpen precisely those features of human experience that seem to represent its ideal archetypical form.

THE EXPERIENCE OF SELF-INCONSISTENCY

It may be useful to start with a fundamental conceptual distinction and then to discuss two different classes of experiences for which one may speak of self-inconsistency.

The distinction is between self-inconsistency and internal contradiction. It is obvious that these two concepts are applied to different cases and used in different contexts. For instance, we can say of a book and of a theory that they are internally inconsistent, but we cannot say that they are self-inconsistent. On the other hand, one who consciously acts against one's own values is said to be self-inconsistent; but it would seem inappropriate, in this case, to speak of internal contradiction or of lack of inner logical coordination. In clarifying this distinction, it would not be sufficient to say that we speak of self-inconsistency when we refer to people and of internal contradiction when we deal with books or theories. One reason is that we may recognize in people both internal contradiction and self-inconsistency; we still would have to clarify which aspects of being a person are precisely involved in self-inconsistency. We try to do so by resorting to some paradigmatic examples.

Probably the clearest cases of self-inconsistency are those in which an action performed by a person does not correspond to a belief about the same action held by the same person. Charles believes that it would be wrong for him to lie to his friend and yet he does lie. We all are personally familiar with this type of situation. But we may not be fully aware of how broad this first category of self-inconsistency can be. Examples of self-inconsistency include acting against one's moral principles, compromising one's ideals in purusing a career or in perfecting one's skills, intentionally betraying one's accepted obligations in one's profession, in one's family or in one's relationships. A dramatic example would consist in verbally betraying, for example through ridicule or simple denial, one's beliefs, ideals, philosophy, or religious convictions out of expediency or for any other motive. But one also should include sycophancy, promising to do what one knows one will not do, lying[1], and, finally, that grey, hard to pin down, area of self-deception: from not wanting to acknowledge what, at some level, one knows to be true to various degrees of dishonesty, bad faith, and lack of intellectual integrity.

In this context, it is useful to point out the importance that beliefs have in all these instances of self-inconsistency. Beliefs seem to play a role that no other human behavior can or does play. It is as if they tied the variety of actions to the center that is the self. There wouldn't be any self-inconsistency without this center and without the beliefs by which it is represented.

However, not all beliefs have the same value and the same effects. One example will clarify the point: John is absolutely convinced that overall Ford is a better car than Chevrolet and yet, when he needs a car, he buys a Chevrolet. This is an example of self-inconsistency, according to the earlier definition. However, this is a *weak sense* of self-inconsistency: The immediate reason is that the belief that Ford is a better car does not necessarily imply buying it, even when one needs a car. In this case, even though the belief belongs to John, John may not be so centrally invested either in cars or in always being rational that he feels a psychological constraint to buy what he judges the best car. On the other hand, one may imagine that John's own identity includes as one of its central characteristics the ideal of absolute rationality, of following in action one's beliefs, whatever they are. In this case, the self is centrally involved, and, within the context of John's identity, believing that Ford is a better car implies buying it. There is no logical implication or necessity: The idea that Ford is the best car does not logically imply the idea of buying it. And yet there is a psychological necessity, because not buying this car would violate the coherence of John's identity. This is the *strong sense* of self-inconsistency, the type on

---

[1]We are not implying that self-inconsistency is the only or the main ground for the immorality of lies and false promises. We are saying that self-inconsistency is a valid additional perspective on these rather common behaviors, even though not many may be aware of, or sensitive to, this aspect.

which we focus. In its strong sense, then, self-inconsistency involves only a subset of a person's beliefs, namely, those, by which one defines one's most central nature, basic self-ideals, most cherished goals and ambitions. Among the examples listed earlier, betraying one's accepted obligation, lying, or making false promises always would involve self-inconsistency; however, there would be strong self-inconsistency in only if the identity of one's self were defined as faithful, truthful, and trustworthy.

So far, we have discussed one group of self-inconsistency examples, those involving a contradiction between an action and its corresponding belief. But there could be a different kind of self-inconsistency, in which action is not directly involved but there is, instead, some sort of conflict in the personality itself, e.g., among different desires, among desires and duties or desires and values, among tendencies, and so on. This type of internal conflict may be experienced as relevant to the self as soon as the child begins to look at him or herself as a set of stable characteristics (traits and tendencies) and no longer as a series of actions. It is possible, then, to become aware that certain stable characteristics are an obstacle in the realization of other equally stable tendencies within oneself.

Internal divisions and their awareness are not limited to the moral domain. The desire to pursue a career and at the same time experience the fulfillment of motherhood, the need to enjoy a certain degree of dependency while protecting the integrity of one's intelligence and the autonomy of one's responsibility have become commonplaces in the psychology of contemporary women. At times the conflict is subtler and may offer no solution. Thomas Mann's (1914/1968) Tonio Kröger felt split between his call to be a writer, to "the redeeming power of the word" on one side, and the realization that "the word" disembodies reality, makes life safe and dull, and renders the writer unable to follow his desire simply to live and to experience, fully unselfconsciously and mindlessly, those everyday pleasures that life offers. In a similar vein, a desire for accomplishment and perfection may appear inextricably tied to a certain degree of elitism and arrogance, which one otherwise despises.

All of these are examples of internal conflict. One could even speak of internal contradiction and lack of internal coordination, at least in the sense that the different elements (traits, tendencies, etc.) of one's personality are not adequately coordinated and subordinated so as to guaranteee a smooth psychological functioning in action and experience. But these are not examples of self-inconsistency, at least not obviously so. There may be conflict, but there is no self-inconsistency in wanting and striving for independence and in desiring to be taken care of, in choosing the lonely and demanding life of an artist and in longing, at the same time, for the simple rewards of family life. In fact, the experience of internal contradiction seems to increase with development (e.g., Loevinger & Wessler, 1970), whereas we should expect self-inconsistency to decrease.

However, there is one case of internal conflict in which it is possible to speak of self-inconsistency: when a trait is a part of a person's self-definition or of the ideal self, when a second trait interferes with the actualization of the first, and when the person could eliminate the conflict but prefers to do nothing. Charles defines himself as a serious writer. He is aware that his need for company and fun seriously interferes with his work, and yet he takes no steps to acquire a reasonable degree of self-control and discipline. In this case, Charles is self-inconsistent, at least from an objective perspective. But, then, this type of self-inconsistency is related to, and derives from, the first type, namely, the contradiction between one's beliefs about oneself and one's actions.

We are able, now, to outline more precisely what is necessarily involved in the strong sense of self-inconsistency. First, from the subject's perspective, there is a contradiction between one's essential definition or one's identity and the expression of one's identity in action; in a derived sense, between one's identity and those tendencies that endanger the fidelity of self-expressions. Second, the perception of agency, namely the understanding that one is responsible for the contradiction, is involved. The third element is a sense of self that allows for the possibility of the experience of self-inconsistency. This prerequisite involves two aspects: first, the perception of identity as a principle of internal unity; second, the understanding of agency as responsible both for the expression of one's self in action and for maintaining those internal conditions that facilitate the fidelity of one's self expressions.

EMOTIONAL RESPONSE TO SELF-INCONSISTENCY

Self-inconsistency, at least in its strong sense, is believed to produce or to be accompanied by emotional reactions, frequently intense in nature. Perhaps one of the best descriptions of such an emotional response is in Joseph Conrad's (1920/1981) *Lord Jim*. As one may recall, Jim had grown up with dreams of adventure and ideals of heroic deeds. In this spirit he enlisted as an officer in the merchant marine, where he considered himself in constant preparation for the difficulties that can be encountered on land and water. The test came when a leak sprang in the ship of which he was second officer. In a moment of confusion and shock, Jim found himself following the rest of the crew and abandoning to their fate the ship and its 800 passengers. The main theme of this novel is the exploration of Jim's affective experience and of the decisions that follow his betrayal of his self ideal. These are shock, dejection, despair, wish to be dead, to disappear; profound feeling of unworthiness together with a stubborn clinging to a very basic sense of dignity; attempt to restore his integrity by searching for an "unworthy" job and, eventually, by dying to affirm his recovered sense of self.

The response is unusual in its intensity. However, uncommon as it might be, this type of emotional response is not unique. In our research,[2] several high school juniors, when presented with hypothetical cases of self-inconsistency, expressed similar feelings: "I couldn't live with myself if I went against my beliefs," ". . . you're not living with the truth of yourself, of what you feel . . . it's not worth living . . .," "If that's where she puts most weight on what she's thinking, she'd feel horrible for the rest of her life, or for a long time doing that . . . because I think her own self should be more important to her . . .," ". . . she'll be hating herself, she'll never . . .; a person starts lying to himself, I guess, he starts going into this fake world . . . you know, they won't be themselves any more, they would be getting worse, lose self-respect of themselves . . .," ". . . if she stands to lose her self-respect by maintaining the lie . . . if she does that and she loses her self-respect, she's going to be sorry . . ."

Two observations seem important about these expressions of emotions. The first is that there is no specific emotional language to indicate self-inconsistency. In a small pilot study, we presented a group of college freshmen with two self-inconsistency situations (one was patterned after *Lord Jim*). They were asked to choose from a list those emotional labels that would correspond to their own feelings in the same situations and to explain the reasons for the choices. The labels selected by these subjects included: guilty, ashamed, disappointed with oneself, embarrassed, having a sense of inferiority, feeling worthless, feeling split or torn, and so on. There clearly is a large variety of terms to describe feelings. Moreover, each of these labels also is used in other contexts, for instance, in comparing oneself to social standards and expectations, in discussing the successful or unsuccessful achievement of one's goals, or in expressing any state of internal conflict. The specificity of one's emotional response to inconsistency is indicated, instead, by *describing* what one has done and by *interpreting* the event within a moral-affective framework. It is the combination of the emotional-evaluative terms and of the description that defines the experience: "I feel terribly depressed, ashamed with myself, disappointed, angry, etc. . . . because I betrayed my trust. I compromised who I am."

The second observation, based on another set of interview data (see Footnote 2), is that an intense moral-affective response to self-inconsistency appears relatively late in development (e.g., only among 15-16 year olds), and even then

---

[2]This particular research project (partially published in Blasi, 1981, 1984) focused on the understanding of responsibility. Children of three age groups (first, sixth, and tenth-eleventh graders) were interviewed individually to explore under what conditions and on the basis of which criteria they recognize a strict obligation to act according to one's moral evaluation. Two of the dilemmas used in this study explicitly involve self-inconsistency. In one (presented to sixth graders and high school students), a city official in charge of assigning contracts had to make a choice between the city laws and his own altruistic concerns. In the other (presented only to high schoolers), a nurse had to decide whether to follow the hospital's rules when they conflicted with her own principles and judgments. In both cases, the issue of self-inconsistency also was addressed by the questions following the presentation of the dilemmas.

it is infrequent. We presented groups of sixth graders and of tenth and eleventh graders with hypothetical situations in which consistency with one's own personal moral standards was pitted against obedience to institutional rules and laws. Briefly, the most important response categories that are relevant to the present discussion were the following:

1. There is no recognition that consistency with one's own moral beliefs has moral value; only objective rules and commands can be the basis for morality.

2. Being consistent with one's moral standard has a genuine moral value. However, this criterion is subordinated to objective criteria and is purely a matter of good will. Thus, even though it may be right to disobey institutional rules and to follow one's own understanding, there is no strict obligation to do so. Accordingly, one should not be blamed for not acting in agreement with one's judgment in this situation.

3. A person's moral judgment and moral standards are among the most important moral criteria. The importance of self-inconsistency, however, lies less in fidelity to one's own self than in its potential to elicit emotions that may impair the subjective sense of well being.

4. Consistency with one's moral philosophy, particularly when it has been carefully thought out, is the ultimate criterion, because one can not go against one's own self.

Sixth graders reasoned mostly according to the first two categories, with emphasis on the first. It should be noted that these children understand quite well what internal conflicts are and frequently describe the emotional tension that they experience when, for instance, a rule is in conflict with a strong desire. They also understand, descriptively, what it means to be self-inconsistent; self-inconsistency, however, is not viewed as a moral issue, nor does it elicit any significant emotional response.

Among high school students, the most frequent responses corresponded to categories 2 and 3: Self-inconsistency is understood, also in its moral value; less understood, instead, is the absolute importance that self-consistency has for the preservation of one's self. Only about 15% of this group saw the issue in these terms and responded emotionally in the way described earlier (category 4). These figures are surprising, because the same adolescents had a strong sense of subjectivity: namely, they saw each person's perspective as the only reasonable one and understood the importance of self-actualization and of achieving personal happiness and a state of peace and satisfaction with oneself.

The difference between the large majority in our adolescent sample and the small group that looked at consistency with one's principles as an absolute for which no compromise is admissible seems to lie in the way the self is understood. For the latter group, the self is so central to the person, one's principles and one's ideals are so central to the self, and fidelity in action is so central to one's identity that self-inconsistency is experienced as total loss, as spiritual death. In Conrad's (1920/1981) novel, Jim concludes his narration of the crucial event: ". . . 'everything was gone and—all was over . . . ' he fetched a deep sigh . . . 'with me'." Marlow then comments: "His saved life was over for want of ground under his feet, for want of sights for his eyes, for want of voices in his ears. Annihilation—hey" (p. 89). In T. S. Eliot's (1952) *Murder in the Cathedral*, Thomas Becket, another hero of fidelity, is begged to leave his church and flee from the king's emissaries who are after his life. In rejecting this suggestion, he says: ". . . Death will come only when I am worthy,/And if I am worthy, there is no danger . . . /No life is sought for but mine,/ And I am not in danger: only near death" (p. 209). The words of some of our subjects are quite similar: ". . . she's not following her own ideas . . . they're individuals, and everybody is, and if you don't, then you are nothing . . . I mean you lose faith in yourself"; "she should have her own principles that she should live by, because if you don't have your own principles . . ., you're not going to really be yourself anymore. You're just going to be one huge mass along with the rest of them."

SELF-INCONSISTENCY AND COGNITIVE DISSONANCE

Having described and tentatively defined self-inconsistency, the questions to be raised now are a more at theoretical level: What can be said about the reciprocal influence of affect and cognition? How should cognition be understood in relation to the emotions that characterize self-inconsistency? We attempt to clarify some of these issues indirectly, by analyzing how two influential views of inconsistency—the social psychological theory of cognitive dissonance and Piaget's equilibration theory—would look at self-inconsistency and the extent to which their understanding is compatible with our common understanding.

As a brief preview of our conclusions, self-inconsistency, as described in the earlier sections, does not seem to be grasped in its integrity either by the theory of cognitive dissonance or by Piagetian disequilibrium. Each of the two views seems readily to represent one important aspect of self-inconsistency and yet to misrepresent another, equally important, aspect of the same experience: The aspect for which one theory is best suited is precisely the one for which the rival theory is most inadequate.

At first look, cognitive dissonance theory seems to provide the ideal framework for the experience of self-inconsistency in its basic characteristics. This theory attempts to predict what people will do when their opinions, attitudes, or beliefs are in contradiction with their behavior (Festinger, 1957). Many of the phenomena that were focused on or that were experimentally manipulated within this paradigm involve a contradiction between what one believes and what one says, or between what one says and what one does, e.g., publicly advocating a political position that runs counter to one's beliefs or trying to convince another person that a certain task is very interesting when one knows it to be boring. Even more important is the specific aspect that is stressed in dissonant behavior. Even though the initial formulation of the theory was meant to be very broad and somewhat ill defined in its extension, important distinctions soon began to be made. Abelson (1968), for instance, differentiated "stresses" from "puzzles," the first being characterized by ego-relevant content. Kelman and Baron (1968) separated, among "stresses," "hedonic dissonance" from "moral dissonance," because of their very different implications for the person.

Briefly, many social psychologists began to recognize that the self and its sense of agency play a crucial role in cognitive dissonance. They hypothesized that the typical cognitive dissonance effects would be especially, if not exclusively, obtained when the self-concept is directly involved and when the individual feels responsible for the inconsistency. Aronson (1968), for instance, writes: "Dissonance theory is clearer . . . when that firm expectancy involves the individual's self concept. . . . Thus, at the very heart of dissonance theory, where it makes its clearest and neatest prediction, we are not dealing with any two cognitions; rather, we are usually dealing with the self concept . . ." (pp. 23–24; see also Bramel, 1968, Brehm & Cohen, 1962; Kelman & Baron, 1968; Secord, 1968).

Similarly, the sense of agency, the realization that dissonance was a result of one's free choice and volition, came to be recognized as an essential factor. This idea soon was crystallized in the concept of commitment, which was operaitonally represented either by public statement or by an irrevocable decision.

Given the similarity between these dissonance characteristics and the basic elements of self-inconsistency, it should not surprise us to find that the emotions that were associated with a typical dissonance situation are very similar to those that we described in the context of self-inconsistency: shame, guilt, feelings of inferiority, and sense of worthlessness (e.g., Bramel, 1968; Kelman & Baron, 1968).

In summation, it seems obvious that cognitive dissonance theory would represent rather well the affective-motivational aspect of self-inconsistency, to a degree that cannot be matched by the theoretical-descriptive tools of the cognitive-developmental approach. However, paradoxically enough, a cognitive-dissonance formulation is inadequate to represent, and tends to distort, the cognitive aspects of self-inconsistency. One could say that the theory of cognitive dissonance, at least in this case, is not cognitive enough, but this statement needs to be explained.

In the cognitive-dissonance formulations, *cognition* refers the verbal or veralizable categorization of certain psychological processes and events (beliefs, opinions, attitudes, values, traits, actions, etc.). There is dissonance every time two different categorial elements or their implications appear to the subject to be incompatible with each other. Not only is this a very limited sense of cognition, but everything else in the cognitive dissonance paradigm is positively noncognitive and frequently irrational.[3]

First of all, in the experience of dissonance, the focus of the theorist is on stress or tension and its motivational characteristics. Self-inconsistency, then, would be important because it generates tension. Once generated, this tension is like any other tension: It produces a drive leading to its own reduction and, as a result, to attitude changes. In summary, the emphasis is on the emotional aspect, cut off from its moral context and its subjective interpretation. However, as we saw earlier, emotional language is inadequate to represent the specific experience of self-inconsistency. Even such terms as guilt, shame, or unworthiness become specifically meaningful only when they are placed in the context of a special understanding of the events and of the self. Of course, this is *a fortiori* true of the grossly generic "stress".

Second, in the categorization of the events or in the cognitive description of the inconsistency, little or no attempt is made to raise questions about the subject's understanding. This theory assumes (correctly in our opinion) that the self is an important and perhaps the central factor in the production of dissonance effects. The self, however, is reduced to self-categories and is thought to operate motivationally through the quantitative variable of self-esteem. Self-categories are modified to maintain a sufficiently high level of self-esteem. The adequacy or truth of these categories is irrelevant. There is virtually no analysis of what it means to understand oneself, to know oneself, and to be convinced of the truth of one's self-knowledge and one's identity.

In fact, self-concepts are present relatively early in childhood, but they do not produce, if they do so at all, the typical response to self-inconsistency until much later. What seems required is the development of the self, by which we are not referring to the accumulation, diversification, and organization of self-categories, but to the experience and the understanding of oneself as an integrated responsible agent. Those who respond to self-inconsistency in the manner described earlier, namely, as a loss of faith in oneself, report that they know the truth of their identity and that, therefore, their integrity cannot be compromised: Self-inconsistency is understood as destroying one's integrity and, thus, one's self.

Consistent with the way cognitive dissonance theory approaches the self is its view of commitment. Whether commitment is operationally defined as public expression of opinion or as strong anticipation of future interaction, there is the sense that it consists of a voluntaristic attitude; once more, how strong one's

---

[3]The literature on cognitive dissonance is enormous. It is indeed possible to find writers that have criticized and have tried to correct the tendency within the theory to construe the phenomena in a rigidly irrational way. Thus, the variety of strategies and of outcomes in dissonance resolution as well as individual and situational differences have been pointed out (e.g., Kelman & Baron, 1968). We feel, however, that our comments are generally accurate. Our purpose, moreover, is not to evaluate the adequacy of this theory, but to bring out important aspects in self-inconsistency, that the theory of cognitive dissonance seems to neglect.

attitude is seems to matter more than one's reasons for acting. In fact, reasons are sometimes regarded with suspicion as if they weakened the strength of one's commitment. In Zimbardo's (1968) words, "As the justifications (be they hedonistic, mystical, or rational) for making a given decision increase, the decision becomes more 'externalized'; the individual can point to circumstances which compel a given course of action, limit his choice, and reduce the risks attendant upon personality" (p. 444). By contrast, our subjects attempt to explain very carefully why in certain cases a person must absolutely take certain decisions and why it is morally necessary for certain individuals to avoid certain actions.

Third, there is the problem of dissonance resolution. In its overall thrust, this theory tends to communicate two basic points: (a) that it is easier to change beliefs than actions and (b) that the typical strategies to resolve dissonance involve distortion of reality. When it has been recognized that certain beliefs, particularly those that concern the self, are highly resistant to change (e.g., Pilisuk, 1968) and that some people, at least in some situations, remain in touch with reality even at the price of maintaining their dissonance (e.g., Aronson, 1968; Berlyne, 1968; Kelman & Baron, 1968), the basic explanatory approach has been to rely on a functionalistic, cost-reward analysis. This point deserves more detailed discussion.

The basic idea is simple: A subject will distort reality if doing so is easy and convenient; a subject will not resort to distorting maneuvers if their effects are unpleasant in the long run. When one's action and its implications for one's self-concept are in contradiction with one's self-ideal, one will change one's self-ideal, if doing so is not too cumbersome conceptually and not too costly emotionally.

But this is not the way people who understand it report the experience of self-inconsistency. Jim, in Conrad's novel, stuck both to his self-ideal *and* to the undistorted perception of what he had done. He paid with his life for his attempt to recover the truth of his own self as one "who does not betray his trust." He did not do so because his course of action was easier or more convenient than getting rid of his guilt. Weston (1975), commenting on the same novel, points out that guilt does not enter Jim's description of the events.

. . . in the way a goal enters the description of reasons: "guilt" enters rather in the fact that to be able *to say and mean* "I betrayed my trust" *is* to feel guilty and consider oneself guilty. . . . His guilt is not *important* to him, and not, of course, *unimportant*. What is important is that he jumped, and this importance is brought out by stating this fact in certain moral terms, that he "betrayed his trust." (pp. 55–56; the author's italics).

This analysis clarifies why it can be so misleading to speak of tension or of dissonance-reduction: If tension has no meaning outside of the description of the event and of the framework within which the event is interpreted, one must deal with the whole experience and not with tension.

In our interviews (see footnote 2) several high school students reasoned that whenever one's personal conscience is involved, the self is involved; and, when the self is involved, no compromise is morally possible. Therefore, they resorted to the irrevocability of certain self-beliefs. In contrast with social psychologists, however, they also tried to show that the basis for the irrevocability is neither a strong emotion nor the high cost of the loss, but the fact that there lies reality, the truth, of the self; and that, if one gives up one's beliefs, there is nothing left. Reality simply is: Truth is not for sale, and neither is the self.

To summarize this section, in cognitive dissonance theory the emphasis is on stress and its drive-arousing nature, independently of its specific psychological or moral meaning. Self-concept is considered an important factor, but without any concern for the specific way self-categories or the self are understood. Commitment is thought to operate in a voluntaristic nonrational manner. The processes involved in dissonance resolution are believed frequently to distort reality, and its outcomes are thought to follow opportunistically the principle of utility rather than the principle of truth.

By contrast, self-inconsistency, as described here, stresses the description of events within a moral-affective interpretation. In order to occur, it requires a certain understanding of the self and of morality, understanding that seems to develop slowly and by steps. It is based on fundamental commitments whose motivational strength lies in the understanding of the self and whose activation depends on specific interpretations of reality and of events. It finally seeks a resolution that does not change the reality of either one's ideal-self or of one's action but, rather, strives to recover a new sense of coherence under the principle of truth.

Empirical data provide enough evidence for the existence of phenomena like cognitive dissonance. On the other side, it seems likely that self-inconsistency as we described it also exists, at least in some people and sometimes. In accounting for the latter, the social psychological theory of cognitive dissonance appears to be entirely inadequate, in spite of its emphases on emotions, commitment, and the self. What is needed is a theoretical formulation that recognizes the importance of understanding, the construction of meanings, and the role of reasons and looks for the ways in which the development of these processes determines both one's emotional responses and one's adjustment to reality.

SELF-INCONSISTENCY AND DISEQUILIBRIUM

Piaget's theory seems to be a most plausible candidate: It is a thoroughly cognitive theory and assigns inconsistency, in the form of disequilibrium, a central role in the explanation of development.

By *disequilibrium* Piaget (1977) refers to a state of cognitive conflict induced by a gap between experience and understanding or by the realization that part of the data cannot be assimilated by one's cognitive system. Disequilibrium is an experience of an active subject engaged in a cognitive project. Therefore, both self-inconsistency and disequilibrium occur in a context of intentionality and awareness. However, despite this similarity, there are radical differences between the two experiences. We focus on four major contrasts between self-inconsistency and cognitive disequilibrium.

The first difference is in orientation. Cognition grasps the world; self-consistency expresses and extends the self. In cognition and self-consistency there is an interaction between the world and the subject, but the focus is quite opposite in each case. In cognition, for example, awareness is directed toward the world, as represented by an object. If there is disequilibrium, the focus of awareness may be redirected toward the workings of the knowledge system, but this is done in the service of assimilating the world. In the case of self-inconsistency, awareness may be focused on the world and on the actions in the world, as illustrated by Jim's obsession with the fact that the ship sank and he jumped. But the underlying focus is on how the self is expressed in those actions in that context.

The second difference lies in the locus of the inconsistency. Whereas disequilibrium essentially concerns the parts of a structure, self-inconsistency is between a center, the self, and its parts.

The metaphors of the ring and of the wheel may help us to grasp the central difference between a cognitive structure and the self. Both the ring and the wheel have, as perimeter, a physical hoop in which concrete parts can be identified; in both cases, one can speak of dynamic and space relations among these parts. But these similarities are less important than the differences. In the ring there is no concrete center; the only physically concrete relations are those among its parts. One can certainly think of the center of the ring and determine it in a very precise way. This center, however, is a mental construction, a purely mathematical abstraction. As such, it remains exactly the same regardless of the physical nature of the ring or of the specific location it occupies in space. Matters are quite different in the wheel. Here the hub is a concrete reality, and the relations between the hub and the parts of the hoop also are concretely real, being mediated by the physical spokes. Dynamically, in fact, these relations are far are important in determining the nature and the function of the wheel than those among the parts of the hoop.[4]

A cognitive structure like the ring is an equilibrated set of relations among parts, which may be concrete mental acts or schemes and concepts. The structure itself is always an abstraction. That is, a structure is not object of or grasped through immediate experience in the way the actual motor or mental operations

---

[4]Barthes (1977) also used the metaphor of the circle to suggest the absence of the self as principle of unity: "To write by fragments: the fragments are then so many stones on the perimeter of a circle: I spread myself around: my whole little universe in crumbs; at the center, what?" (pp. 92–93).

are. Instead, a structure is known through a process of comparing a variety of operations and abstracting from them the principle of logical unity. For this reason, the subject has no special advantage over other people in knowing his or her own cognitive structure.

Because cognitive structures consist of logical relationships among parts, disequilibrium is internal contradiction or lack of internal coordination. Contradictions and gaps can occur anywhere within the system, without reference to a center; but, as was argued earlier, internal contradiction is very different from self-inconsistency.

The self, on the other hand, is not an abstraction; it is a concrete subject, concretely and immediately experienced in every action as the central source of agency. Behaviors and operations, like the parts of the wheel's hoop, are much less revealing of the self than the relations or the stances that the self establishes toward them: stances of distancing, of agency and appropriation, of unification and separateness (Blasi, 1983). Thus, from the perspective of the subject, the unity among a person's behaviors and mental operations does not depend on their sharing the same logical principle, as is the case for cognitive structure, including self-concepts. It depends, instead, on their being perceived as produced by the same concrete agent (metaphorically, as radiating from the same hub), as being appropriated by the same self, and as being recognized as expressons of its identity. Agency, appropriation, and identity are not concepts (even though self-concepts and self-descriptions may be based on them); they are experienced primarily as stances, as relations established between the self as center and the periphery.

Self-consistency and inconsistency, therefore, always concern the relations between this concrete center and the periphery, namely, the actions that express it, and not the relations among the parts themselves, as is the case in the equilibrated cognitive structure. Self-inconsistency always is a problem of fidelity of one's actions in expressing the identity of one's self. For example, if I lie, believing that I should not lie, I may suffer great guilt because of my self-inconsistency; yet there is no disequilibrium because my understanding of the situation remains internally consistent with my general moral understanding. There is no gap in my knowledge; there is only a discrepancy between my self and its expressions.

The third difference between self-inconsistency and disequilibrium lies in an aspect of agency, responsibility. Cognitive activity may indeed be intentional. However, disequilibrium itself is not sought after and falls outside the scope of the cognitive intentional project; it simply happens to the knower in interaction with the world, a byproduct of just the opposite intent.

Self-inconsistency is another matter. To be self-inconsistent, the agent must intend to act contrary to his or her belief. If I do not intend to not tell the truth, I do not lie; I make a mistake. If I intend to keep my promise to help a friend move, but my car breaks down and I do not show up, my action is not self-inconsistent. So, unlike disequilibrium, self-inconsistency implies that I intended it and, consequently, that I am responsible for it.

The final, and for our purpose central, difference between the two kinds of inconsistency is in the emotional responses associated with them. The typical emotions of disequilibrium are "sense of gap," surprise, puzzlement, confusion, and so on, whereas the emotions characteristic of self-inconsistency are guilt, shame, "feeling torn", and the like. At the phenomenological level, there is no doubt that these are distinct emotional experiences; but we can go further and consider how these feelings are understood in a cognitive context.

Surprise, confusion, and the other emotions of the same family are understandably linked to disequilibrium because they reflect an appraisal that an expectation, perhaps tacit, or a certain understanding of the world has not been fulfilled. For this reason, J. M. Baldwin referred to surprise as "that logical emotion" (quoted by Décarie, 1978). Children are surprised when they release a balloon and see it rising to the ceiling—other objects have fallen to the floor. When questioned about moral dilemmas, adolescents may feel confused, as they contradict what they said only moments earlier, and may find this experience of disequilibrium quite disturbing, as they may not know how to resolve the contradiction.

Surprise and confusion are reactions to failures of knowledge, to mistakes. They are not found in self-inconsistency. In fact, it would be ridiculous to speak of puzzlement and surprise in this case. The reason is that, in self-inconsistency, knowledge concerning the self, concerning what one believes, what one has done or should have done, is not at issue.

Guilt and similar feelings, by contrast, are tied to self-inconsistency through agency and responsibility as well as through identity and that sense of self which demands fidelity to one's identity. The inconsistency, in this case, is intentional—it is a misdeed, not a mistake—and so the violation of one's ideals and beliefs is morally reprehensible.

Piaget's theory of disequilibrium fails to account for the emotional experience of self-inconsistency. It fails because this theory does not have conceptual tools to explain either the self and its identity or the responsibility aspect of agency. As we pointed out, these are precisely the aspects of self-inconsistency that cognitive-dissonance theory emphasizes. However, there is a large gap between using concepts and understanding or explaining them. In some real sense, the theory of cognitive dissonance ends up by distorting both responsibility and the self, precisely because of its noncognitive bias.

It is here that Piaget's contribution to the understanding of self-inconsistency lies, despite its real and unresolvable inadequacies. Piaget's contribution is both specific, in his theory of equilibration, and general, in his emphasis on cognitive orientations, ideals, and motives.

Whatever the self is, it is also is an object of understanding and knowledge, an organization of concepts, ideas, and ideals that are acquired in interaction with one's own experience, but also in interaction with other people and with the social world in general. Even though cognitive structures alone cannot adequately account for the development and transformations of one's identity, there seems to be little doubt that identity relies on cognitive competencies and uses all the knowledge that a person possesses. Therefore, the development of the self also is partially influenced by the dialectic between disequilibrium and equilibration, in which relevant terms include all of one's experiences with the world, not only one's own actions, thoughts, and emotions. What one knows about oneself cannot be separated from what one knows in general.

This framework offers a much better understanding than does the theory of cognitive dissonance of what has been called the irrevocability of self-concepts and self-ideals and of its limits. Even though the gap between identity and action is, most frequently, a result of failure in action, there may be cases in which the inconsistency follows from a much too restrictive identity and from unrealistic self-ideals. For example, having gone through a long series of what could be considered "self-betrayals" of artistic identity, a person begins to discover at the same time a lack of artistic talent and other genuine interests, all of which slowly leads him or her to the construction of a new identity. In such cases "truth" may be on the side of action and not on the side of identity. It is here that the theory of disequilibrium becomes relevant.

Piaget's general contribution also to our understanding of self-inconsistency is no less important. It consists in having made plausible the ideas that a significant part of human activity is directed at constructing knowledge of the world and that, in doing so, one is motivated not by immediately utilitaristic considerations, such as the satisfaction of needs and the elimination of unpleasant emotions, but by curiosity and respect for the way things objectively are.

CONCLUSION

Although every conclusion is expected to bring some closure on a topic, we, instead, end our discussion by opening new perspectives and by shifting our present emphases.

In inquiring about the relations between affect and cognition, we perhaps have been asking the wrong kind of question. Formulating the question as we have does not seem to take seriously enough the fact that both cognitions and emotions belong to a person, are cognitions and emotions of a subject, and therefore take place in the context and as part of an integrated personality structure. It is reasonable, then, that there are no immediate relations between affect and cognition, as one part to another part, but that their mutual interacton is mediated by the overall personality. This is probably one reason why Loevinger

(1976) so stubbornly refuses to separate different dimensions (cognitive, inter-personal, moral, or affective) within her concept of ego.

Within this perspective, more appropriate questions are: In what way do certain cognitive competencies affect personality as a whole? What kind of personality structure is required for certain cognitions to produce certain kinds of emotions? Or, equivalently, in what way does the emotional response to the understanding of a situation differs with different personality structures? In the context of self-inconsistency, as we saw, the emotional response is a much better indicator of the nature of the self, of the way the self is lived and understood, than of the conceptual categorization of the event. Of course, we still speak of understanding the self or self-inconsistency. But, in this context, *understanding* refers to a much more comprehensive and complex type of psychological reality than when we speak of understanding conservation or theoretical possibility.

The second, and much more radical, way in which the terms of the question could be fruitfully changed concerns the meaning of cognition. In more than one instance, in the process of analyzing the experience of self-inconsistency, clear cognitive elements were pointed out that could not adequately fit the Piage-tian cognitive paradigm. For instance, we mentioned, on one hand, distortions of reality and bad faith and, on the other, being true to oneself and being faithful to one's identity. Even if one allows that self-concept and identity could be rendered in Piagetian terms, one still may wonder what "being true to oneself" might possibly mean within this theory or why it should be an important ideal.

This problem does not apply only to Piaget's theory but is present in most, if not all, of contemporary cognitive psychology. Contemporary cognitive approaches limit themselves to concepts and focus on the way these become differentiated and organized into increasingly complex systems. A few years ago, Kaplan and Crockett (1968), commenting on cognitive dissonance theory from a Wernerian perspective, focused on "the cognitive means that are employed to bring order and coherence into one's world" (p. 663) and noted that, "An analysis and genetic ordering of these means must, therefore, ignore the sec-ondary, and here unadjudicable, issue of veridicality and correctness and concern itself with the ways in which subjects organize information . . ." (p. 665).

But to understand self-inconsistency in cognitive terms, we need such concepts as veridicality, truth, fidelity, distortion, and bad faith. Truth and untruth, although requiring concepts, are located on a different plane and need a different level of analysis.

In comparing the present preoccupation with conceptual systems with the cognitive orientation toward truth, two observations can be made. First, the average person, in daily life, refers to the latter when thinking of knowledge and knowing. Second, the language of truth and untruth has a very wide range of applications; in fact, it also can be used in many areas for which concepts do not strictly apply. Thus, we can speak of the truth of myths and fables, of the truth of poetry and music; we can intelligibly say that a painter or a writer is true to his or her inspiration and understanding or that the painter or writer has compromised art to fashion, political pressure, or commercial demand.

If we accept that there is something in common in all these different uses of "truth" and that in all these instances we do indeed deal with knowing and knowledge, we also realize how narrow and limited, and in many cases irrelevant, is the meaning of cognition that has been adopted by the different varieties of contemporary cognitive psychology. It is clear to us that cognition is relevant to personality, including affects and emotions. However, we may have reached the limit in usefully extending cognitive conceptual views to personality. We may need now to focus on a different understanding of cognition, one that includes as central elements orientation to the truth, fidelity to it, and responsibility in its discovery and affirmation; and to study in which ways the study of personality is clarified by it.

REFERENCES

Abelson, R. P. (1968). Comment: Uncooperative personality variables. In R. P. Abelson, E. Aronson, W. J. McGuire, T. M. Newcomb, M. J. Rosenberg, & P. H. Tannenbaum (Eds.), *Theories of cognitive consistency: A sourcebook*. Chicago: Rand McNally.

Aronson, E. (1968). Dissonance theory: Progress and problems. In R. P. Abelson, E. Aronson, W. J. McGuire, T. M. Newcomb, M. J. Rosenberg, & P. H. Tannenbaum (Eds.), *Theories of cognitive consistency: A sourcebook*. Chicago: Rand McNally.

Barthes, R. (1977). *Roland Barthes by Roland Barthes*. New York: Hill & Wang.

Berlyne, D. E. (1968). The motivational significance of collative variables. In R. P. Abelson, E. Aronson, W. J. McGuire, T. M. Newcomb, M. J. Rosenberg, & P. H. Tannenbaum (Eds.), *Theories of cognitive consistency: A sourcebook*. Chicago: Rand McNally.

Blasi, A. (1981). Kognition, Erkenntnis und das Selbst [Knowledge in social cognition]. In W. Edelstein & M. Keller (Eds.), *Verstehen der Sozialen Welt*. Frankfurt an Main, FDR: Suhrkamp Verlag.

Blasi, A. (1983). *The self as subject: Its dimensions and development*. Unpublished manuscript, University of Massachusetts, Boston.

Blasi, A. (1984). Autonomie im Gehorsam [Autonomy in obedience]. In W. Edelstein & J. Habermas (Eds.), *Soziale Interaktion und soziales Verstehen*. Frankfurt an Main, FDR: Suhrkamp Verlag.

Bramel, D. (1968). Dissonance, expectation, and the self. In R. P. Abelson, E. Aronson, W. J. McGuire, T. M. Newcomb, M. J. Rosenberg, & P. H. Tannenbaum (Eds.), *Theories of cognitive consistency: A sourcebook*. Chicago: Rand McNally.

Brehm, J. W., & Cohen, A. R. (1962). *Explorations in cognitive dissonance*. New York: Wiley.

Conrad, J. (1981). *Lord Jim*. New York: New American Library (Original work published 1920.)

Décarie, T. G. (1978). Affect development and cognition in a Piagetian context. In M. Lewis & L. A. Rosenblum (Eds.), *The development of affect*. New York: Plenum.

Eliot, T. S. (1952). Murder in the Cathedral. In *The complete poems and plays: 1909–1950*. New York: Harcourt & Brace.

Festinger, L. (1957). *A theory of cognitive dissonance*. Stanford, CA: Stanford University Press.

Kaplan, B., & Crockett, W. H. (1968). Developmental analysis of modes of resolution. In R. P. Abelson, E. Aronson, W. J. McGuire, T. M. Newcomb, M. J. Rosenberg, & P. H. Tannenbaum (Eds.), *Theories of cognitive consistency: A sourcebook*. Chicago: Rand McNally.

Kelman, H. C., & Baron, R. M. (1968). Determinants of modes of resolving inconsistency dilemmas: A functional analysis. In R. P. Abelson, E. Aronson, W. J. McGuire, T. M. Newcomb, M. J. Rosenberg, & P. H. Tannenbaum (Eds.), *Theories of cognitive consistency: A sourcebook*. Chicago: Rand McNally.

Loevinger, J. (1976). *Ego development: Conceptions and theories*. San Francisco: Jossey-Bass.

Loevinger, J., & Wessler, R. (1970). *Measuring ego development. I. Construction and use of a sentence completion test*. San Francisco: Jossey-Bass.

Mann, T. (1968). *Tonio Kröger*. New York: Blackwell. (Original work published 1914).

Piaget, J. (1977). *The development of thought: equilibration and cognitive structure*. New York: Viking.

Pilisuk, M. (1968). Depth, centrality, and tolerance in cognitive dissonance. In R. P. Abelson, E. Aronson, W. J. McGuire, T. M. Newcomb, M. J. Rosenberg, & P. H. Tannenbaum (Eds.), *Theories of cognitive consistency: A sourcebook*. Chicago: Rand McNally.

Secord, P. (1968). Consistency theory and self-referent behavior. In R. P. Abelson, E. Aronson, W. J. McGuire, T. M. Newcomb, M. J. Rosenberg, & P. H. Tannenbaum (Eds.), *Theories of cognitive consistency: A sourcebook*. Chicago: Rand McNally.

Weston, M. (1975). *Morality and the self*. New York: New York University Press.

Zimbardo, P. G. (1968). Cognitive dissonance and the control of human motivation. In R. P. Abelson, E. Aronson, W. J. McGuire, T. M. Newcomb, M. J. Rosenberg, & P. H. Tannenbaum (Eds.), *Theories of cognitive consistency: A sourcebook*. Chicago: Rand McNally.

10 Affect, Cognition, and Self in Developmental Psychology

William Damon
Clark University

Developmental psychology, like any other social science, offers a set of conceptual tools for understanding certain features of human life. Of the many aspects of human life that we need to understand, developmental psychology can help with only some because it focuses primarily on behavioral formation that takes place in a progressive manner over time. Consequently, developmental psychology is best suited for analyzing the aspects of human behavior that do "improve" or that can be ordered on some scale relative to other aspects of behavior. Behavior that neither advances nor is developmentally scalable according to some reasonable criteria is best understood within another conceptual framework.

For example, we may expect developmental psychology to shed light on how and why an individual's thought, affect, and conduct change over time. It also might tell us something about how the individual's thought, affect, and conduct are interrelated, at least with respect to each other's development. To take the case of the moral behavior cited in Blasi and Oresick's chapter: An illuminating developmental analysis might help us see how Lord Jim's actions and feelings were connected with his current moral beliefs, which in turn could be placed in the context of his life history. Or, it might help us understand how the important changes in Jim's moral beliefs were triggered by key affective or social experiences. These are issues that can be understood by examining how cognitive and behavioral systems change over time in an ordered manner. Developmental psychology is ideally suited for such analyses.

We could not, however, look to developmental psychology for an answer to the question of whether Jim was a good or an evil person in a moral sense. Nor could we determine whether Jim was capable of becoming good or evil, even though on the surface this question seems more like a developmentalist's task.

167

Blasi and Oresick do not attempt this, nor could any persons limited to psychological tools of analysis, for two reasons. First, of course, defining good and evil is a matter of faith. Any attempt to construct developmental directions based on such notions would create even more confusion and controversy than exist in the usual debates about the ordering implicit in developmental directions. Because developmental analyses rely above all on the sense that such directions are based on legitimate ordering principles, it is essential to start with constructs that can be defined and ordered according to criteria that are explicit, precise, and compelling. These criteria must reflect values—all developmental directions do—but the values must be defensible as ordering assumptions.

The second reason that the question of good or evil personhood lies beyond the scope of developmental psychology is that developmental analyses are inappropriate for assessing the moral worth of individuals. Behavioral systems, cognitive structures, even emotional experiences can be ordered developmentally with profit. The values underlying the ordering principles can be derived from the function served by the behavioral system. For example, if we wish to examine logical thinking in terms of how well it yields quantitative accuracy, it is a straightforward enough task to derive a behavioral sequence representing steps toward this end. Developmental psychologists have always proceeded this way, whatever their area of focus. But when whole individuals rather than behavioral systems become the focus of assessment, a developmental analysis is precluded. Individuals are too varied in their goals and too complex in their functioning to be ordered in any consistent way. In fact, the very mention of such an enterprise would no doubt strike us as repugnant, a sentiment that attests to the inappropriateness of applying developmental values in this way. Although we legitimately could examine Jim's moral behavior from within a developmental framework, we could not assess his progress toward a good or evil personhood. Blasi and Oresick, fortunately, do not attempt this either.

Within the constraints of its own essential assumptions, developmental psychology as a field of inquiry has had its share of successes and failures. there is no point to dwelling on the successes here. They are adequately represented in our vast and expanding literature. The field's failures, not surprisingly, are mentioned less frequently, but Blasi and Oresick's chapter goes to the heart of several of them. These—at least the ones that Blasi and Oresick touch upon—are worth noting here.

First, as the authors imply, developmental psychology has never adequately addressed the relation between cognition and affect. There has been plenty of valuable work on cognitive development, and, as this volume demonstrates, there are a number of promising initiatives in the area of emotional development. It is when we consider one in relation to the other that we run into problems. Piaget's (1962) classic manner of dealing with this relation was to assert that structure belongs to cognition, that affective experience reflects this cognitive structure, and that otherwise affect adds a kind of undifferentiated energizing force to cognition and action. The virtue of this solution is that is direct and comprehensible. It is not, however, very satisfying; for one thing, it does not allow for the possible contribution of a unique affective experience to cognitive structuring. Further, once we veer even slightly from this formulation, it becomes less direct and comprehensible. This is because we then unavoidably are faced with some unconfortable questions. If affect does not mirror cognitive structure, what is the nature of its own unique organization? What is it about affective experience that *develops*, beyond one's cognitions about affect? Other than through informal and speculative discussions within the psychoanalytic tradition, no one to my knowledge has seriously tackled these questions.

The second problematic issue that Blasi and Oresick raise concerns the nature of developmental processes. Blasi and Oresick implicitly ask two questions about developmental processes: (a) Is there more than one basic process responsible for developmental change? and (b) Is there an intrinsic relation between developmental processes and developmental structures? The two questions are related; for, if the answer to the second is yes, the answer to the first must be yes also. The authors confront these questions in trying to adapt Piaget's equilibration model to their construct of self-inconsistency. Piaget's equilibration model is essentially a one-process model, with some hierarchically ordered subprocesses. Self-inconsistency, they tell us, is a "rather rare" disequilibrating process that is experienced at the "end or . . . highest stage" of development. By implication, less-advanced forms of self-reflection, therefore, must be perturbed and changed through different sorts of developmental processes—processes that are somehow less advanced than the experience of self-inconsistency. Does this mean that processes, like structures, develop? Is the development of the one connected with the development of the other? What does this mean about the relations between developmental structures and processes? In Blasi and Oresick's chapter, as in the field at large, we see the collison of a one with a many-process model. The authors try to make the best of both, but the theoretical problem remains, as it does for many developmentalists today.

The third problem that the authors uncover is how to conceptualize the self. Part of this problem has to do with what the self actually is, and part of it has to do with the role of the self in psychological development. The authors suggest that Piaget's theory—and we probably can read any cognitive theory in here—does not need a concept of self. This is true if we make two assumptions: (a) that the self can be conceptualized only as a "homunculus" with its own energies, motives, and insight, operating in an executive capacity as a controller of the individual's behavior and cognitions; and (b) human cognition can be explained on its own terms, without reference to executive or motivational functions outside the cognitive system. Most developmentalists accept at least one of these assumptions and thus rarely refer to the self.

But a concept of self as a cognitive construct, focusing on one's experience of individuality and identity and seen as a vital part of one's conceptual make-up, would fill a critical gap in developmental theory. Do we need a more full-bodied self than "merely" a conceptual system focusing on individuality and identity? Judging from the way the term *self* is used in discursive writings throughout the other areas of psychology, it seems that our intuitive answer to this is "yes." But what are the boundaries of the self, what does it do exactly, and what does it not do? Is it simply synonymous with the term *person*, and is the study of self simply the study of personality? There is enormous ambivalence and little clarity about this in the field. Blasi and Oresick's chapter is no exception and raises the issue by virtue of its evident concern (and difficulties) with it.

What makes Blasi and Oresick's presentation so interesting is that not only do they wrestle with these critical problems, but also their theoretical struggles yield insights into some other puzzling aspects of human behavior. For example, the authors show how their self-inconsistency paradigm could be used to explain moral emotions. This in turn could help us solve the old riddle of how (and whether) moral reasoning becomes translated into conduct.

Blasi and Oresick report that they find a developmental difference in how one's moral principles are viewed in relation to one's self-identity. Only some of their older subjects, adolescents in their mid to late teens, see morality as an essential part of their identities. Further, only their oldest subjects viewed them-selves as responsible for the consistency and "unity" of their self-expressions. In other words, only the adolescents felt bound by an overarching principle that the authors call "fidelity" to oneself. The implication is that this principle, available only at a relatively advanced level of development, impels consistency between moral judgment and conduct. Blasi and Oresick cite a number of emo-tional experiences associated with this advanced state.

My own current studies (Damon, 1984) of self-understanding in children and adolescents are yielding findings that confirm much of what Blasi and Oresick report. I, too, have observed a tendency in late adolescence for morality to become an increasingly central part of an individual's self-definition. This is based initially on a tendency for adolescents to construe themselves in terms of their sociability. From this tendency emerge concerns like being considerate of others, caring for one's friends and relatives, displaying virtues like trustwor-thiness, generosity, or loyalty, and so on. Later in adolescence the focus shifts to one's psychological processes and beliefs. There emerges a tendency for adolescents to define themselves in terms of the values and ideologies that they most cherish. With this tendency comes a sense of earnestness about one's morality per se. Both of these adolescent tendencies—and particularly the second—lead the adolescent to adopt morality as a central aspect of the self. This, I believe, is the developmental phenomenon that Blasi and Oresick describe while discussing adolescent morality.

Further, in accord with Blasi and Oresick's claims, my self-concept research (Damon, 1983; Damon & Hart, 1982) has found that, with development, children and adolescents become increasingly aware of their own volitional capacities. By the mid teens, adolescents normally acquire a sense that they themselves determine the shape of the self. This new sense of personal agency is based in part on a developmental advance in the self-concept: The self is now viewed as a matter of subjective experience and belief, which generally is under one's own control (at least to the extent that mental life is ever controllable). The adolescent's enhanced sense of personal agency naturally translates into a greater sense of moral responsibility for the adolescent's beliefs and actions. It also brings home the need for consistency in one's beliefs and goals, for one likely would not feel responsible for contradictory or incoherent principles. This awakened need for self-consistency is what Erikson (1968) described as the "identity crisis" and what the current authors call the motivating orientation toward fidelity.

Although I am impressed by the richness of Blasi and Oresick's approach and fascinated by its potential to grapple with some of developmental psychology's critical problems, I wonder if there may not be more direct routes to some satisfactory solutions. I do not see the need, for example, to deal with the self as anything more embodied than a conceptual system—as long as we recognize it for the unique conceptual system that it is. The problem for cognitive-developmental theory has not been in reducing the self to a concept, but rather in treating it as indistinguishable from the concept of "persons" in general. Those who make the self into more than a concept invariably fail to explicate exactly *how much* more of exactly *which* human processes to include. I suspect this is because it is not possible to conceptualize a "full-bodied" self short of *personality*— and psychology does not need *another* construct called personality.

How can we forge a construct that does justice to the uniqueness and complexity of the self-concept? For a cognitive self-concept suited to a developmental analysis, we can look back to the philosophical writings of James (1892), Baldwin (1902), and Mead (1934). From these writings emerge two unique features of self, neither of which is found in any other concept. First is the notion of the dual self, the "I" and the "me," as James called it. The self alone, as Mead wrote, is "reflexive" because it views itself both as a subject and as an object. Second is the notion that the emotions associated with "self-regard"—emotions like self-esteem, pride, shame, and so on—have no parallels in other conceptual experience. These two unique features require developmentalists to construct a structural analysis especially tailored to the self-concept instead of assimilating it to other conceptual frameworks. This, admittedly, is a challenge that few have undertaken. (Broughton, 1978, is one exception; and my own current work is also directed toward this goal—see Damon & Hart, 1982.)

The self-concept, treated in all its uniqueness and complexity, covers all the concerns expressed by Blasi and Oresick. It allows for the volitional as well as the organizational aspects of self and requires them to be analyzed according to distinct conceptual principles. It also avoids the unnecessary burden of analyzing the whole person. This, as I indicated at the beginning of this chapter, is a task for which developmental psychology is not equipped. I wish to add one further, ideological note. This position is not as antihumanistic and coldly scientific as it may sound. As I see it, the danger in taking on this unnecessary task would be to distort the very "whole person" that we are trying to understand by viewing him or her through too narrow a lens. A developmental analysis, with all of its inherent value presuppositions concerning the end-point and goals of development, is a fine tool for understanding functions and structures of behavior, but cannot do justice to the human worth of individuals.

Finally, there is a metatheoretical issue involved. What is the wisest way to proceed with theory building in developmental psychology? In order to approach unsolved problems like the role of affect or the nature of the developmental process, do we need new theoretical constructs, or should we instead redefine or extend some existing theoretical constructs?

This question brings us back to the issue that I raised at the beginning of this chapter: the proper use of a developmental analysis. As implied earlier, I do not believe that developmental psychology can offer an insight into every area of human life. It is far better suited for some sorts of analyses than for others. In particular, because it relies on assumptions of order and progression, it is best suited to those aspects of life that do indeed show a tendency to advance in some ordered manner over time. This certainly applies to conceptual systems, as well as to conceptual aspects of an emotional state. Apart from the conceptual aspect, though, it is doubtful that it applies to other aspects of emotion.

For example, there is no reason to believe that happiness in an emotive or quantitative sense is or should be considered a developmental phenomenon. Part of the reason is that, like goodness, happiness is hard to define. But the real issue is locating something that can be developmentally analyzed apart from the conceptual underpinnings of the emotion. If there is a sense in which persons regularly advance in their happiness over time, can we ever isolate this from the person's cognitive strategies and conceptual interpretations? I doubt it. The implications are that, for the sake of developmental analysis, emotions must be seen in terms of their cognitive or behavioral structures. However, this does not preclude our treating emotions as unique constructs with special conceptual and behavioral features. Nor does it preclude others' analyses of human emotions within a nondevelopmental framework, for whatever purposes nondevelopmental psychological analyses legitimately have. In this sense, the reduction of affect to a cognitive construct within a developmental framework is by no means total and follows the same logic as our treating the self as a cognitive construct: The uniqueness of each construct must be preserved in the cognitive analysis. The rationale behind such treatment is fundamental. The developmental approach is stronger, and more readily serves its goals, by virtue of our recognizing its limits and building upon its unique assumptions.

REFERENCES

Baldwin, J. M. (1902). *Social and ethical interpretations in mental development.* New York: MacMillan.

Broughton, J. (1978). Development of concepts of self, mind, reality, and knowledge. *New Directions for Child Development, 1,* 75–100.

Damon, W. (1983). *Social and personality development.* New York: Norton.

Damon, W. (1984). Self-understanding and moral development in childhood and adolescence. In J. Gewirtz & W. Kurtines (Eds.), *Moral development and moral behavior: New directions and recent research.* New York: Wiley.

Damon, W., & Hart, D. (1982). The development of self-understanding from infancy through adolescence. *Child Development, 53,* 831–857.

Erikson, E. H. (1968). *Identity: Youth and crisis.* New York: Norton.

James, W. (1892). *Principles of psychology: The briefer course.* New York: Holt.

Mead, G. H. (1934). *Mind, self, and society.* Chicago: University of Chicago Press.

Piaget, J. (1962). *Affectivite et intelligence.* Presses universitaires de Paris.

11

Cognitive Controls, Metaphors, and Contexts: An Approach to Cognition and Emotion

Sebastiano Santostefano
McLean Hospital and Harvard Medical School

To guide studies of cognition and emotion, a model is proposed that conceptualizes cognition as a mobile set of mental and sensorimotor actions. These actions coordinate the responses required by the context and task stimuli with which a person is dealing and by the person's fantasies and affect that interpret the same context and stimuli. The model subscribes to one of Piaget's (1981) hypotheses: that, in reality situations, cognitive and affective aspects of behavior always are present simultaneously, and one aspect does not result from or cause the other. But the model also departs from Piaget's second hypothesis (functional parallelism of intellectual structures and emotions) because this hypothesis, it seems, leads to one set of concepts and methods for cognition and to another for affect, thereby segregating the two domains and opposing the first hypothesis.

If cognition and affects are viewed as inseparable, then the same model and methodology should apply whether one is interested in the experience and expression of emotions or in the experience and actions taken when one circle is perceived as larger than another, an issue articulated by Bruner (1951) 30 years ago. One such model, described here, is framed by three concepts: cognitive controls, metaphors, and contexts. After these, we present laboratory findings and clinical observations to illustrate the heuristic value of the model. In comparing the model with others, the conclusion articulates issues important to the problem of the relation between cognition and emotion.

THE CONCEPTS AND MODEL

Cognitive Controls

The concept of cognitive controls views cognition as a set of strategies, each iinvolving a particular mental process, each consisting of levels of organization from global to differentiated, and each reorganizing so that the attributes of internal stimuli (fantasies) and external stimuli (task at hand) either are assimilated or avoided in serving adaptation and learning.

Cognitive controls have the status of intervening variables that define principles by which motoric behavior, perception, memory, and other aspects of cognitive functioning are organized as an individual coordinates him or herself with the environment. Specifically, cognitive controls are defined as mechanisms that: (a) govern and determine the amount and organization of information that becomes available to an individual perceiver; (b) are activated by the individual's intention to use and adapt to information; (c) vary in the extent to which they operate in the cognitive functioning of individuals; (d) evolve as a function of maturation and life experiences and become autonomous from their origin of development; (e) mediate the influence of personality and motivation in the individual's cognitive encounters with the environment; and (f) become enduring aspects of an individual's cognitive functioning and adaptive style, thus giving shape to his or her subsequent experiences (Gardner, Holzman, Klein, Linton, & Spence, 1959; Klein, 1951, 1954; Klein & Schlesinger, 1949; Santostefano, 1978).

Five such mechanisms have been identified in the cognitive functioning of children and adults, and each has been observed to follow a developmental course throughout childhood.[1]

1.   The cognitive control mechanism, *body-ego tempo regulation*, defines the manner in which an individual uses images/symbols to represent and regulate body motility. When asked to walk on a pathway at slow and fast tempos, the young child moves with one tempo and assigns global images to represent the tempos (e.g., a turtle and a bug). With development, the child moves on a pathway with increasingly differentiated tempos and assigns more differentiated images to represent them (e.g., a horse walking and a horse galloping).

2.   The cognitive control mechanism, *focal attention*, defines the manner in which an individual scans a field of information. The young child scans slowly and directs attention at narrow segments of a field of information. With development, the child scans more actively and at broader segments of the field.

3.   The *field articulation*[2] cognitive control defines the manner in which an

---

[1]The discussion of cognitive controls that follows represents an elaboration of the concept by the author and relies upon numerous investigations detailed elsewhere (Santostefano, 1978).

[2]The cognitive control principle of field articulation is related to, but not synonymous with, Witkin's style of the same name (see Santostefano, 1978).

individual attends to and articulates a field of information in terms of relevance. The young child attends nearly equally to information that is relevant and irrelevant to the task at hand. With development, the child directs attention more selectively at relevant information while actively ignoring irrelevant information.

4. The *leveling-sharpening* cognitive control defines the manner in which the individual constructs images of information and compares these images with present perceptions. The young child constructs global images and fuses them with present perceptions so that changes in information are not readily noticed. With development, the child constructs more differentiated images and articulates them from present perceptions, noticing subtle changes in information.

5. The *equivalence range* cognitive control defines the manner in which an individual categorizes and conceptualizes information. The young child constructs narrow categories (the group contains only a few members) and conceptualizes them in concrete terms. With development, the child constructs more broad categories that are conceptualized in more abstract terms.[3]

A brief comparison of cognitive control mechanisms with the more familiar schema in Piaget's model may serve to articulate the view of cognition used here. A cognitive control, like a schema, is a behavioral analog of structure in biology and conceptualizes a pattern of behaviors that include overt actions, perceptions, mental images, thoughts, and words. However, several important differences distinguish the two. The processes of schemas change throughout development from actions on objects (sensorimotor schema) to mental imitations of these actions (cognitive schema), to classifications (symbolic schema), to logical-hypothetical thinking. A different schema process dominates each stage in development. In contrast, each cognitive control process, while undergoing differentiation from infancy to adulthood, maintains its essential form. Further, all cognitive controls are viewed as operating simultaneously throughout development, although one may dominate the manner in which a person assimilates information at one developmental phase or in a particular situation. Finally, cognitive controls, unlike schemas, are conceptualized as assimilating and accommodating to information from both external stimuli and fantasies, coordinating requirements of the two domains so that the associated emotions are balanced to permit efficient functioning.

Of special relevance to the topic of cognition and emotion are propositions that define how cognitive controls are structured in long-term adaptation and restructured in short-term adaptation. Each cognitive control mechanism is structured continuously throughout development as a person's cognition accommodates to the pace and complexity of stimuli unique to his or her *usual* environments.

---

[3]The extreme ends of each control are not taken as synonymous with bad (e.g., leveling) and good (e.g., sharpening); any control level could represent adequate or inadequate adaptations depending upon the requirements of the situation and individual (Santostefano, 1978).

For example, a child whose home is regularly chaotic and ever changing and whose family routine does not include discussions of past events develops the habitual mechanism of forming global images of information that are fused with present perceptions.

In addition, each control mechanism is temporarily restructured whenever a person is confronted with stimulation that is *unusual* given his or her history. During these short-term changes, a cognitive control restructures to coordinate both the requirements of external stimuli and of fantasies, and associated affect in ways that permit effective handling of the task at hand.

The restructuring of cognitive control mechanisms in response to short-term changes in stimulation was proposed by Klein (1954) as a central explanatory construct for studies of cognition, emotion, and motivation in his initial formulation of cognitive control theory. In his classic Thirst Study, Klein (1954), employed young adults who habitually used extremes of the field articulation mechanism, i.e., either they attended to relevant and irrelevant information or they attended selectively to relevant stimuli while ignoring the irrelevant. Half of each group was served a thirst-inducing meal, and all subjects were then administered various tasks that included thirst-neutral and thirst-related stimuli (e.g., estimating the sizes of standard disks on which were placed various symbols). Subjects high in field articulation handled all tasks more successfully, withholding attention from irrelevant stimuli of all types. The presence of thirst-related stimuli in each task intensified the mechanism of field articulation characteristic of the individual. Compared to their nonthirsty controls, thirsty subjects high in field articulation were more successful with tasks containing thirst-related stimuli, suggesting that fantasies and affect associated with being thirsty were articulated and subordinated even more. In contrast, thirsty persons characteristically low in field articulation performed less successfully than their nonthirsty controls, suggesting that the requirements of fantasies and affect associated with being thirsty were attended to at the expense of successfully handling the task.

From the start, then, cognitive controls were conceptualized as mechanisms that shifted in response to changing stimulation, responding simultaneously to task stimuli and associated fantasies and affect, i.e, the inner environment. However, this conceptualization did not receive attention in cognitive control research (Wachtel 1972; Wolitzky & Wachtel, 1973) except for studies of perceptual defense (Erdelyi, 1974). As a result, the concept of inner environment was not elaborated further nor adequately operationalized. The model proposed here addresses this need and designates the inner environment as its second major concept.

Metaphor: A Conceptualization of Inner Environments

Two earlier formulations of the inner environment in cognitive-psychoanalytic theory contain the historical backdrop for the conceptualization proposed here. Stimulated by his study of cognitive control mechanisms and emotion, Klein

(1970) proposed a cognitive reformulation of the psychoanalytic view of drives, pointing out that internal stimuli or "drives" become motivation only when they are cognitively represented in a wish, image, or memory. To conceptualize the inner environment, he outlined a cognitive-motivational construct, "train of thought," which he located in a hypothetical "primary brain region of imbalance." A train of thought defined a closed feedback loop beginning with a wish, image, or memory and ending with some experience or action. Klein stressed that the final actions deriving from a cognitive train *balance* rather than reduce tension, anxiety, and affect.

Holt (1976) attempted to free Klein's model from the vague, anatomical metaphor of primary region of imbalance by introducing the more behavioral concept of *perceptive-evaluative mismatch*. This concept defined a cognitive process that evaluates the degree to which a perception of information fits with the expectations of a memory/image/wish of related information and experiences. When a large discrepancy exists between the values assigned to the perceived information and to the related memory/image, a mismatch exists that motivates behavior. The mismatch is corrected by acting in reality, either by assimilating or by avoiding the perceived information. Holt also proposed that the standards used to evaluate the match between perceptions and images/wishes derive from the values and behaviors displayed by adults important to the person, behaviors that are assimilated throughout childhood becoming representations of standards of ideal behavior (ego ideal in psychoanalytic theory).

In spite of these earlier conceptualizations of the inner environment, there still was the need to operationalize further how images/memories/wishes played a role in cognitive and emotional functioning and in the actions taken by an individual. As Richardson (1983) emphasized in discussing various definitions of imagery, researchers must clarify how the term is used, including the conditions that give rise to imagery and the information images make available. To approach this task, the author has integrated the Piagetian concept of symbolic schema and the psychoanalytic concepts of psychic reality and of ego modes, within a reformulation of the concept of metaphor (Ortony, 1979).

Because metaphor as used here departs appreciably from usual usage in the psychological literature, we should first remind ourselves of current views. As detailed elsewhere (Santostefano, 1985), it is generally accepted that metaphor, along with its close relatives, simile and analogy, involves the transfer of meaning, i.e, something is described in terms of properties that belong to something else. For example, when a child tells a newly enrolled classmate, "The school principal is a general," a linguistic metaphor is transferring the attributes rigid-authoritarian from the general to the school principal. Relevant to this discussion, reviews of research on metaphor report that results are inconclusive and theory incomplete in part because of the questionable assumption that a verbal expression is the exclusive locus of metaphor. Accordingly, these reviewers emphasize the need to extend the definition of metaphor to include the processes of play and imaging (Billow, 1977; Ortony, Reynolds, & Arter, 1978). The reformulation of metaphor proposed here to conceptualize the requirements of a person's "inner world" responds, in part, to these promptings.

A Definition of Metaphor.[4]   Phenomenologically, a *metaphor* is a persistent organization (pattern) of mental pictures, symbols, words, emotions, postures, and physical actions that synthesizes, conserves, and represents a person's experiences with negotiating key developmental issues vis-a-vis the self, other persons, material objects, and situations. Examples of these issues are: bonding–trusting–loving; receiving–giving; individuating; controlling–being controlled; depending–being independent; self-serving–reciprocating; asserting–initiating; aggressing.

In addition to conserving and representing past negotiations with these issues, metaphors are distinguished by two additional attributes. When a metaphor is imposed on a situation, selected ingredients of that situation are emphasized (centered) and serve to construe the entire situation (see Schön, 1979, and the notion of cognitive myopia). Also, when imposed on a situation, the metaphor contains a plan of action; i.e., prescriptions for the behavioral mode and emotions to be used in coping with the situation as construed.

The Origin and Development of Metaphors.[5]   The behavioral roots of metaphors are given at birth in the capacity for body and sensory perceptions to override established links between stimuli in favor of novel ones. (For laboratory support of this proposition, see Wiener, Wapner, Cicone, & Gardner, 1979). These behavioral roots, coupled with innately given cognitive-behavioral structures, determine the infant's initial experiences negotiating with caretakers in determining the pace, complexity, and meaning of environmental stimulation (see Sander, 1969, for one such model).

From these initial negotiations, the first metaphors are constructed and then restructured during subsequent development. And, at the same time, new ones are constructed. Different principles define the restructuring of existing metaphors and the construction of new ones. Existing metaphors are reformed as they continuously construe a range of environments and prescribe cognitive, emotional, and physical exchanges with them. In normal development, unique ingredients from these experiences, especially behaviors displayed by idealized adults, are assimilated, reforming the original metaphor, which then contains a new plan of action. In abnormal development these ingredients are not assimilated, and metaphors (with their plans of action) remain fixed. Experience with the environment, then, plays a specific role in restructuring existing metaphors.

The following illustrates how the same metaphor could be expressed in different situations, but remain unchanged. A 9-year-old construed each of several

---

[4]The discussion that follows borrows from and was stimulated by recent writing on metaphor (e.g., Ortony, 1979). The writer assumes responsibility for the modifications introduced.

[5]This formulation was influenced in particular by Mounoud's (1982) conception of revolutionary periods in development.

events with the metaphor, "I am deprived by others," which prescribed the same action (running off) and the same emotion (crying): She was waited on last when in a restaurant with her family; she was standing in line to receive a workbook from the teacher; and she was given a balloon containing less air than most at a birthday party. A new metaphor is constructed with the development of new coding capacities in the child. Here the developmental course of a metaphor defines stages, and the environment plays a relatively nonspecific role. An example from Piagetian theory of the emergence of new coding capacities would be the shifts from grasping objects, to constructing mental copies of concrete reality, to constructing symbols of reality. An example from psychoanalytic theory would be changes in psychosexual excitation that contribute to the meaning given an experience: from oral (receiving–trusting) to anal (being dominated–controlled) to phallic (asserting–competing).

Although newly constructed metaphors contain ingredients determined by intrinsically emerging coding capacities, they also contain ingredients assimilated from earlier metaphors. However, although integrating previous metaphors, a new metaphor does not replace earlier ones, which remain potentially active. Therefore, any given situation could be construed and acted on in terms of developmentally early metaphors that prescribe regressive behaviors or in terms of developmentally more advanced ones that prescribe stage-appropriate behaviors.

The following example illustrates how metaphors, constructed at developmentally different points in psychosexual development, could be expressed in a single event, each metaphor providing a unique definition of the way in which the child represented and experienced bonds between herself and others. While listening to her mother read her a story, a 7-year-old girl experienced a sense of intense satisfaction when she construed the event as like being fed the same amount of milk her infant brother had been given. At another time, she experienced a surge of anger, now construing the event as one in which she is being controlled, because she had to go to bed after the story was read. And, at another time, she experienced competitive aggressiveness, construing mother as jealous and therefore reading to her only to keep her from daddy's lap and the "special time" she spends with him.

Metaphors As Plans of Action: The Ego Modes of Action, Fantasy, and Language.   As previously noted, in addition to conserving past experiences, metaphors that are experienced center on selected ingredients of a present situation that are used to construe it and also prescribe behaviors to deal with the situation as construed. The behaviors a metaphor prescribes, including emotions, and the attributes of an event on which it centers follow a developmental sequence (for related studies, see, Santostefano, 1970, 1977b, 1978).

Acting, imaging (fantasy), and verbalizing are conceptualized as alternative coding systems (modes of construing) as well as alternative modes of behavior. An object or a person, then, could be represented and engaged by a verbal label, an image, or an action. For example, to represent his father's "superhuman strength," a child could stand under a table, raise his arms in the posture of a superhero, and play at lifting the table; or the child could imagine his father is lifting a car to rescue someone pinned beneath it; or the child could explain with pride, "My father is superman!" Similarly, in engaging a school bully, a child could hurl a snowball at him, or stand and imagine a snowball crashing into the bully's head, or say, "I'll smash you with a snowball!"

Although all three coding systems and modes of behaving are potentially available, a young child construes things and events with the action coding system, centering on the action ingredients of an event, and engages the situation using the action mode. With development, the fantasy coding system emerges as dominant, subordinating and integrating the action system so that things and events are construed more by increasingly elaborated images; and, at the same time, the situation is engaged more by fantasying along with acting or by fantasying with no actions taken. With further development, the language system emerges as dominant in coding events and behaviors, subordinating and integrating the fantasy and action systems. Now words alone or words accompanied by fantasies and actions are used to construe and engage things and events.

This developmental sequence in the behavioral expression of metaphor is conceptualized as an ontogenetic shift from concrete behavioral processes (direct–immediate) to abstract (i.e., indirect–delayed). The action mode is viewed as most concrete because it involves physically manipulating an object here and now. The fantasy mode is less concrete, because an image is manipulated rather than the object itself, and more delayed, because action is postponed at least for the duration of the fantasy. The language mode is most abstract (i.e., most indirect and delayed), because a verbal expression does not physically represent its referent, and is typically associated with the greatest delay of physical action.

The same progression governs the expression of metaphors within each mode. In early development, action metaphors are immediate and tied to a narrow set of goals (more direct). For example, a 4-year-old boy, negotiating assertiveness and aggression, repeatedly charged his older brother like a bull while wearing one of his father's neckties. With development, actions become tied to a wider range of goal objects and are more delayed. Now, at the age of 7, the same child engages his older brother in a range of competitive activities, such as kick-ball, king-of-the mountain, form board games, and so on. In the same way, fantasies initially are more concrete and gradually become more indirect and delayed, and words shift from concrete to more abstract forms (e.g., "I'll punch you," to "I'll beat you in race").

At this point in our discussion it is necessary to reintroduce the proposition, noted earlier, that existing metaphors also are restructured in part when behaviors of idealized adults are assimilated. If an ontogenetic sequence of modes determines which ingredients of an event are centered, it follows that different behaviors displayed by idealized models are centered and assimilated at different points in development. When the action mode dominates, the actions and associated emotions of idealized models are centered and, when assimilated, become especially potent in restructuring the prescriptions and representations of a metaphor. As one example, a young adult given to sudden, unprovoked, violent behavior revealed in treatment that his metaphors about aggression included memories, assimilated at the age of 4 or 5, of father suddenly exploding at dinner time and hurling a dish or silverware across the room.

In a similar fashion, when the fantasy mode emerges as dominant, fantasies and pretending displayed by idealized adults, when internalized, become especially potent in restructuring the child's fantasy metaphors; and when the language mode dominates, verbalizations by idealized authority now play a more critical role in restructuring language metaphors.

The Issues of Present/Past; Conscious/Unconscious; and Dreams.   Metaphors are not synonymous with past information. One child described a trip the family took last summer, the details forming a photocopy of the event with no metaphor at work. The same child slithered a stick toward the therapist using a metaphor (attacking snake) to transform the present information.

A dream is not automatically a metaphor. A child could describe a dream of a building as he or she would a picture and not include any hint of a metaphor construing the information. In contrast, while describing the dream, the same child could stack blocks and topple them and, offering the first hints of one meaning imposed on the dream, comment that the teacher had discussed a plane that crashed into a building.

Also, metaphors are not synonymous with the unconscious. A child could be aware or unaware of a metaphor at work. For example, an encopretic boy modeled clay (e.g., sausage-like shapes, small balls) showing no evidence that he was conscious of the possible meaning of his activity. Then, at one point, he made soupy clay and oozed it between his fingers. Grinning with pleasure and excitement, he said, "A BM," suggesting that he was becoming aware of his equation between clay and feces. Still later he took sections of clay and angrily "exploded" them against the wall. Although he made clear that he was aware that clay now equalled bombs exploding, he was not yet conscious of the possible equation between defecation and destruction.

The Definition of Metaphor Revisited   The several issues discussed elaborate the definition of metaphor proposed at the start: (a) when metaphors are constructed to represent experiences, a developmental sequence is followed from centering and assimilating action to fantasy to language ingredients of events; (b) the same developmental sequence defines the behaviors and emotions displayed by idealized adults, which, when assimilated, are especially potent in restructuring existing metaphors; (c) the behavior and associated emotions metaphors prescribe to deal with a situation could be primarily actions, fantasies, language, or some combination; (d) metaphors serve normal development when their representations and prescriptions for behaving assimilate and accommodate to an increasingly wide range of environments, resulting in the child's constructing a wide range of metaphors (from highly personal to conventional ones) and in the child's gradually developing the capacity to use alternative behaviors to achieve the same goal, and to accept alternative goals to satisfy the same behavior, thereby permitting adaptive, flexible responses to changing opportunities; (e) metaphors interfere with normal development whenever their representations and associated prescriptions for behavior fail, over an extended period of time, to assimilate and accommodate to available, relevant experiences, resulting in behaviors that are highly inappropriate for existing contexts and/or are mismatched with developmental expectations, leading to anxiety, guilt, and conflict with others; (f) a person could be unaware or become aware of the meaning of a metaphor and the behaviors it prescribes.

Contexts and the External Environment

Thus far we have considered cognition as changing in response to changing environments and metaphors as interpreting and prescribing behaviors to deal with them. Here we consider contexts, the third and final concept framing the proposed model. Renewed interest in the psychology of situations (e.g., Magnusson, 1981; Shapiro & Weber, 1981; Zimmerman, 1983) has emphasized the contextual dependency of behavior, the need to study cognition in naturalistic settings, and that events are holistic phenomena, i.e., experienced as a unified whole and not as discrete stimuli.

Several principles from the psychology of situations are integrated into the model proposed here. A person's behavior is determined by the context and stimuli, and the context, in turn, is determined by the person's fantasies and behaviors, the total meaning of the event resulting from an interaction of person and context. This interaction is a reciprocal process, with each system attempting to influence the other to achieve a mutually agreed upon degree of coordination. The person presents the environment with an evolving series of behaviors prescribed by metaphors and that usually are suited to deal with the requirements of various contexts. The environment, in turn, presents the person with a continuous series of stimuli and requirements for particular actions that usually fit the person's metaphors and behavioral capacities. (McGrath, 1976; Sarason & Sarason, 1981).

But the environment is not always matched with the requirements of a person's metaphors, sometimes abruptly changing its demands. In dealing with these fluctuations, the person shifts from one level of responding to another in order to maintain a degree of person-situation coordination in the service of adaptation and development. These shifts in responding are mediated by situational variables (e.g., environmental restraints or permissions to engage in particular behaviors), by person variables (e.g., the individual's appraisal of a situation as under his or her control, Sarason & Sarason, 1981), and by the degree of anxiety/fear/ anger signaling danger/stress as prescribed by metaphors interpreting the context.

All situations are not interpreted by metaphors to the same degree. The more a situation is unusual for a particular person and/or limits the individual in engaging the information actively, the more likely the situation would be interpreted in terms of the requirements of highly personal metaphors rather than socially shared ones. The degree of match, then, between the demands and limits of a situation and the competence and usual actions a person brings is an important factor in the degree to which a situation is construed (e.g., Holt, 1976; Hunt, 1981; Santostefano, 1978).

Whereas individuals may differ in the way a situation is interpreted, persons raised in the same environment and/or who share key personal variables are likely to share a representation of some situation (Rommetveit, 1981). And individuals may be conscious or unaware of the unique way they are perceiving information in a situation (Gardner, 1959; Pervin, 1978; Santostefano, 1978) and, therefore, of the elements they are subjecting to some interpretation (Bowers, 1981; Nisbett & Wilson, 1977). Finally, contexts are defined as a range of settings from molar (e.g., school) to molecular (e.g., test stimuli) and in terms of whether the setting is average and usual for a person given his or her history or whether it is unusual (Hartmann, 1958).

A Model and Methodology to Study Cognition and Affect

The concepts of cognitive controls, metaphors, and contexts are integrated to guide studies of cognition and affect, an integration that attempts to place cognition in the center and to hold cognition and affect as inseparable. In this integration, a person's cognitive control functioning is observed to deal with at least two contexts/stimuli. In one, the requirements of stimuli are usual and/or neutral in terms of the person's history, and, in the other, unusual and/or not neutral. The cognitive functioning, actions, and emotions observed in each situation are then compared.

Figure 11.1 presents a diagram of the model and methodology. One or more cognitive control mechanisms are assessed while a person is dealing with a context that is usual and/or neutral (Time–Environment 1). The cognitive control functioning that takes place is conceptualized as assimilating the requirements of the context/stimuli and, at the same time, those of the metaphor interpreting the stimuli. The level of cognitive control functioning the person displays, along with emotions and physical actions, are presumed to derive from the coordination that the cognitive control achieved between the two sets of requirements (Action/ Emotion 1).

The *same* cognitive control mechanism is then assessed while the person is dealing with a context that is unusual and/or not neutral (Time–Environment 2).

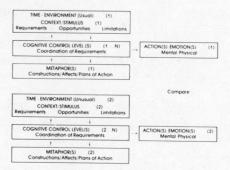

FIG. 11.1 A methodology to Study Cognition/Affects

The cognitive control functioning in this situation also is conceptualized as assimilating the requirements of this context and, at the same time, the requirements of the new or different metaphor interpreting the new situation. The level of cognitive control functioning that the person displays, along with physical actions and emotions, also are presumed to derive from the coordination cognitive controls achieved between the requirements of these nonneutral stimuli and associated metaphors (Actions/Emotions 2).

By comparing the cognitive, motoric, and emotional behavior observed in both environments, one can draw inferences about shifts in cognitive control functioning that take place in response to changing events (unified phenomena integrating stimuli and metaphors) and intended to balance emotions so that adaptation is not disrupted.

At this point, the concept that a person's cognitive control functioning is defined both by a single level and by a range of levels requires elaboration because of its central position in the model and in interpreting studies to be reported. The single level pertains to the control organization a person employs when dealing with average and/or neutral environments. In these contexts, cognitive control organization tends to be stable. The range of levels pertains to a range of cognitive control organizations through which a control mechanism moves either regressively or progressively whenever the person deals with a situation that is unusual, or not neutral, and that is especially potent in activating personal metaphors. In these contexts, cognitive control organization tends to be highly mobile.

The direction and degree of cognitive control reorganization observed from usual to unusual situations is judged successful on two interrelated counts: (a) whether the cognitive level employed coordinates the requirements of stimuli and metaphor so as to foster mastery, development and learning, and (b) whether the coordination prescribes a type and intensity of affect that serves rather than restricts the adaptive/learning process. Accordingly, cognitive control reorganizing is evaluated as unsuccessful whenever the coordination employed results in situational requirements' dominating (stimulus bound) or those of metaphors (distortion of reality) so as to limit mastery and learning, and whenever the type and intensity of affect prescribed interferes with effective adaptation.

At this point we turn to selected studies intended to illustrate how observations made in two situations permit an exploration of the role cognitive controls play in coordinating the requirements of stimuli and metaphor so as to balance emotions in the service of adaptation. In our work to date, we focused intially on demonstrating whether or not consistent cognitive changes are observed in response to changes in molar and molecular environments presumed to evoke common metaphors/affect in the populations compared. To gather information about the restructuring of metaphors as a function of experience and/or maturation, we have relied, thus far, on systematic observations of children in psychoanalytic treatment.

Studies in Molar Environments

Parachute Jumping. The leveling-sharpening cognitive control of novice parachutists was compared in their home environments and at an airport within an hour of a scheduled jump (experimental group: $N = 22$) or when no jump was scheduled (control group: $N = 22$) (Guthrie, 1967; Santostefano, 1978). The groups were comparable in age (19 years), education (13 years), and experience with prior jumps (a maximum of two). Both groups stated that along with excitement in the sport, anxiety/fear and jeopardizing their lives were associated with jumping.

As noted earlier, the principle of leveling-sharpening defines the manner in which a person compares images of past information with perceptions of present, ongoing information. When detailed images of information are constructed and articulated from present perceptions, changes that occur are noted in the information being examined. When less detailed images of information are constructed and fused with present perceptions, few correct changes are noticed or incorrect changes perceived in the information examined.

To assess this control mechanism, three test procedures were used, one consisting of neutral stimuli and the others, stimuli related to parachute jumping. The Leveling-Sharpening House Test (LSHT) consisted of 60 lined, achromatic drawings of a house, presented in succession, 5 sec each display. From the first drawing to the last, 19 details were omitted cumulatively. Each new configuration, representing some combination of omissions, was displayed three successive times. The Leveling-Sharpening Parachute Test, Form A (LSPTA) depicted a parachutist in free fall (the chute not yet deployed), and the Leveling-Sharpening Parachute Test, Form B (LSPTB) depicted a parachutist descending with chute fully deployed. As with the House Test, details in each form were omitted cumulatively from the first to the last displays.

Half of each group received Form A followed by Form B, and half the reverse order. The House Test was administered immediately after one of the Parachute

Test forms. With each test the men were asked to look at each picture and to report "anything that changes or looks different." The number of correct and incorrect changes detected and the recency of each detection were examined by means of a group x test x session ANOVA. Here we consider the effects of airport versus home environments.

Experimentals detected a significantly greater number of correct changes, and more quickly, when at the airport than when in the home environment, i.e., more differentiated images of test stimuli were constructed and efficiently compared with present perceptions. Viewed in terms of cognitive levels, the leveling-sharpening process reorganized progressively when the subjects were at the airport intending to execute a jump. This was interpreted as a change in coordination maintained by the leveling-sharpening control in the service of successful adaptation. Requirements of fantasies of injury/annihilation, including the accompanying fear/anxiety, were balanced so as to minimize the degree to which these fantasies and affect interfered with perceiving changes in external stimuli that could serve executing a jump. Further, because of the significant differences observed with all three tests, the results supported the hypothesis that a change from home environment to airport resulted in a fundamental reorganization of the leveling-sharpening control with the effect that external stimuli of any type were organized in more differentiated, stable images.

One finding provided indirect evidence that subjects imposed different metaphors on the situations assessed and therefore experienced different emotions. Experimentals who, at the airport, viewed the free-fall scene (a suspenseful situation none of the men had experienced) showed a significantly greater shift toward sharpening than those who received the "more benign" scene of a slow descent. The control group did not perform differently with the two parachute tests. This result permitted the speculation that the free-fall scene was more potent in activating a metaphor of self-annihilation/anxiety/fear and, together with the requirements of the situation, called for more sharpening of information.

Together, these data were interpreted as follows: When dealing with an elected, unusual environment, construed as threatening survival and in which the individual could make active use of external stimuli, the leveling-sharpening control reorganized progressively (increased sharpening) so as to coordinate the requirements of the metaphor of annihilation (including associated fear/anxiety) and those of the task/situation (articulating changes in external stimuli), a coordination that should serve learning to execute a jump successfully.

Children Undergoing Surgery.   Another study (Shapiro, 1972; see also, Santostefano, 1978) explored more directly the role of the leveling-sharpening control in coordinating molar environments, metaphors, and affect and whether cognitive regression could be associated with successful adaptation. The experimental group consisted of boys evaluated at home, again in a hospital bed hours before undergoing surgery for hernia repair, and again at home 30 days after discharge. Comparison groups consisted of children evaluated at home, at a dentist office, and at home again; and children evaluated only at home at three comparable points in time. There were 15 boys in each group matched for age (mean 8 years), IQ, and SES.

In addition to the LSHT to assess leveling-sharpening, the following personality/affective measures were used: (a) Fisher and Cleveland's Rorschach barrier score—the degree to which the inner world (metaphor) is accessible; (b) the Rorschach genetic index—the degree of differentiation and integration reflected by the images constructed (cognitive maturity); (c) Friedman's fables—assessments of fantasied castration and bodily injury; (d) TAT ratings of fantasied aggression; and (e) behavioral ratings by mothers of children in the surgical group.

With the LSHT, the surgical children detected *fewer* correct changes and detected changes later in the series when in the hospital than when at home. Viewed in terms of cognitive levels, the leveling-sharpening process reorganized *regressively* when the children were at the hospital. To explore the significance of this finding, the degree to which each child shifted in leveling-sharpening functioning was correlated with the differences observed in the child's personality measures when at home and when in the hospital. Children who shifted most toward increased leveling, from the home setting to the hospital, produced fewer Rorschach images containing body barriers (indicating that personal metaphors were more accessible), constructed more fantasies depicting aggression and bodily injury, and organized more differentiated–integrated Rorschach images (cognitive maturity when in the hospital). Moreover, these same children were rated by their mothers as adjusting best after surgery.

The results were interpreted in terms of the following hypothesis: When children facing surgery were in a hospital situation that limited the extent to which they could make active use of external stimuli, leveling-sharpening reorganized so that external stimuli were avoided (leveled); whereas those of fantasied castration and aggression were assimilated. This coordination was associated with constructing more differentiated fantasy metaphors that concretely expressed and rehearsed imagined castration/aggression and anxiety. The correlation of mothers' ratings suggested that these rehearsals in fantasy resulted in some resolution of the emotional upset and imagined body injury. Thus, when responding to the demands of a hospital situation and the meaning imposed on it, cognition turned away from environmental stimuli, over which the child had no control, and focused on internal metaphors.

Studies in Molecular Environments

The next studies are intended to illustrate cognitive control reorganization in response to changes in molecular environments defined as test stimuli. The metaphors activated by these stimuli are inferred from differences observed between populations that share some key variable relevant to the stimuli.

Parachute Test Stimuli and Leveling-Sharpening. In the study previously described, recall that the House Test was administered either at home or at the airport immediately after *either* Parachute Test A (free fall) or B (slow descent). A significant test sequence effect was observed. Individuals administered the House Test following an experience with Form A showed significantly more sharpening with the House Test than did those administered the House Test after Form B. Given results discussed earlier, the following interpretation is possible: Forms A and B represented different "environments," activating different metaphors and associated affect. The requirements of Form A (free fall) and of the metaphor activated, contained more elements of stress and danger and prescribed a greater degree of sharpening external information (i.e., the same reorganization observed in response to the molar environment of the airport).

Aggressive Test Stimuli and Leveling-Sharpening. Children hospitalized in a psychiatric facility were assigned to high aggression ($N = 70$) or low aggression ($N = 90$) groups on the basis of their performance with an action test of aggression (Santostefano & Rieder, 1984a). The variables, high or low aggression and age, were compared with two tests of leveling-sharpening: the LSHT, presenting nonaggressive test stimuli and a parallel form presenting a scene of two cowboys in a fist fight, a stimulus that usually aroused fantasies of violence (Leveling-Sharpening Fight Test - LSFT).

Two preliminary observations emphasize the significance of the main finding. First, high- and low-aggressive children did not show differences in performance when types of test stimuli were ignored. Second, the aggressive and nonaggressive test stimuli resulted in different leveling-sharpening functioning when the groups were combined. With aggressive stimuli, all children shifted significantly toward increased leveling (i.e., were less likely to detect picture omissions). This finding was interpreted as follows: The aggressive fantasies that were aroused in all children, including anxiety and conflict about aggression, required that the aggressive test stimuli be avoided (leveled).

In terms of the main finding, when group differences were compared, high-aggression children were significantly more efficient in maintaining images of aggressive stimuli in memory and comparing them with present perceptions (sharpened), whereas low-aggression children leveled aggressive stimuli and sharpened nonaggressive stimuli. This difference was interpreted in terms of the hypothesis that the requirements of aggressive fantasies of high-aggression children (which included low anxiety about aggression) were concordant with those of aggressive stimuli, prescribing a coordination that called for the ready assimilation of aggressive test stimuli. Conversely, the requirements of aggressive fantasies of low-aggression children (which included high anxiety and conflict with aggression) were discordant with those of aggressive test stimuli, prescribing a coordination that avoided (leveled) the attributes of aggressive test stimuli.

Aggressive Test Stimuli and Focal Attention.   This study (Santostefano, 1983) is reported to illustrate the approach with one of the other cognitive controls. As noted earlier, focal attention concerns the breadth and vigor with which an individual visually scans a field of information. The Scattered Scanning Test (SST) was used to evaluate this control in groups of hospitalized children designated as high or low in aggression (30 in each group) on the basis of their performance with an action test of aggression. The SST consisted of multiple forms on which were printed, in random arrays, 50 drawings of one or another type of stimulus: geometric shapes, familiar "neutral" objects (e.g., chair), oral objects (e.g., bottle of milk), aggressive objects (e.g., pistol). With each form, the child was asked to begin anywhere and, for a period of 30 seconds, to mark as quickly as possible only the designated stimuli (e.g., circles and crosses, chairs and shoes). The location and sequence of markings were recorded.

To score and interpret this test, the distances from one correct marking to the next are summed. The greater the distance covered by the markings, the greater the vigor of visual scanning. In addition, the total distance traversed by markings made is divided by the number of markings (minus 1). The greater this averaged distance, the greater the average width of single sweep.

The scanning of high-aggressive children covered less total distance (less vigorous scanning) and resulted in a smaller average distance (more narrow scanning) when surveying aggressive stimuli, whereas that of low-aggressive children became more vigorous and broad. If this finding is related to the previous study (leveling-sharpening in aggressive children), there is the suggestion that although aggressive children sharpen aggressive test stimuli (detect more changes in ongoing information) they also survey narrow segments of a field of aggressive information. This suggested relationship between two controls relates to the concept of cognitive style that is defined as the *pattern* of multiple cognitive controls revealed by a population or individual. In previous studies (Santostefano, 1978), the cognitive style of pathological groups was characterized by a pattern of controls interpreted as uncoordinated. That is, these groups showed maturity in one control and immaturity or inefficiency in another. In the sample noted here, the mechanism of sharpening and narrow scanning are uncoordinated, the former reflecting a mature level of functioning and the latter an immature level. Normal children reveal coordinated patterns of controls, e.g., sharpening and broad scanning. The significance of uncoordinated cognitive styles for efficient learning and adaptation awaits further study.

Multiple Controls in Decoding Nonveral Affective Cues.   This study explored whether and how all five cognitive controls of tempo regulation, focal attention, field articulation, leveling-sharpening, and equivalence range (see previous section definitions) are implicated in decoding affective cues (Rieder, Santostefano, & Wertlieb, 1979, 1983). Eighty-three public school males were administered tests of each cognitive control: (a) the LSHT, the LSFT, and the SST (each described earlier) to assess the leveling-sharpening and focal attention control mechanisms respectively; (b) the Fruit Distraction Test, assessing the field articulation control, required the child to name as rapidly as possible the colors of pictures of 50 fruit (e.g., yellow banana) arrayed in 10 rows (5 each row) in three conditions—when no distracting stimuli were present on the test card and when pictures of food objects (e.g., bottle of milk) or weapons (e.g., pistol), defined as irrelevant to the color-naming task, were located around the colored fruit; (c) the Object Sort Test, assessing the equivalence range control, required the child to form groups of 44 common objects and then explain (conceptualize) how the objects in each group belong together; (d) Fine Motor Delay Test, assessing tempo regulation, required the child to move a pencil along an S-shaped pathway at three different tempos—regular, fast, and slow.[6] In addition, the children were administered the Profile of Nonverbal Sensitivity Test (PONS) (Rosenthal, Hall, Di Matteo, Rogers, & Archer, 1979), which presents photographs of an adult female enacting positive emotions (e.g., expressing love; helping someone) or negative emotions (e.g., threatening someone; expressing anger). With each picture the child selected one of two statements that best described what the girl was feeling.

A factor analysis was conducted of the cognitive control test scores (44 variables) to abstract the basic dimensions, and their relative weightings, unique to this population. The factors obtained resembled factor structures observed with a number of other populations (Santostefano, 1978) and defined each of the cognitive control principles: i.e., regulating motility, scanning, selective attending, comparing present perceptions with images of past information, and categorizing. Factor scores were computed for each child, and each PONS score was regressed on each control factor score. Of the control principles, efficient selective attention (field articulation), with both neutral and aggressive test stimuli, was most powerful in predicting accurate decoding of positive affects (e.g., expressing love). A shift to sharpening when dealing with aggressive test stimuli predicted best accurate decoding of negative affect (e.g., expressing anger).

Critique of Studies.   Before proceeding, it is helpful to summarize the conclusions that could be drawn from these several studies and that relate to the proposed integration of cognitive controls, metaphors, and contexts.

When the leveling-sharpening mechanism was assessed while a person dealt with a neutral molar or molecular context (i.e., home; test stimulus of a house) and then assessed again in another, less neutral context (i.e., airport, hospital, test stimuli of parachutists and fist fighters), the control mechanism restructured,

---

[6] For a complete description of these tests and evidence of validity and reliability, see Santostefano (1978).

shifting from that level of organization associated with usual contexts and neutral stimuli to another level associated with unusual or less neutral stimulation.

The directions in which the control mechanism shifted could be conceptualized in terms of three broad principles that define the balance that the mechanism achieved in assimilating or avoiding the requirements of external and internal stimulation. One principle concerns whether or not the context permitted the person to be active with external stimuli and have some control over them, or required the person to be passive. Another concerns the degree to which the content/requirements/value of external stimuli and those of the associated metaphor are concordant or discordant. The third concerns the degree to which a context/stimulus is unusual given a person's life history.

When the airport situation required and permitted that external stimuli be used actively, the control mechanism reorganized constructing a balance that assimilated external stimuli more while, at the same time, avoiding anxiety and threat of possible body injury prescribed by metaphors. And the mechanism reorganized to prevent such metaphors from disrupting the efficient perception of external stimuli which they were interpreting. When the hospital situation defined that the person could not control or make active use of external stimuli, the cognitive mechanism reorganized to achieve a balance that avoided external stimuli while, at the same time, assimilating and expressing the requirements of associate metaphors concerned with anxiety and threat of body injury. In both instances, the reorganization achieved by the control mechanism coordinated the requirements of the context and metaphors so as to foster mastery of the situation at hand and balance the associated affect in ways that served rather than restricted successful adaptation.

With regard to the second principle, in some instances studied there was a higher degree of concordance between the content/requirement/value of stimuli and those of related metaphors. One example is illustrated by the relation between the free-fall parachute test stimuli and presumed metaphors of the parachutists requiring efficient use of stimuli concerned with jumping and preventing danger and injury. Another example is illustrated by the relation between the fist-fight test stimuli and the metaphors of violent children that are presumed to have an affinity for aggressive stimuli. In other instances studied, there was greater discordance between test stimuli and associate metaphors. This is best illustrated by the relationship between the fist-fight test stimuli and the associate metaphors concerning violence presumed to characterize low-aggressive children. Discordance also is illustrated by the relation between the test stimuli of a parachutist in slow descent (a more benign scene than the free fall) and the associated metaphors presumed to characterize parachutists.

We observed that the violent children assimilated the aggressive test stimuli more than the neutral house test stimuli, whereas non-violent children assimilated the house test stimuli more than the fight test stimuli. The parachutists assimilated the stressful free-fall test stimuli more than the slow-descent test stimuli. Taken together, these observations suggest that, when there is a high degree of concordance between the content/requirement/value of external stimuli and those of the associated metaphor, the cognitive control mechanism reorganizes and achieves a balance that is associated with less anxiety, stress, and conflict and that more readily assimilates the external stimuli. When there is a high degree of discordance, the cognitive mechanism reorganizes and achieves a balance that is associated with anxiety and conflict and that avoids external stimuli while permitting the requirements of metaphors to dominate.

In terms of the third principle, the observations made suggest that the more unusual or provocative the contexts/stimuli, relative to a person's life history, the more likely that the requirements/values of the associated metaphors dominate in the balance constructed by a control mechanism between stimuli and metaphor. Some support for this concept was provided by the finding that the parachutists perceived more changes *when at the airport* with the free-fall test stimuli than with the slow-descent test stimuli, and they perceived more changes with the latter than with the house test. In the surgical study, the control group of children, when assessed in a dentist's office, showed less of a shift towards perceiving fewer changes (leveling) than did the children assessed in the hospital.

How these three principles correlate requires further study. The many possible combinations are illustrated by the following questions. If there is concordance between stimuli and metaphor, would a cognitive control mechanism reorganize differently if, in one context, children are required/permitted to be active (e.g., play at performing surgical procedures on dolls), and in another context they are required to be passive (e.g., undergo surgery)? If there is discordance between test stimuli and metaphor, would a cognitive control mechanism reorganize differently if nonviolent children are required/permitted to be actively aggressive (e.g., engage in boxing matches) vs. passive (e.g., sit and witness boxing matches)? Are there differences in the restructuring of a cognitive mechanism in groups of children who differ in the number of hospitalizations experienced or in the number of times the family has moved from one city to another?

These principles and the questions they raise relate to observations of a single control mechanism undergoing change in response to changing stimulation. Also in need of further study is the question of the pattern of cognitive restructuring observed when multiple cognitive controls (i.e., cognitive style—see previous) are assessed in response to the same change in context/stimuli. We noted here that, when measures of several control mechanisms were obtained from a group of boys, selective attending (field articulation mechanism) with both neutral and aggressive test stimuli was implicated most in decoding the affect of affection, whereas the restructuring of the leveling-sharpening principle (so that aggressive stimuli are articulated in images and assimilated more) was implicated most in decoding the affect of hostility. We also noted that, when dealing with neutral and then aggressive test stimuli, violent children revealed in one study that the

leveling-sharpening principle reorganized progressively (i.e., a more differentiated image of aggressive stimuli was constructed), whereas in another study,
violent children revealed the focal attention mechanism reorganized regressively
(shifted from broad to narrow scanning in response to a shift from neutral to
aggressive stimuli).

These observations relate to studies reported elsewhere in which unique patterns of multiple cognitive controls have distinguished public school children,
latency children versus adolescents hospitalized because of emotional disturbances (Santostefano, 1978) and suicidal and nonsuicidal children (Santostefano
& Rieder, 1983). In general, clinical populations reveal patterns of controls that
are conceptualized as noncoordinated in contrast to the pattern of normal children.
That is, the pattern consists of cognitive maturity in one control mechanism
associated with cognitive immaturity in another.

Although these studies support the view that unique patterns of control mechanisms distinguish populations, they say nothing about whether and how multiple
cognitive controls restructure simultaneously in response to changing environments. A more comprehensive application of cognitive control theory, then,
would consist, for example, of a study assessing all five cognitive control mechanisms, as well as personality variables, when children are at home and again
when they are in a hospital for treatment. We have some evidence that leveling-
sharpening reorganizes regressively in response to this change in environments.
But, what of scanning, attending selectively, and conceptualizing?

The Expresson, Repetition, and Restructuring of
Metaphors in a Child's Therapeutic Analysis

To this point, studies reviewed emphasize cognitive changes observed in groups
responding to changes in molar and molecular situations presumably construed
by a shared metaphor with its prescribed emotions. The model also indicates the
need for studies of unique metaphors an individual imposes on situations, the
changes these metaphors undergo, the role they play in the actions taken and
emotions experienced. One type of laboratory that might permit such studies
would be a professional treatment situation[7] in which the child and therapist
estabish unconditional trust and meet frequently over a long period of time, with
the mutual understanding that the child is free to express behaviors, fantasies,
thoughts, and emotions, however primitive or civilized.[8]

---

[7]These observations come from children whose course of development is significantly derailed.
Thus they say little about the repetition of metaphors in normal development, insights gained might
serve studies of children not in need of psychological treatment.

[8]Tower (1983) discusses other conditions necessary for the emergence of fantasies in children.

Method.   Accordingly, the author has regularly recorded narrative descriptions of each treatment session held with a child. Once the therapeutic analysis is completed, these descriptions are reviewed by at least one independent rater and the analyst, to address several questions: What key metaphor is revealed in the child's play activity when examined in terms of organization of physical actions, emotions, fantasies, words, and symbols? Is the metaphor, with its plans of action, a major factor in the child's psychological illness, construing self, others and current situations in ways that impede adequate functioning and development? As this organization of activity is repeated, does the metaphor undergo restructuring as a function of the child's internalizing the analyst's behavior, especially standards? Does each restructuring provide the child the opportunity to redefine his/her concept of self and others in ways that advance development? When the key pathological metaphor is reformed, does it restructure to a higher developmental level with the emergence of new coding capacities, resulting in developmentally more advanced constructions of experiences and more adaptive plans of action and affect?

To answer these questions, the configuration of play the child repeats is established following the definition of metaphor, i.e., (a) theme, (b) roles the child construes for himself or herself and for the analyst, (c) whether or not a figure/symbol is included representing standards of conduct (superego), and (d) the dominant mode implicated in the activity, labeled as: *macroaction*, child moves through total space available; fantasy and language behaviors are subordinate to the activity; *macrofantasy*, an elaborate fantasy is expressed which is not a literal statement of the child's actual experiences, but a representation of them. and which is accompanied by little action; *macrolanguage*, statements about things, people and events in the child's reality, past and present; and *microactions*, fine motor activity that is always subordinate to and in the service of elaborate fantasies or discussions of reality experiences.

The metaphor suggested by the identified configuration is noted, as well as the number of sessions over which the configuration and metaphor are repeated. The metaphor is viewed as having been restructured to a significant degree when changes are observed in the theme or plot, roles assigned to child and analyst, type of superego figure, behavioral mode employed, and type and intensity of emotions experienced. Successive restructurings are examined to determine whether theoretically expected developmental lines are being followed (e.g., from play acting mythical figures to human figures; from including an undifferentiated, excessively punitive superego figure to one more differentiated and realistic; from macroactions dominating to discussions of real experiences (especially those concerning the child's difficulties and cause for psychological suffering), and from using private symbols to more socially shared ones.

Case Illustration.   These questions and methods were used to organize observations made in the 4-year therapeutic analysis of a 7-year-old boy. From the psychoanalytic view, the boy's key pathological metaphors prescribed egocentrism, self-righteousness, struggles for control and pleasure and excitement in sadism, all ingredients of the anal stage in which he appeared fixated, judging from his history and presenting problems. These pathological metaphors were expressed and restructured repeatedly over a 3-year period and eventually resolved. Then the boy constructed new metaphors with new coding capacities associated with the phallic stage that prescribed behavior that included socially shared codes of conduct and pleasure in reciprocating and competing.

To aid the reader in following the case material in terms of the questions discussed earlier, the major observations made are summarized in Table 11.1. As shown, the entire therapeutic analysis could be divided into four phases, inferred from an inspection of the changes in play activity, each phase defining a long-term underriding theme: (a) in Phase I, a period of 6 months, the boy repeatedly displayed hostile, aggressive, self-serving behaviors that significantly interfered with his functioning in school and at home; (b) in Phase II, a period of 9 months, the boy gradually identified with the therapist as an ally and as an idealized source of strength to cope with pathological metaphors; (c) in Phase III, a period of 20 months, the boy expressed in highly personal and graphic symbols the pathological metaphor that had arrested his personality development and that defined him and his relations with others in terms of hostile control versus masochistic submission and pleasure in anal-sadistic behavior; and (d) when the pathological metaphor was resolved, the boy constructed a new metaphor (Phase IV) that defined him and his relationships with others in terms of new coding capacities associated with the phallic stage of psychosexual development and that included asserting, competing, reciprocating, and genital excitement.

During each of these phases, the boy displayed various patterns of play activity, repeating and sustaining each one for some time. Table 11.1 also lists the sequence of these patterns of activity. For example, after Phase I, in which the boy directed diffuse, hostile-aggressive behavior at the therapist as himself, the boy organized a pattern of activity that defined the therapist as a *Giant Rat* attacking a victim, played by the boy (the beginning of Phase II). This pattern of activity was then followed by another in which the boy prescribed that the therapist play the role of a *King Rat* battling a character named *Batman*, played by the boy. This activity was followed in turn by a pattern of play in which the therapist as King Rat and the child, as Batman, joined forces and searched for energy pills, and so on.

To the right of each pattern of play activity, Table 11.1 also lists: (a) the characters involved in that activity, whether human, animal, or mythical, or the person of the child and therapist; (b) the behavioral mode that dominated the play, whether action, fantasy or language; (c) the metaphor suggested by the pattern; and (d) the major emotion displayed by the child within the play theme.

Table 11.1
Restructuring of Metaphors and Associated Affect in the Therapeutic Analysis of a Child

Long Term Theme	Play Activities	Characters	Dominant Behavioral Mode	Metaphors	Dominant Affect
Phase I. Preparation	Form Board War Games; Cheating; Tantrums	Child & Therapist	Macro & Micro-Action	I am frightened to learn about myself; I am enraged and terrified if I do not control others and situations.	Fear/Rage
Phase II. Establishing Alliance/Trust and Commitment to Reveal Key Metaphors	Giant Rate (TH) attacks victim (CH)	Rats	Macro-Action	I am a helpless victim of powerful forces	Fear/submission
	King Rat (TH) & Batman (CH) battle	Rats	Macro-Action	Evil force battles the good force	Hostility
	King Rat (TH) & Batman (CH) search for energy pills	Rats	Macro-Action	I need strength to battle the evil in me	Alliance/Trust/Determination
	King Rat (TH) & Kings Highest Servant (CH) capture & punish bad rats	Rats	Macro-Action	I am beginning to identify with rules & authority; I am disgusted by infractions	Affiliation/Allegiance/Disgust
	General Bolthead (CH) places tail glands into his anus	Rats	Macro-Action	My anus is my power and center of my life	Pride/Excitement/Dominance

Phase	Description	Character	Type	Interpretation	Emotion
Phase III. Pathological Metaphors Revolve/Reform on Horizontal Plane	Highland Rat Policeman (CH) Punishes Rats Stealing Tail Glands	Rats	Macro-Action	It is a crime to seek power for the anus	Recrimination/Disgust
	Scientist (TH) controls "dirty" monsters with assistant (CH)	Mythical Humans	Macro-Fantasy & Micro-Action	I struggle to control my primitive anal wishes & actions	Excitement/Turmoil
	Leader of Silver Stallion Squadron (CH) & friend (TH) civilize Rat Land	Mythical Humans	Macro-Fantasy	I am a new self, civilizing and controlling anal wishes & actions	Pride/Assertiveness/Dominance
	(a) Carving Wooden Swords	Humans	Micro-Action	I identify with the power & rules of idealized authority	Pride/High Self-Esteem
	(b) Story Telling (CH): Teddy & the Ass Club punish & strive for Penis Peak	Humans	Macro-Fantasy	I reveal my anal behaviors & wish to advance my development	Humiliation
Phase IV. Metaphor Spirals to Phallic Stage—Insight	Child makes encyclopedia about sharks and rates "Playboy" pictures	Child	Macro-Fantasy Micro-Action	I am very excited by genital stimulation; but I am frightened of being castrated or harmed in some way	Fear/Excitement
	(a) Child discusses past anal activities, fantasties, & interests	Child	Macro-Language	None—autobiographical	Humiliation/guilt
	(b) Child constructs Origami designs & plays musical instrument	Child	Micro-Action	I find pleasure in accomplishments & industry	Pride/Achievement/Pleasure

Preparation (A Phase of 6 Months).   The reasons why Tom required treatment are readily seen in behaviors that he displayed during a preparatory period of two sessions per week. These behaviors mirrored those observed at home and at school. His frantic, hostile, play activity and high-pitched, rapid speech (punctuated with stuttering) indicated that he continually experienced intense anxiety, fear, and rage. Of the various materials available, he typically played form board games involving armies at war, and he regularly argued and cheated, altering the rules to suit his situation. During each session, Tom usually ruptured these games by hurling or spilling the materials on the floor and shouting vindictives. His tendency to project responsibility for his behavior was reflected in his comments about peers—who always got into trouble, swore, liked to pull down the pants of children, steal, damage property, and put objects in the anuses of stray dogs and cats, all behaviors accurately describing Tom's presenting problem.

Gradually we worked on his first metaphor, the meaning he gave to therapy that produced intense anxiety and fear—that his secrets would be discovered. As Tom repeatedly staged armies, each fighting to learn the secrets of the other, I play-acted that the armies did not have to battle each other for secrets but could join each other to learn about them. As Tom assimilated this behavior, staging games that integrated our armies, the frequency of sessions was increased to four per week.

Establishing Alliance and Trust (A Phase of 9 Months).   There occurred a major shift in activity that suggested that, although receptive to exploring and sharing his secrets, Tom was at the same time terrified of sharing because he now construed his relationship with the therapist in terms of attack and submission. He asked me to pretend that I was a Giant Rat attacking him, a captured rat, whose arms and legs were tied. I lunged forward, snarling and growling, while Tom twisted on the floor, screaming in agony. Tom asked that the attacks be repeated in the following sessions, and with each he played a captured rat, prescribing various tortures (chop off his head, pour hot oil over him). While struggling to keep control over captured rats, I, as Giant Rat, enacted fear of the possible collective power of all uncaptured rats and over whether it was possible ever to capture all of them.

Tom soon transformed our roles. I became King Rat, King of Ratland in charge of "all evil forces," and Tom became Batman, who was in charge of "the good force." If Ratman gained control he would have Batman "do all kinds of dirty things." If Batman gained control he would have rats "do good things" (e.g., clean up trash; help put out fires). King Rat and Batman battled repeatedly, with Tom displaying vicious hostility. Throughout the metaphor, King Rat worried that allies might come to Batman's aid and give him the power to win.

With this, Tom introduced a new activity that defined an alliance and trust between us for the first time. Batman discovered that energy pills, which he needed to maintain his strength to fight the evil forces, and the machine that made them, had been stolen by bad rats. Batman asked King Rat if he would help him find the pills and the machine in "rat cave," which was pitch dark. Tom added that Batman could see in the dark, though he was extremely weak; King Rat could not see in the dark but was strong. As we crawled about the playroom in search of the pills and machine, Batman enacted joining his power of sight with King Rat's strength, guiding him to the pills and the machine.

Following this statement of alliance and trust, Tom again restructured the activity and metaphor. Now the metaphor prescribed allegiance to rules and disgust with any infraction. King Rat was assisted by the "King's Highest Servant" (enacted by Tom) in punishing rats who committed crimes. Tom presented captured rats to the King for punishment, detailing the crimes committed. Tom was disgusted by and uncompromising in what he called a crime ("A crime is a crime; even stealing a stone off the streets of Ratland is a crime.") and insisted the King behead any bad rat who stole a stone (many rats were beheaded— played by Tom). The King Rat began to ask about the age of each offender, and meted out punishments accordingly, emphasizing that expectations were different for different ages and that a list of punishments was needed to fit various crimes.

To this point Tom, for the most part, had been struggling to define himself as allied with and trusting of an authority figure and as committed to rules. With this construction achieved, he was able to introduce a metaphor that represented a major pathological source of his maladaptive behavior.

Pathological Metaphors Expressed and Restructured (A Phase of 20 Months). Tom introduced a new character *General Bolthead*, armed with a "big gun" (a car vacuum cleaner he brought to the office). Bolthead crawled through "underground tunnels" and fought rats that attacked him. Then he cut out "tail glands" from the anus of each defeated rat and placed them into his own anus. Bolthead also directed his buttocks toward passing rats and "sucked up" their tail glands, and his "ass" became "very nervous" if it did not obtain glands. Tom elaborated that Bolthead had a "computer gland" in his anus to direct his many tail glands and a special "life gland" that he was afraid of losing. Other rats were envious of Bolthead's many tail glands, and stealing tail glands became rampant throughout Ratland.

The therapist enacted that something had to be done about all of this stealing. Tom responded with a brief shift in activity that recycled the issues of the previous phase of crime and punishment, rules and regulations. In this revolution, however, the standards used were closer to reality symbols, and punishments were more fitted to crimes. Tom introduced an elite corp of "Highland Rat Police." As a policeman, Tom marched around the playroom in a military posture and firmly and efficiently captured rats that had stolen tail glands, taking them to the chief of police (analyst) for punishment.

Tom replaced this theme with an activity that, although another repetition of the same metaphor, contained a significant new element. For the first time, macroaction was subordinated by fantasy, with Tom sitting still on the floor (manipulating materials) and elaborating increasingly differentiated fantasies.

Tom obtained a set of plastic monster figures from his cupboard (placed there many months before and never used). The figures were "dirty, wild savages" who spit, urinated, defecated, and wallowed in filth and who were stupid and had no language. I placed a sheet of construction paper on the floor as the place where the monsters lived and Tom called it "the wild house." He then selected one of the more human-looking figures and named it "a scientist" who lived within a plastic container that he set next to the wild house. The scientist called the monsters from the wild house, put ideas in their minds, and sent them to the village to suck blood from people. As this theme repeated, the scientist had difficulty controlling the monsters.

Tom selected another figure, "a human monster—Dracula," who helped the scientist control the monsters. Tom located Dracula's house, another sheet of paper placed next to the scientist's house, and a "punishment chamber" (a fourth sheet of paper), where monsters were punished when they disobeyed the scientist's wishes. Tom also elaborated fantasies such as the "finger monster," who enjoyed sticking his finger into the anus of the "ass monster" as well as in his own. Whenever I was assigned the role of the scientist, I asked Dracula if he longed to be free; if I was assigned the role of Dracula, I wondered what I could do to be free of the filthy monsters who dragged me into the wild house.

Following this, Tom introduced *David Barcelona*, (an ego ideal) who would help Dracula gain freedom. David was strong, honest, intelligent, and the leader of the "Silver Stallion Squadron." He was "not a Christian and not a Jew," but "a new religion." With his elite "Italian Batallion," David (played by Tom) and his friend (played by the analyst) hunted savages created by the scientist. As he marched about the playroom leading his troops with pride, Tom made clear the the Squadron was organized "to rid the village of dirty rats forever."[9]

The form and content of activity then restructured, assuming symbols closer to reality and illustrating that multiple metaphors could operate simultaneously. With one, Tom defined himself as identified with power and rules of idealized authority and as deriving self-esteem from this identification. With a simultaneous activity, he repeated the metaphor of anal conflicts but in a form that more closely approximated his own maladaptive behaviors.

Tom borrowed a jack knife from the analyst and asked the analyst to help him carve a series of swords, each one larger and more decorative than the last. Tom proudly waved each sword, discussed the relative power of each and noted

---

[9]Here we have an example of possible unconscious symbolic references that contribute to the construction of ego ideals. There are as many letters (22) in Silver Stallion Squadron as in the analyst's first and last names and the letter S begins each word in each of the two labels. Further, the name David Barcelona, and the two religions assigned to him, appear to relate to the patient's Jewish background and the writer's Italian background. The ego ideal now formed appears to integrate aspects of Tom's heritage and the standards perceived in the analyst.

that he was making them for the "Italian Batallion," the fantasied police force of the previous phase. He also frequently referred to the analyst's person, pointing out, for example, that he and Tom were wearing the same kind of trousers.

While carving, Tom began telling "stories" about "Teddy." Teddy would stand nude before a mirror, look at his buttocks, and get "all kinds of exciting ideas and feelings." Teddy made huge, decorative cakes from his feces, assigning stars to the best one. Teddy was editor of the "Ass Times," which contained descriptions and pictures of the "perfect ass." Teddy organized an "Ass Club," whose members played with each other's buttocks.

Tom gradually included fathers who discovered their children during these meetings and punished them. Initially punishments resembled torturing performed by the Giant Rat at the start of the analysis (e.g., dipping the children in hot oil), but gradually they became more realistic. Teddy was "humiliated" when caught. Tom also noted that "Teddy's ass was the most important part of his life," and we recalled this was also true of General Bolthead of some months ago. When invited to tell a story, I included that everyone goes through a phase where the ass is the most important part, but then they go on to other phases. Tom then narrated that Teddy "was stuck in the ass phase" but wanted to climb to the top of "Penis Peak." In story after story, as Teddy climbed, either he slipped to a ledge below ("Sometimes Teddy still does his ass things") or he searched for short cuts, but there were none. Through storytelling I wondered what was it that blocked Teddy from reaching the top of Penis Peak; was he afraid of some danger there or was it that he didn't want to reach it?

Metaphor Spirals to Phallic Stage with Autobiographical Discussions (19 months). With this phase the original key metaphor, with its anal elements, spirals to another stage with the emergence of new coding capacities that include genital excitement and its associated castration fear.

Tom replaced storytelling when he brought in reference books about sharks. Over many weeks, he wrote "chapters" on the habits and physical anatomy of sharks, focusing in particular on reviews of reports of sharks injuring or killing people. The effort resulted in a 70-page manuscript.

Tom also brought *Playboy* pictures to the sessions and, alternating with his writing project, he engaged the analyst in constructing "rating scales" that were applied to the pictures. The scales included variables such as "vulgar," "artistic," "animalistic." When rating pictures, Tom displayed genital excitement and pleasure, frequently touching his genitals.

As these activities phased out, Tom began to make fleeting references to his past anal behaviors and fantasies, gradually returning to them, adding details and raising questions. He talked about these experiences with considerable guilt and embarrassment, but without anxiety escalating to levels that interfered. We made connections between his behaviors, fantasies, and concerns and those of General Bolthead and Teddy, who were stuck in the ass phase. We referred to

Teddy's wish to reach the top of Penis Peak, and we discussed ways to reach it that involved risks, aggressiveness, competition, and reciprocating (e.g., school work, sports).

Following these discussions, he became occupied with constructing Origami designs. He also occasionally brought in a musical instrument and played for the analyst, activities suggesting that he was increasing his capacity for pride in achievement and for sublimating impulses.

This case study illustrates several principles concerning the development of metaphors: (a) the plans of action of metaphors restructured following a sequence from actions, to fantasies, to language, which implicated developing multiple means-ends and increasing degrees of delay; (b) within this course, the symbols employed reorganized from highly personal (primary process) to socialized ones (secondary process; e.g., characters/roles shifted from animals, to mythical humans, to humans; (c) the construction of an ego ideal preceded each major reconstruction of the key metaphor; (d) as the pathological metaphor resolved, new coding capacities emerged, and the metaphor spiraled to a new structure; (e) affect was experienced as prescribed by the metaphor/context, e.g., Tom, as Bolthead, experienced pride in possessing many tail glands, and, as David Barcelona, pride in the beauty and power of his sword.

CONCLUDING REMARKS

In the model and methodology proposed here, and in the studies reported to illustrate their heuristic value, cognition and affect are viewed as inseparable and not as parallel or interacting psychological systems. A person could deal with an interpersonal-molar situation (hospital) or a discrete stimulus (e.g., perceiving the volume of water poured from one beaker to another) as both relatively neutral and usual stimuli because the person has been hospitalized many times and because the person perceives the water as water. Or the person could deal with these same stimuli as unusual and emotionally provocative because she was never hospitalized before and she construes the water being poured as blood a technician removed from her arm with a syringe. In both instances the person is conceptualized as experiencing and coping with an holistic event constructed by the coordination that the person's cognition achieves between the requirements of the external context/stimuli and those of personal metaphors that interpret the former and prescribe actions to be taken, including affect to be experienced. When other approaches to cognition and affect (e.g., Clark & Fiske, 1982; Lewis & Rosenblum, 1978) are viewed through the lens provided by the proposed model, several issues are brought into view.

Defining Cognition as One with Emotion and as Reorganizing in Response to Changing Stimulation.   When cognition and emotion are conceived as separate but interacting systems, investigators frequently are cornered into taking a position that either cognition (e.g., Arnold, 1960) or emotion (e.g., Bower & Cohen, 1982; Mower, 1960) is more important in this interaction. Related, Izard (1977) argued that models that see emotion as arising from cognition tend to evaluate reason and rationality as good and emotion as bad and thus view reasoning as a control and substitute for emotion. The debate over the relative dominance of cognition and emotion becomes meaningless and dissolves when the two systems are conceived as one.

In addition conceptual and methodological problems emerge when cognition and emotion are viewed as parallel but interacting systems (e.g., DeCarie, 1978; Izard, 1978; 1982; Leventhal, 1982; Royce, 1973). As one illustration, Royce (1973), in defining *style linkages* between cognition and emotion, proposed one cognitive principle (scanning) as a *cognitive style*; another, reflective-impulsive, as an *affective style*; and still another, field articulation as a *cognitive-affective style*. Moreover, these style linkages are conceptualized as stable, inflexible traits or structures. In a similar way, Izard (1978) posited affective-cognitive structures, *trait-like characteristics*, which in homogeneous sets form basic, static personality orientations (e.g., passive; anxious).

When cognition and affect are related with an emphasis on the meaning given stimuli by the person interacting with them (constructivist/contextualist approaches[10]), the same issue of cognition as static processes also emerges. For example, Mandler (1982) introduces the structure of value into schema as representations of experiences, including values that give meaning to stimuli. These schemas play a role in "descriptive cognitions" (judgments that depend on what is out there) and "evaluative cognitions" (judgments of, for example, threat to one's self-esteem that do not depend on what is out there.)

Whether cognition is defined in terms of Mandler's descriptive cognitions (which resemble cognitive control mechanisms acting on environmental stimulation) or evaluative cognitions (which resemble metaphor) or in terms of values, beliefs, conservation, and classification, cognition is not operationalized as mobile levels responding to changing stimuli. As a result, constructivist/contextualist approaches also tend to result in a relatively static picture of constructions imposed on situations.

In contrast, cognition in the present proposal has been conceptualized and operationalized as a set of particular, highly mobile, processes (cognitive controls) shifting from one level of organization to another in response to changing requirements of both external stimuli and personal metaphors. As a result of this conception, each cognitive control mechanism is not viewed as primarily affective or cognitive or some combination, but all mechanisms participate in coordinating internal and external requirements, whether these call for little or no affect (e.g., judging the sizes of circles) or for considerable affect (e.g., dealing with parachute jumping). Further, in the writer's view, not only do constructivists and interactionists tend to conceptualize cognitive behaviors as static events, but

---

[10]Zimmerman (1983) provides a concise historical review of contextualist formulations.

neither approach assigns to cognition the role of coordinating requirements from changing contexts with those of changing representations, a coordination achieved by a continuous process of cognitive regressions and progressions.

Metaphors as Representations that Prescribe Appraisals and Plans of Action. The concept of metaphor relates directly to the various uses made of appraisal theory in studies of emotion. Like Mandler's schemas, metaphors are not carbon copies of an event but representations which result in a readiness for certain information and which prescribe particular actions and affect. However, most conceptions of appraisal, including Mandler's, conceive of schema as being structured only by experiences with the environment. Further, these schemas, though centering the individual on particular information, are not conceptualized as prescribing, according to developmental principles, the behavioral modes in actions taken (Scheier & Carver, 1982; Leventhal, 1982, are exceptions).

As we have seen, two of the features which distinguish metaphors involve these very issues. With one, metaphors are structured not only as a function of experiences, but also as a function of intrinsic development. The heuristic value of this conception, demonstrated by the case study reported, is illustrated by the approach it offers to a problem Mandler acknowledges is left unattended by his notion of appraisal—namely, if one considers that a horse could be judged as beautiful at one time and ugly at another, when there have been no experiences with horses that could account for this change in appraisal. Could the reason be that the metaphor, activated by and associated with horses, is undergoing intrinsic change as new coding capacities participate in the metaphor's construction? Another example is illustrated by a dilemma posed for Piagetian theory by Bever (1982). When 2- and 4-year-olds were asked to conserve rows of candy (which they were allowed to eat), 2-year-olds solved the problem perfectly whereas 4-year-olds tended to select and eat the longer row (i.e., containing fewer candies). Is a metaphor intrinsically developing that construes the clay and candy differently for 4-year-olds than for 2-year-olds?

With the second feature distinguishing metaphor as defined here, representations are viewed as condensing and prescribing action, fantasy, and language behaviors in terms of particular developmental relations. One illustration of the possible heuristic value of this concept is the approach it provides to a question Piaget (1973) raises as to why some sensorimotor schemas become conscious (by a translation into representative concepts or verbal ones) whereas others remain unconscious. He offers one possibility that some action schemas remain unconscious because they are in conflict with, and incompatible with, conscious ideas. The case study reported here illustrated the behavioral consequences and suffering that result from such a conflict. But, of more importance, the case study illustrated why and how the conflict should be resolved by facilitating a particular sequence of restructuring or translations in Piaget's terms: that widespread roots from action metaphors (sensorimotor schemas) should be connected first with fantasy representations (symbolic schemas) and then to "conscious ideas" (language mode)—that without this system of roots to integrate the three modes, insights (words, concepts) would float detached as intellectualizations, fantasies would be deprived of experimentation and fulfilment in reality experiences, and actions would remain automatons without the breadth, psychological economy, and meaning provided by thought and fantasy.

The conception of repeating or revolving metaphors' playing a role in prescribing emotions experienced and expressed in various situations also brings into focus Izard's (1982) proposal that no evaluative or symbolic process is required "for sensing pain or sexual pleasure." But the view outlined here, again illustrated best by the case study, suggests what clinicians have long held as a dictum, that what is pain for one is sexual pleasure for another and visa versa. How do we understand that Tom experienced and expressed intense pride in accumulating tail glands and in making elaborate cakes of feces and, at another time, experienced and expressed equally intense pride in swords he carved and waved about. The concept of metaphors' repeatedly interpreting and assimilating a range of experiences, and continually restructuring as a result, provides one approach to this question.

Cognition/emotion and Psychopathology.   The proposed model also permits a view of psychopathology that emphasizes the role of cognition. Psychopathology could result from inflexible cognitive controls' failing to shift in response to changing environments, and from inflexible metaphors' failing to restructure, as a function of experiences and/or with the emergence of new coding capacities. This view has guided studies of pathological individuals (Santostefano, 1985) of pathological groups (Santostefano & Rieder, 1983; 1984, a & b) and the formulation of a form of psychodynamic psychotherapy, called cognitive control therapy (Santostefano, 1978; 1984), which attempts first to restructure controls diagnosed as inflexible and inefficient in copying information and then to rehabilitate the capacity of controls to coordinate requirements of metaphor and contexts.

Nearly a century ago James (1890) suggested that, rather than dissected into static parts, the human mind should be studied "in motion," as a person copes with changing environments. The theory of cognitive controls, which emerged among the New Look approaches some 30 years ago (Bruner & Klein, 1960), subscribed to this position. Elaborations of this view and the cognitive/emotional model presented here are an attempt to continue in the same spirit. Although there is much to be learned by examining where Freud and Piaget meet (Furth, 1983), the two masters who themselves are metaphors of emotion and cognition respectively, the writer believes it would be more fruitful if we constructed a new metaphor of cognition and emotion, a metaphor that assimilates earlier ones but is shaped by new coding capacities. Cognition as a set of mobile functions coordinating changing contexts and everchanging metaphors is suggested as one possibility (Holt, 1976; Klein, 1970; Santostefano, 1977a, 1980).

REFERENCES

Arnold, M. B. (1960). *Emotion and personality, Vol. 1, Psychological aspects*. New York: Columbia University Press.

Bever, T. G. (1982). Introduction. In T. G. Bever (Ed.), *Regressions in mental development* (pp. 1–4). Hillsdale, NJ: Lawrence Erlbaum Associates.

Billow, R. M. (1977). Metaphor: A review of the psychological literature. *Psychological Bulletin*, 84, 81–92.

Bowers, K. S. (1981). Knowing more than we can say leads to saying more than we can know: On being implicitly informed. In D. Magnusson (Ed.), *Toward a psychology of situations* (pp. 179–194). Hillsdale, NJ: Lawrence Erlbaum Associates.

Bower, G. H., & Cohen, P.R. (1982). Emotional influences in memory and thinking. In M. S. Clark & S. T. Fiske (Eds.), *Affect and cognition* (pp. 291–332). Hillsdale, NJ: Lawrence Erlbaum Associates.

Bruner, J. S. (1951). Personality dynamics and the process of perceiving. In R. R. Blake & G. V. Ramsey (Eds.), *Perception: An approach to personality* (pp. 121–147). New York: Ronald.

Bruner, J. S., & Klein, G. S. (1960). The functions of perception: New look retrospect. In B. Kaplan & S. Wapner (Eds.), *Perspectives in psychological theory* (pp. 61–77). New York: International Universities Press.

Clark, M. S., & Fiske, S. T. (Eds.). (1982). *Affect and cognition*. Hillsdale, NJ: Lawrence Erlbaum Associates.

DeCarie, T. G. (1978). Affect development and cognition in a Piagetian context. In M. Lewis & L. A. Rosenblum (Eds.), *The development of affect* (pp. 183–204). New York: Plenum.

Erdelyi, M. H. (1974). A new look at the new look: Perceptual defense and vigilence. *Psychological Review, 81*, 1–25.

Furth, H. G. (1983). Symbol formation: Where Freud and Piaget meet. *Human Development, 26*, 26–41.

Gardner, R. W., Holzman, P. S., Klein, G. S., Linton, H. B., & Spence, D. P. (1959). Cognitive control: A study of individual consistencies in cognitive behavior. *Psychological Issues, 1* (4, Whole No. 4).

Guthrie, G. D. (1967). *Changes in cognitive functioning under stress: A study of plasticity in cognitive controls*. Doctoral dissertation, Clark University, Worcester, MA.

Hartmann, H. (1958). *Ego psychology and the problem of adaptation*. New York: International Universities Press.

Holt, R. R. (1976). Drive or wish? A reconsideration of the psychoanalytic theory of motivation. *Psychological Issues, 9* (4, Whole No. 36, 158–198).

Hunt, J. M. (1981). The role of situations in early psychological development. In D. Magnusson (Ed.), *Toward a psychology of situations* (pp. 323–342). Hillsdale, NJ: Lawrence Erlbaum Associates.

Izard, C. E. (1977). *Human emotions*. New York: Plenum.

Izard, C. E. (1978). On the ontogenesis of emotions and emotion-cognitive relationships in infancy. In M. Lewis & L. A. Rosenblum (Eds.), *The development of affect* (pp. 389–414). New York: Plenum.

Izard, C. E. (1982). Comments on emotions and cognition: Can there be a working relationship? In M. S. Clark & S. T. Riske (Eds.), *Affect and cognition* (pp. 229–242). Hillsdale, NJ: Lawrence Erlbaum Associates.

James, W. (1890). *The principles of psychology*. New York: Holt.

Klein, G. S. (1951). The personal world through perception. In R. R. Blake & G. V. Ramsey (Eds.), *Perception: An approach to personality* (pp. 328–355). New York: Ronald.

Klein, G. S. (1954). Need and regulation. In M. R. Jones (Ed.), *Nebraska symposium on motivation* (Vol. 2, p. 224). Lincoln: University of Nebraska Press.

Klein, G. S. (1970). *Perception, motives and personality*. New York: Knopf.

Klein, G. S., & Schlesinger, H. J. (1949). Where is the perceiver in perceptual theory? *Journal of Personality, 18*, 32–47.

Lewis, M., & Rosenblum, L. A. (1978). Introduction: Issues in affect development. In M. Lewis & L. A. Rosenblum (Eds.), *The development of affect* (pp. 1–10). New York: Plenum.

Leventhal, H. (1982). The integration of emotion and cognition: A view from the perceptual-motor theory of emotion. In M. S. Clark, & S. T. Fiske (Eds.), *Affect and cognition* (pp. 121–156). Hillsdale, NJ: Lawrence Erlbaum Associates.

Magnusson, D. (1981). *Toward a psychology of situations*. Hillsdale, NJ: Lawrence Erlbaum Associates.

Mandler, G. (1982). The structure of value: Accounting for taste. In M. S. Clark & S. T. Fiske (Eds.), *Affect and cognition* (pp. 3–36). Hillsdale, NJ: Lawrence Erlbaum Associates.

McGrath, J. E. (1976). Stress and behavior in organizations. In M. D. Dunette (Eds.), *Handbook of industrial and organizational psychology* (pp. 1351–1395). Chicago: Rand McNally.

Mounoud, P. (1982). Revolutionary periods in early development. In T. G. Bever (Ed.), *Regressions in mental development* (pp. 119–132). Hillsdale, NJ: Lawrence Erlbaum Associates.

Mowrer, O. H. (1960). *Learning theory and behavior*. New York: Wiley.

Nisbett, R. E., & Wilson, T. D. (1977). Telling more than we can know: Verbal reports on mental processes. *Psychological Review, 84*, 231–259.

Ortony, A. (Ed.) (1979). *Metaphor and thought*. New York: Cambridge University Press.

Ortony, A., Reynolds, R. E., & Arter, J. A. (1978). Metaphor: Theoretical and empirical research. *Psychological Bulletin, 85*, 919–943.

Piaget, J. (1973). The affective unconscious and the cognitive unconscious. *Journal of American Psychoanalytic Association, 21*, 249–266.

Piaget, J. (1981). *Intelligence and affectivity: Their relationship during child development*. Palo Alto: Annual Reviews.

Pervin, L. A. (1978). Definitions, measurements and classifications of stimuli, situations, and environments. *Human Ecology, 6*, 71–105.

Rieder, C., Santostefano, S., & Wertlieb, D. (1983). *Cognitive controls and decoding nonverbal affective cues*. Unpublished manuscript.

Richardson, A. (1983). Imagery: Definition and types. In A. A. Sheikh (Ed.), *Imagery: Current theory, research and application* (pp. 3–42). New York: Wiley.

Rommetveit, R. (1981). On the meaning of situations and social control of such meaning in human communication. In D. Magnusson (Ed.), *Toward a psychology of situations* (pp. 151–168). Hillsdale, NJ: Lawrence Erlbaum Associates.

Rosenthal, R., Hall, J. A., Di Matteo, M. R., Rogers, P. L., & Archer, D. (1979). *Sensitivity to nonverbal communication. The Pons Test*. Baltimore: Johns Hopkins University Press.

Royce, J. H. (Ed.). (1973). *Multivariate analysis and psychological theory*. New York: Academic.

Sander, L. W. (1969). Regulation and organization in the early infant-caretaker system. In R. Robinson (Ed.), *Brain and early behavior* (pp. 78–92). London: Academic Press.

Santostefano, S. (1970). Assessment of motives in children. *Psychological Reports, 26*, 639–649.

Santostefano, S. (1977a). New views of motivation and cognition in psychoanalytic theory: The horse (id) and rider (ego) revisited. *McLean Hospital Journal, 2*, 48–64.

Santostefano, S. (1977b). Action, fantasy, language: Developmental levels of ego organization in communicating drives and affects. In N. Freedman & S. Grand (Eds.), *Communication structures and psychic structures* (pp. 331–354). New York: Plenum.

Santostefano, S. (1978). *A biodevelopmental approach to clinical child psychology: Cognitive controls and cognitive control therapy*. New York: Wiley.

Santostefano, S. (1980). Cognition in personality and the treatment process: A psychoanalytic view. *Psychoanalytic Study of the Child, 35*, 41–66. New Haven: Yale University Press.

Santostefano, S. (1983). *Changes in focal attention in response to changing stimuli*. Unpublished manuscript.

Santostefano, S. (1984). Cognitive control therapy with children: Rationale and technique. *Psychotherapy: Theory, Research and Practice, 21*, 76–91.

Santostefano, S. (1985). Metaphor: An integration of action, fantasy and language in development. *Imagination, Cognition and Personality, 4*, 127–146.

Santostefano, S., & Rieder, C. (1983). *Cognitive controls and cognitive styles in suicidal children and adolescents.* Unpublished manuscript.

Santostefano, S., & Rieder, C. (1984a). Cognitive controls and aggression in children: The concept of cognitive-affective balance. *Journal of Consulting and Clinical Psychology, 52*, 46–56.

Santostefano, S., & Rieder, C. (1984b). The structure of fantasied movement in suicidal children and adolescents. *Journal of Suicide and Life-Threatening Behavior, 14*, 3–16.

Sarason, I. G., & Sarason, B. R. (1981). The importance of cognition and moderator variables. In D. Magnusson (Ed.), *Toward a psychology of situations: An interpersonal perspective* (pp. 195–210). Hillsdale, NJ: Lawrence Erlbaum Associates.

Scheier, M. F., & Carver, C. S. (1982). Cognition, affect and self-regulation. In M. S. Clark & S. T. Fiske (Eds.), *Affect and cognition* (pp.157–184). Hillsdale, NJ: Lawrence Erlbaum Associates.

Schön, D. A. (1979). Generative metaphor: A perspective on problem-setting in social policy. In A. Ortony (Ed.), *Metaphor and thought* (pp. 254–283). Cambridge: Cambridge University Press.

Shapiro, I. F. (1972). *Cognitive controls and adaptation in children.* Unpublished doctoral dissertation, Boston College.

Shapiro, E. K., & Weber, E. (Eds.) (1981). *Cognitive and affective growth.* Hillsdale, NJ: Lawrence Erlbaum Associates.

Tower, R. B. (1983). Imagery: Its role in development. In A. A. Sheikh (Ed.), *Imagery: Current theory, research and application* (pp. 222–251). New York: Wiley.

Wachtel, P. L. (1972). Cognitive style and style of adaptation. *Perceptual Motor Skills, 35*, 779–785.

Wertlieb, D. L. (1979). *Cognitive organization, regulations of aggression and learning disorders in boys.* Unpublished doctoral dissertation, Boston University.

Wiener, E., Wapner, W., Cicone, M., & Gardner, H. (1979). Measures of metaphor. *New Directions for Child Development, 6*, 67–75.

Wolitzky, D. L., & Wachtel, P. L. (1973). Personality and perception. In B. B. Wolman (Ed.), *Handbook of general psychology* (pp. 826–857). Englewood Cliffs, NJ: Prentice-Hall.

Zimmerman, B. J. (1983). Social learning theory: A contextualist account of cognitive functioning. In C. J Brainerd (Ed.) *Recent advances in cognitive-developmental theory* (pp. 1–50). New York: Springer-Verlag.

12

Cognition-Affect: A Psychological Riddle

Irving E. Sigel
Educational Testing Service

INTRODUCTION

Clarification of the roles and relationships between cognition and affect is of theoretical and practical importance. The theoretical significance rests on the assumption that understanding the cognition-affect connection is a crucial building block to understanding human functioning because *cognition* and *affect* are labels denoting two basic sets of human actions. With such understanding we would be able to enhance our theoretical and practical approach to human development. On such bases, we could develop practical (clinical and/or educational) ways to help individuals function effectively, particularly by keeping thoughts and emotions functioning in harmony.

The issue of how cognition and affect interact, coupled with conceptualization of each, is not new (see Kagan, 1978, for an historical perspective). In spite of the age of the problem (2,000 years or more), we still struggle to construct solutions that, when proferred, continue to create controversy (see Zajonc's [1984] debate with Lazarus [1984]). This chapter adds another perspective, using Santostefano's chapter as a backdrop. I direct my comments to Santostefano's conceptualization and then proceed to describe a developmental model, essentially a new constructivistic Piagetian developmental perspective.

In this chapter I show that the cognition-affect dichotomy is an artifact of our conceptualization and that it refers to an indissociable whole. The dichotomy must be rejected in favor of a holistic approach. Then I discuss Santostefano's model, which seeks to overcome the dichotomous cognitive-affect argument, and finally, I present still another approach that is more akin to that of Piaget.

PERSPECTIVES ON THE RIDDLE

Is the relationship between thought and affect one of reciprocal influence as some might suggest (Lewis & Michalson, 1983), or are there two different but parallel systems (Zajonc, 1980), or does cognition influence affect (Lazarus, 1982), or are they two aspects of the same whole, indissociable, as Piaget (1951) suggests? Answers to these riddles have been forthcoming from biologists, philosophers, sociologists, psychologists, and even theologians for many years. In spite of this concerted, albeit disparate, set of efforts, vast disagreements still exist. Each generation of investigators has produced data or arguments supporting particular perspectives, which have been subsequently modified or rejected or assimilated into the general body of knowledge. Although different conceptualizations of affect development have waxed and waned over the years, we have in the past 2 decades witnessed a paradigmatic and conceptual revolution in the behavioral sciences, especially developmental psychology (Sigel, 1981), which has attempted to reintegrate affect into the larger unit of the person.

The apparent renewed interest in the cognition-affect connection is probably due to increased limitations of the cognization of much psychological theorizing in recent years (Sigel, 1981). The problem that has arisen is how to conceptualize and study the interaction between cognition and affect, recognizing the fact that both are ever present characteristics of the whole individual. My argument is that the one reason we perpetuate the problem is that we insist on the cognition-affect dichotomy, where affect or emotions refer to nonrationale feelings, whereas cognition refers to the thought, the rational human functions.

Evidence for the belief in the cognition-affect distinction. A number of writers have addressed the issue and I quote from some to illustrate how the relationship between cognition and affect has been described:

Cognition and affect are conceptualized as two distinct domains by Izard (1977). For him:

> Affect is a general nonspecific term that includes . . . motivational states and processes . . . the affective domain includes the fundamental emotions, patterns of emotions, drives, and their interactions. The affective domain also embraces states or processes in which one of the affects (emotions, drives) is linked with or interacting with perception or cognition. (p. 65).

As for the affective-cognitive relationship, Izard (1977) writes: "An affective-cognitive structure or orientation represents a bond, tie or strong association of one of the affects (or a pattern of affects) with images, words, thoughts, or ideas" (p. 65). It is clear from these quotations that Izard employs categorical distinctions between cognition and affect. This perspective seems to be congruent with a logical positivistic, or a *heuristic orientation.*

Of particular significance is Izard's contention that "emotions constitute the primary motivational system for human beings" (p. 3). For Izard affect is a superordinate category, a subset being emotion, which is a "complex phenomenon having neurophysiological, motor-expressive, and experiential components" (p. 64). Emotion is presumably specific, e.g., anger, fear, joy, whereas affect appears to be a free-floating state—perhaps feelings that are expressed emotionally. If one thinks hierarchically, emotions are on a concrete level with physiological substrates; affect is viewed at a higher, more abstract level.

Zajonc (1980) argues for the cognition-affect distinction:

> A number of experimental results on preferences, attitudes, impression formation, and decision making, as well as some clinical phenomena, suggest that affective judgments may be fairly independent of, and precede in time, the sorts of perceptual and cognitive operations commonly assumed to be the basis of these affective judgments . . . It is concluded that affect and cognition are under the control of separate and partially independent systems that can influence each other in a variety of ways . . . (p. 151).

Not to belabor the issue, the reader should note the qualifiers in Zajonc's statement, e.g., partially independent.

Lazarus (1982), who disagrees with Zajonc on the issue of primacy of affect or cognition in determining responsivity, holds that cognition and affect are fused. He writes that although cognition and emotions are usually fused, there are conditions in which the two can be dissociated. Cognitive processes serve in appraisal capacities. The summative statement of Lazarus is as follows: "*Cognitive activity* is a *necessary* as well as sufficient condition of emotion (p. 1019). The task for psychology, according to Lazarus (1982), is "to formulate rules about how cognitive processes generate, influence, and shape the emotional response in every species that reacts with emotion, in every social group sharing values, commitments, and beliefs and in every individual member of the human species" (p. 1024).

Admirable as Lazarus' effort is, there are some logical problems in his formulation. If something is fused, a physical metaphor, is he arguing that the fusion is destroyed by the action (energy) of some emotion, or is the defusion a function of some intense cognitive judgment? Is the cognition-affect fusion different in kind than when they are "de-fused"?

Piaget (1981), on the other hand, does attempt to justify his approach to cognition and affect as indissociable. He concludes as follows:

> Behavior cannot be classified under affective and cognitive rubrics. If a distinction must be made [which by the way, Piaget makes] . . . it would be more accurate to make it between *behaviors related to objects and behaviors related to people*. Both have a structural or cognitive and energetic or affective aspects . . . In behaviors related to people, the energetic element is made up of inter-personal feelings. Ordinarily, these are emphasized exclusively [Piaget writes emphasized which is merely accentuation not exclusively affective]. They contain a structural

element, however, which comes from taking consciousness of interpersonal relationships and leads, among other things, to the constitution of value structures [a
cognitive-type evaluation]. (p. 74)

Yet it is interesting to note that the bulk of Piaget's research was directed at
the epistemological level of how the child comes to know such phenomena as
space, time, number, causality (physical), and how perception, memory, and
intelligence develop. In none of his writings does Piaget concern himself with
the affective features inherent in the child's performance on the various tasks,
nor does he incorporate "affect" in his interpretation of findings. Ironically, most
of the American research using the Piagetian paradigm also excludes affect, not
even attempting to incorporate involvement in Piaget's considerations of affectivity and intelligence.

Although Piaget writes of the significance of the child's interest (affect) and
will (ego control) in task performance, is it not reasonable to assume that he
should deal with interest and will? Are these factors not relevant to the child's
performance on tasks Piaget and his co-workers used on hundreds of Genevan
children? Could any of the results have been influenced by either the lack or the
presence of interest and will to perform? Piaget never addresses these issues in
the context of his experiments.

What can we conclude from this brief survey? First, the cognition-affect
dichotomy is alive and well. Zajonc and Lazarus are still in the throes of their
debate. Other writers are proceeding to develop new approaches, but still persist
in dealing with the categories of cognition and/or affect as distinct and *as if* there
are categories in nature. There are no categories in nature. We construct the
categories, define their parameters, and strive to discover legitimate instances
representing the categories. Is there a pure affective category—that is, a category
with no indication of cognitive awareness? Is there a category of pure cognition?
It all depends on whom one asks and what criteria and definitions are used as
bases for seeking answers. For example, Zajonc (1984) uses a neuroanatomical
model, arguing that because separate neuroanatomical structures can be identified
for affect and cognition, it is possible to infer "pure sensory input requiring no
transformation into cognition that is capable of bringing about a full emotional
response involving visceral and motor activity" (p. 119).

It should be pointed out, of course, that Zajonc, Lazarus, and Izard provide
evidence for their perspective. Lazarus and Zajonc refer to data from infant
developmental studies to support their differing cases. Interestingly, Zajonc argues
that infants are not capable of cognitive appraisal and hence their responses of
fear, joy, and surprise are affective and do not involve cognitive appraisal.
Lazarus (1984) argues that it is doubtful if a good case can be made that infants
are not capable of making cognitive appraisals. So, the developmental data are
used essentially to infer, and hence to maintain, the basic position of the respective investigators.

What none of the investigators seem to grapple with is their fundamental epistemology that in my view is at the heart of the problem. The investigators previously described are not emancipated from the Aristotelian categorization. Thus the current categorization of events, e.g., cognition and affect, is derived from the existing social categorization system. As Gergen (1982) so aptly states, "The units of understanding human action do not appear to be furnished by observation, but rather through participation in the cultural system of understanding" (p. 23). Both the culture and the historical nature of our perspectives, coupled with generally accepted theory, combine to generate a category system used to describe human actions. Perhaps because of the commitment to an Aristotelian-type categorical system that seems endemic to our daily lives, we struggle with relationships between two perceived distinct yet related categories of emotion and thinking.

DEVELOPMENT

Much of the discussion of cognition and affect has been derived from work with adults. Piaget and Erikson are exceptions, but they do not inform us of the particular developmental pattern of affect. Piaget rejects a causal relationship between cognition and affect and stresses, according to Décarie (1978), "the existence of a functional parallelism" (p. 185) that is, cognitive and affective stages are concordant—i.e., for each cognitive stage there is a corresponding affective stage. However, the affective stages are considered as social feelings involving morality, rather than what is commonly thought of as emotion, e.g., joy, sorrow, feeling good about self, and so on. Unfortunately, Piaget's effort at systematizing affective development was aborted in 1954. However, Piaget also writes of the indivisible nature of cognition and affect. Thus, if they cannot be separated, how can he write of the functional parallelism? I think Piaget never did resolve the cognition-affect question in his theory.

If we turn to the psychoanalysts for a theory to conceptualize cognition and affect (especially Erikson), we discover that the terminology and language are no longer in the genre of *cognition* and *affect*, but rather, in terms of language units of the personality. It seems clear that thought and feelings are labels used for heuristic purposes. Basically there is a dynamic wholeness where at times thought seems preeminent but is never divorced from the dynamic affective overtones and vice-versa.

While Piaget employs affect in a special social interpersonal context, writers like Erikson (1950) and Lidz (1968) employ psychoanalytic concepts that are ostensively personal and affective, yet do involve cognitive operations. These cognitive operations are implicit and embedded in a psychoanalytic framework. For example, Lidz (1968) incorporates cognition and affect in his definition of ego. He writes of ego as:

A construct used to designate decision-making, self-directing aspects of the self or of the personality. Ego functions depend upon the use of language to construct an internalized representation of the world which can be manipulated in trial-and-error fashion to weigh potential outcomes and to contain gratification of wish, drive, and impulsion in order to cope with "reality" and the pursuit of ultimate objectives. (p. 87)

Note the explicit cognitive concepts, e.g., representation, decision-making. In other words, the psychoanalytic system encompasses affect (gratifications) and cognition-decision making.

The psychoanalytic model is developed as a life-span approach by Erikson who in his developmental model focuses more explicitly incorporating cognition-affect under one umbrella construct. For example, Erikson (1959) describes an initiative stage when the child is between 3 and 6. He writes: "Both language and locomotion permit him to expand his imagination over so many things he cannot avoid frightening himself with what he has dreamed and thought up" (p. 75).

Again, reflecting on these and other descriptions of Erikson's stages, one asks whether he provides an explicit cognitive model that defines the operations involved in the individual's coping. The answer is no. Rather, cognition and affect are conceptualized in the broader context of development, with social or interpersonal indicators used as linguistic referents (e.g., basic trust, sense of autonomy, self-control). Erikson and other psychoanalysts do provide broad sweeps describing development in general with varying degrees of specific reference to particular cognitive operations (in contrast to Piaget).

To this point, I have set out to demonstrate that the cognition-affect dichotomy reflects a categorical perspective. I believe the separation leads nowhere because the distinctions are social-historical artifacts. There are alternative approaches that ostensively eschew the effort to link cognition-affect as separate systems, but, rather, conceptualize these functions in a holistic way. Santostefano's approach (this volume) is an excellent example of an organic holistic approach in the psychoanalytic mode, in which cognition and affect are embedded as integral to the whole. However, as we proceed to discuss Santostefano's model, remnants of the cognition-affect dichotomy are evident, indicating he is still tied to the dichotomous viewpoint.

SANTOSTEFANO'S MODEL

Santostefano organizes his model around three fundamental constructs: *cognitive-control*, *metaphor*, and *context*, each of which contributes to the creation of a whole model. Let me briefly provide a perspective regarding each of these concepts in its historical context.

Cognitive Control. The cognitive control construct is conceptualized by Santostefano (this volume) "as mechanisms that shifted in response to changing stimulation, responding simultaneously to task stimuli and associated fantasies and affect, i.e., the inner environment" (p. 178). The cognitive control concept has been in the psychological literature since the 1950s, emerging from early studies of Klein (1958) and associates who investigated the relationship between needs and perceptions among adults. They conducted a series of studies using an array of cognitive and perceptual tasks. In the course of this effort they identified six distinct processes which they referred to as *cognitive controls*, which in their totality are classified as cognitive style, an individual difference concept denoting characteristic ways individuals cope with the environment (Gardner, Holzman, Klein, Linton, & Spence, 1959).

Gardner and Moriarty (1968) applied similar control complements to a study of preadolescent children. In their view, affect is not integral to cognitive control; rather, cognitive control is conceptualized as a defense—a way to cope with anxiety. The relation between cognition and affect, however, is as follows: "Affect is more fundamental and of greater causative significance in behavior" (Gardner & Moriarty, 1968, p. 305) than has generally been accepted even in psychoanalytic theory. They write that: "Feeling states, and individuality in the organization of feeling states, must in part be referable to the nature and inter-action of a wide variety of behavioral structures, including defenses, cognitive controls, intellectual abilities, the little-explored patternings of motoric behavior, and others" (Gardner & Moriarty, 1968, p. 305). For these psychoanalytically oriented writers, then, affect is identifiable and is a fundamentally reactive system that influences adaptive functioning.

The beginnings of the research by Klein and Gardner in the 1950s and 1960s showed great promise. Because cognitive controls were seen as "a form of cognition that is thought to be dynamically related to aspects of impulse control and affective expression" (Zimiles, 1981, p. 57), they seemed capable of pro-viding the organizing constructs for parsimonious conceptualization of the cognitive-affect relationship.

The organizing cognitive control construct that seems to undergird all sub-sequent conceptualization and research is as follows: "The organism must not only bring needs, impulses, and wishes into continual harmony; it must also resolve the many independent claims of reality" (Gardner et al., 1959, p. 3). Thus, cognitive controls are adaptive mechanisms enabling the individual to cope with anxiety.

There has, however, been a shift away from cognitive control research, per-haps based on a rejection of its psychoanalytic origins, since cognitive control was judged as a defensive reaction rather than as a cognitive (thinking-reasoning) construct. Further, the de-emphasis on psychoanalytic theory, with the concurrent *cognization* of developmental theory, especially among developmental psychol-ogists, resulted in the movement away from studying cognitive controls.

Santostefano, however, was one of the few investigators that persisted in cognitive control research in an effort to study cognitive controls in their affective contexts.

Santostefano's Control Construct.   Santostefano presents us with a developmental model that reflects a structural-functional conceptualization. Five controls are identified and defined as mobile structures that can change in their interrelationship as a function of environmental conditions (see Table 12.1). A major way cognitive controls seem to function in the service of adaptation is to coordinate, or in my terms, mediate between inner fantasies and emotions and environmental (outer) variables.

Cognitive controls are defined as mechanisms that (a) govern and determine the amount and organization of information that becomes available to an individual perceiver, (b) are activated by the individual's intention to use and adapt to information, (c) vary in the extent to which they operate in the cognitive functioning of individuals, (d) evolve as a function of maturation and life experiences and become autonomous from their origin of development, (e) mediate the influence of personality and motivation in the individual's cognitive encounters with the environment, and (f) become enduring aspects of an individual's cognitive functioning and adaptive style, thus giving shape to his/her subsequent experiences. (Santostefano, this volume, 176).

Cognitive controls maintain a balance between inner forces such as feelings, fantasies and outer environments. Cognitive controls function to maintain a balance between affect and cognition and hence are "viewed as fostering adaptations, psychological development, and learning" (Santostefano, 1984, p. 78). Each of the five cognitive controls changes qualitatively with age.

At first blush cognitive controls appear to be volitional, reflective cognitions that serve as a means to adapt to various trials and tribulations of living. There is on the one hand the implication that the individual deliberately selects particular

Table 1
Cognitive Controls and Their Definitions

Body Ego-Tempo Regulation: The manner in which an individual constructs images representing the body and regulates body motility.

Focal Attention: The manner in which an individual scans a field of information.

Field Articulation: The manner in which an individual deals with a field of information that contains both relevant and irrelevant elements.

Leveling-Sharpening: The manner in which an individual constructs images of information and compares them to present perceptions.

Equivalence Range: The manner in which an individual categorizes and conceptualizes information.

Note. Definitions are from Santostefano (1984), p. 78.

controls to help cope with environmental experiences. Yet the thrust of Santostefano's argument is that the cognitive controls are employed virtually automatically to adapt to particular life events. For example, in one experiment Santostefano reports that, when individuals are faced with an anxiety-provoking situation, in this case parachutists waiting at the airport, they respond to cognitive tasks more in terms of levelling than they did in a benign context. The question is, are the responders aware of this shift?

I read cognitive controls as types of defense mechanisms because, judging by their defined characteristics, there is no indication of the conscious volition elements, in spite of Santostefano's stating: "controls are activated by the individuals' *intention* [italics added] to use and adapt to information" (p. 176). Is this statement to imply that the individual is aware that he or she has to adapt to a situation but is unaware of the controls that he or she has to use? Basically my questions are, do cognitive controls comprise a repertoire of adaptation strategies that are differentially, appropriately, and *intentionally* used, or are the controls part of a repertoire of response mechanisms that are automatically activated (i.e., without awareness)? The answer to this question is not in Santostefano's chapter in this volume, but some answers may be inferred from Santostefano's (1984) recent publication on cognitive control therapy. The aim of this therapy is to help the patients (usually children and adolescents) restructure the cognitive affective balance, thereby becoming more efficient to promote "integrating internal and external information, and assimilating the results of actions into cognitive schema . . ." (Santostefano 1984, p. 176). The implication of developing a therapeutic approach to modify an individual's cognitive controls is that cognitive controls are subject to change, enhancing their coping mechanisms—literally influencing how the individual learns and/or copes. Two questions then arise: One, is the level of awareness of one's controls usage enhanced so that adaptations via controls are in awareness?; and a second, related question, what drives the controls?

The implications of the therapeutic approach are theoretical and practical. The theoretical implications revolve around increased understanding of the function, and perhaps structure, of cognitive controls in the adaptive system. If through therapy patients become more flexible, i.e., open to alternative control strategies in the service of problem solving, then the practical ends will be well served.

A related issue refers to the relationship between cognitive control and metacognitive processes that function as superordinates, encompassing such internal processes as reflection, judgment, and evaluation in the service of responding to the array of experiences. To put it another way, what functions do the intellectual processes serve as mediators between inner and outer experience?

Conceivably, the developmental changes in cognitive structure that Piaget describes may well influence the kinds of cognitive controls and metaphors children develop and which they are able to use. Does the children's cognitive structural status influence the pattern of cognitive controls? For example, does the fact that children are capable of solving class inclusion problems have any relationship to cognitive controls used, and if so, in what context?

Although at first reading the cognitive control construct appears to come to terms with the cognition-affect dichotomy, on reflection from my perspective, it avoids coming to grips with the issue of whether cognitive controls are cognitively or emotionally driven. Santostefano's research suggests they are driven by emotional factors, because the cognitive control changes occurred in contexts that are charged with anxiety and fear. For example, the task for the subjects in the parachute study was to make judgments—a cognitive task. Hence the subject's response and the task demands generated cognitions. These cognitions seem to be driven by affect; namely, the anxiety people feel while waiting to make parachute jumps.

The cognitive control then, for me, is a label for those processes that mediate between cognition and affect, rather than integrating the two. Affect and judgment may be reciprocal in cognitive control. The cognition serves to control the affect. For Santostefano, on the other hand, the cognitive control construct is integrative—defining in effect the action (cognition) and the function (control) but instigated by the affect-arousing properties in the context.

If cognitive controls are not under the individual's conscious control, then what does regulate the controls? There are no data provided by Santostefano, nor any of the other researchers, to answer this question. Rather, the argument is based on inference, i.e., individuals perceive threat and employ particular controls as defense. On the more general level, according to the cognitive control theorists (Gardner et al., 1959), everyone employs control patterns that serve as adaptation techniques. Thus, we can conclude from Santostefano's perspective that affect and cognition are intimately related. However, if my interpretation of his position is correct, the affect is aroused by some cognitive evaluation (but not necessarily conscious), and the intensity of the anxiety induced by the event is filtered through the ego which activates cognitive controls.

The Metaphor.   In Santostefano's system the metaphor, a second critical construct, reflects the content and the thematic aspects individuals employ in organizing their worlds of experience. He writes of a metaphor as spiraling from one plane to another and taking on a new structure with the intrinsic emergence of new coding capacities for the child. He uses the metaphor concept to incorporate Piagetian transitions in development, as well as changes attributed to psychosexual development. The overarching role of metaphor has appeal. It allows for maximal flexibility in defining its references, facilitates communication, and allows for defining aspects of the human condition difficult to denote in our everyday language. However, Santostefano's use of the metaphor, although intriguing, poses some conceptual and analytical problems. Santostefano uses the definition of metaphor proposed by Schön (1979), who holds that a metaphor functions as a mediator between inner and outer forces or between self and others.

As the notion of metaphor is used by Santostefano, it becomes clear that virtually *all* experience can be considered metaphorical. Does this mean the individual constructs his experience in metaphorical terms, or does it mean that the experience is *reported* in metaphorical terms? Apparently Santostefano would agree with Petrie (1979) that "experience is never directly of the world as it is, but always in part constituted by our modes of representation and understanding" (p. 440). If this is the case, then it is likely that a metaphor is in the reporting, not in the experiencing. The distinction between the inner experience of a metaphor and its expression suggests that understanding of the meaning of the metaphor may be ambiguous, because it resides in what Polanyi (1967) refers to as the tacit dimension; that is, in essence, "*that we can know more than we can tell*" (p. 4). We often use metaphors to capture and to communicate because we have difficulty telling what we know. Poetry, art, and music use metaphors just for those reasons.

In effect, all experience is transformed into some internalized representation in the form of a symbol or a sign and is expressed in comparable or diverse symbolic form that may be metaphorical. For example, the child experiences a trip to the orchard. This experience may be stored as images, but the child may act out the trip in play or tell a story. In each instance, these representations are transformations of experience. To refer to these activities as metaphorical stretches the metaphor concept; we are left to conclude that virtually *all* human activity is metaphorical. If this is the case, then the concept may lose its power as a viable, researchable construct, because a concept is of value only if it can be identified as a separate phenomenon. The metaphor idea is but one approach to understanding the cognition-affect relationship. The following constructs function in the same conceptual role as Santostefano's idea of metaphor, e.g., Kelly's (1955) personal constructs, Witkin's cognitive style (Witkin & Goodenough, 1981), Piaget's (1951) schema or scheme, Schank and Abelson's (1977) scripts, Sigel's (1985) beliefs. What these theoretical concepts have in common with Santostefano's is that each is proposed as a construct for organizing experience. These are metaphors also, except that Santostefano, introducing his metaphor idea from the phenomological perspective, suggests that metaphors are private and personal organizing schemes and include not only the content of the environment, but also personal relevant actions. However, the distinctions among these constructs and their function have to be made to demonstrate the uniqueness of metaphor.

There are two issues in the way the metaphor construct is used by Santostefano: One concerns the subject's phenomenological experience expressed in metaphors; the other concerns the phenomenological experience of the observer and his or her expression in metaphor. Thus, we have two metaphoric communication systems functioning in synchrony; i.e., that of the patient and that of the therapist. Santostefano constructs his metaphors in the therapeutic context from a psychoanalytic perspective of human functioning. These are his working constructs. The metaphors he attributes to the child then derive from these perspectives. In other words, Santostefano uses psychoanalytically-oriented metaphors as a means of constructing his view of the child. What Santostefano hears and sees then is transformed into metaphors reflective of his preformed belief system.

This poses some interesting and challenging questions regarding constructions of reality, communication and conjoint understanding of meaning. Lakoff and Johnson (1980) describe the process succinctly when they write:

> Metaphors may create realities for us, especially social realities. A metaphor may thus be a guide to future action. Such actions will of course fit the metaphor. This will, in turn, reinforce the power of the metaphor to make experiences coherent. In this sense metaphors can be self-fulfilling prophecies. (p. 156)

Metaphors are symbols, as Santostefano argues. Symbols, however, have a particular function, denoting cognitive-affective relationships. As Piaget (1951) contends, a metaphor "is a symbol because there is a relationship . . . which is not due to social convention but directly experienced by the mind of the individual" (p. 169). Focusing on the symbolic definition of the metaphor narrows the construct and facilitates relating it to other conceptualizations. Piaget (1951) defines symbol, and consequently metaphor as "an image which has a meaning distinct from its immediate content, and in which there is a more or less direct resemblance between signifier and signified" (p. 169). Symbols may be conscious (i.e., where there is a clear meaning for the subject and the unconscious symbol whose meaning is hidden from the subject). For Piaget, affect is expressed in symbols: "The symbol will . . . be used in 'affective language,' to express feelings and concrete experiences, rather than in 'intellectual language' to express impersonal thoughts" (p. 169). Santostefano, in his case study, describes the child's symbolic representation, and Santostefano, as the investigator, strives to understand the referents. There is then an interaction between the metaphors of each participant. To understand what the child's phenomenal world is all about is to come to understand the hidden meaning of the symbols employed. Santostefano's conception of metaphor provides a heuristic for conceptualizing the cognition-affect connection.

Metaphors characterize much of our conceptual thought (Lakoff & Johnson, 1980). Santostefano's *cognitive control* is a metaphor. Piaget's *structuralism* is a metaphor. The term *constructivism* is a metaphor. Obvious as this observation is, its value is that it accentuates the degree to which we organize our social realities in ways which are not necessarily templates of social or physical reality, but of our constructed experience. However, there are those who take the objectivist position not realizing they too are using metaphors. They act as if " there is an objective reality, and we can say things that are objectively, absolutely, and unconditionally true and false about it" (Lakoff & Johnson, 1980, p. 187). The metaphor of an objective world contains properties independent of the person and the knowledge of these properties comes about through experience. Metaphors are constructions of these experiences.

Although Santostefano has brought metaphor, context, and cognitive control into a conceptual whole, and generated a three-dimensional model subsuming cognition and affect, there remains the issue of how to integrate cognition and affect in the developing child. Before I develop my argument, the reader may accuse me of speaking in terms of a cognition-affect dichotomy in spite of my earlier protestations to the contrary. I do not deny that cognitive processes can be identified, processes that are employed in the service of thought. However, this is not to say these processes are independent from affect. In a subsequent section I return to the issue, but for now I would like to show how Santostefano's model does not appear to take into account children's cognitive structural level.

Santostefano has not integrated the knowledge available on children's cognitive processes that function operatively in processes of the child's adaptation. Cognitive operations, or thinking, or reflective thought, particularly from a Piagetian perspective, develop structurally. Conceivably, cognitive structural developmental changes can influence the cognitive controls children employ. Also the quality and rate of change of cognitive operations are influenced by social-cultural factors. Experience, then, broadly conceived in the broader culture as well as at home, may combine to influence the cognitive controls children develop. Related to this issue is the meta-thinking of the child, i.e., the increased awareness of self as a conscious thinker—one who can reflect on one's own and other's actions and intentions.

We can conclude from this discussion of Santostefano's work that the cognitive controls, the metaphors, and context form a triumvirate that in their totality help explain how cognition and affect interact. However, I feel this perspective needs a sharper developmental focus. Further, there is need to integrate a cognition-affect model more explicitly.

SUMMARY OF THE ISSUES

My brief review of some of the investigators addressing cognition and affect issues provides a sample of the *au courant* thinking. The issues addressed deal with the primacy of affect and/or cognition as instigators of behavior, the facilitative or disruptive role of affect on cognition, the control functions of cognition relative to affective expression, and the relative significance of cognition/affect as predictors to behavior. Santostefano provides a comprehensive model drawing on philosophical (metaphors), psychological (cognitive control), and social (context) concepts to generate a holistic model. The multidisciplinary approach, for Santostefano, rests on a psychoanalytic base. Nevertheless, there are a sufficient and impressive number of overlapping themes to suggest that in time there may be increased rapprochement by future investigators. In fact, the proposed model was stimulated by Santostefano. His concepts of metaphor, control, and context can be embedded in the foregoing. In the following section I present a viewpoint that incorporates much of the foregoing.

A UNITARY COGNITION-AFFECT PERSPECTIVE

The conceptualization to be presented leans primarily, not exclusively, on the theories of Piaget (1951), Freud (1937/1946), Kelly (1955), and Polanyi (1966). From each of the theorists, a particular emphasis was abstracted to create a new model. Its basic assumption is clearly stated by Piaget (1981) where he writes:

> It is impossible to find behavior arising from affectivity alone without any cognitive elements. It is equally impossible to find behavior composed only of cognitive elements. Nevertheless, cognitive functions, from perception and sensorimotor schemes to abstract intelligence with formal operations will be distinguished from affective functions. This seems necessary because, although cognitive and affective factors are *indissociable* [italics added] in an individual's concrete behavior, they appear different in nature. (pp. 2-3).

Piaget presents a paradox—how is it that cognition and affect are indissociable in behavior and yet appear different in nature? Piaget resolved the paradox by virtually ignoring affect in his studies. I accept the indissociable nature of cognition and affect but recognize that we can observe, and hence infer affective and/or cognitive features. There is an assumed functional relation between affect and thought, and there is a conjoint influence on behavior.

The next issue to be addressed is the conceptualization of affect and cognition from a transformational developmental perspective. Posing this question accepts the notion that, although indivisible in nature, there is a synchronous developmental course for affect that is coterminious with the developmental descriptions of cognitive development. If there is such a developmental relationship, how does affect function in the context of cognitive growth?

What develops? The rationale for segregating *affect* from cognition as an identifiable component of the human organism is that affect refers to a biopsychological set of functions—feelings and emotions. It is clear that there is a biological basis required for emotional expression as well as arousal when appropriate stimulators occur (Izard, 1977). There also is ample evidence that emotions are aroused differently, even in infants. Does this imply that emotions can be aroused only by specific stimuli, or does the individual learn how and when to respond in an emotional way? Knowing that disease is spreading in a community, individuals become fearful and anxious. Such responses depend on knowledge of the event and its meaning. Whether this is the case for infants is still an issue under study (Lewis & Michalson, 1983). Over time individuals *learn* how, when and what to respond to affectively, and how to label the arousing aspects of the stimuli as well as their own internal feelings. If emotional responses essentially are contingencies and learned responses, can we not hold that affective expression is more than a conglomerate of physiological reactions, that it is tied to experience? What accounts for the differentiations in affect expression and arousal may well stem from the judgments (cognition) the child makes about the nature of the situation. If this is the case, cognition and affect are intertwined, each significant to a varying degree as the child engages different contexts.

The child learns how to distinguish stimuli by their pleasant or unpleasant arousal qualities. If we push the question of *what is learned*? in this context we come to the issue of *how* the learning process is conceptualized, especially in regard to affect. For some, learning in this context can be described in a non-cognitive contingency way; whereas for those with a constructivistic cognitive perspective (that is my position), the child is continuously constructing experience, employing those cognitive operations available at his or her developmental level. Experience, however, is total—it includes feelings and thoughts. Consider the analogy of field forces where particles are in motion generating tensions and collisions as they proceed through a unitary space. Similarly, for the individual, feelings and thoughts can be conceptualized as moving in a unified space where the space is indissociable. The space is the schema.

Two propositions are proposed on which my formulation is based: (a) cognition (referring to such processes as thought, judgment, reasoning), and affect (feelings and emotions) are organized in schemas, and (b) the components of the affective-cognitive schema are, by definition, in a configuration where cognition and affect function together and yet as identifiable separates.

The degree of togetherness and/or separateness of cognition and affect depends on the particular activity and the relationship of the activity to one's self, especially one's habitual way of responding. The self moderates, through central executive processes, whether affect and/or cognition is dominant and identifiable. However, both are operative in varying intensities and obviousness. Affective-cognitive schema evolve from one's own experience as an *actor*, where actor is used in the sense of being active, as described by Boesch (1983). The schema serves to regulate the individual's *action*, action being an activity in pursuit of a goal. For example, an individual is striving to solve a problem in mathematics. The activity required involves the use of mathematical schema that contain skills (cognition) and the concomitant affective aspects assimilated in the course of development of that mathematical schema. This assertion is based on the premise that knowledge is never assimilated in a totally nonaffective way. The intensity level could range from minimal to maximal and could have a positive or negative valence. Irrespective of intensity or directionality, there is no neutrality. Affect and cognition serve as regulating functions and as major influential sources determining the quality and directionality of an activity relative to the goal.

A second factor is the quality of the engagement between the person and the task. In the mathematics example, the individual is positively (affect) involved in efforts to solve the problem but finds the problem difficult. Depending on the individual's evaluation of the context, the goals, and his ego controls, he might persist. The positive affect may contribute to maintaining the activity. As the tensions between the initial positive affect and negative ongoing experience interface, and depending on the intensity of the negative experience relative to the positive, the individual's activity may be disrupted. How the disruption will be handled depends on other personal-social coping strategies.

It is reasonable at this point to propose that equilibration, as an active process, controls the individual's capability to exert conscious control (ego), in part by nonconscious cognitive controls, i.e., the controls become automatic and, hence nonconscious, in the course of development. For example, an individual's ability to reflect and to inhibit actions for conscious reasons are examples of conscious control. Effective establishing of equilibration depends on the intensity level of the stimulation (be it external or internal) interacting with the cognitive operational level of the child.

I so far have emphasized the equilibration of cognition and affect as influenced by developmental level of cognition and of the psychological bases of affective arousal. Arousal of feeling does occur on a physiological basis when particular events occur, stimulating the central or autonomic nervous system. In some cases such activation may be on the conscious level, e.g., loss of a loved one; or nonconscious or reflexive, such as a sudden noise. I see no point in debating which is primary—cognition or affect—but rather, that the issue has to be examined in terms of the class of stimuli and the appropriate response mechanisms. A sudden, bright, blinding light arouses different classes of receptors than a sarcastic demeaning comment. Activation of emotion and/or cognition is a function of the appropriate interface between the particular stimulus event and the receptivity of the individual. Of import here is determining the thresholds necessary for activation as well as the interaction between psychological sources regulating cognitive-affective responses and physiologically based determinants (Levenson & Gottman, 1983).

In summary, cognition and affect are embedded in schemas that are not solely cognitive but "contain" affective components. Essentially, no developed schema evolved without cognitive-affective constituents. Particular experiences activate one or the other components, which also activate the other, or both, depending on the event in question. The metaphor of the Siamese twins may describe the construct I am referring to. Cognition and affect function in tandem; neither can or does function independently. Cognition involves affect, and affect interacts with cognition. Disruptions of schemas can occur when the equilibrated relation between cognition-affect within the schema is stressed. Cognitive controls, as Santostefano suggests, influence the cognitive-affect balance within the unified space. The efficacy of control depends on the developmental competence level of the child. If there is a cognitive affective schema functioning as a whole, why the need for the cognitive and affective categories? I agree with Piaget in this instance that, although cognition and affect are parts of a whole, each part has characteristics that can be distinguished and labelled with high reliability. Distinctive features of a coin, heads and tails, comprise the totality of coinness. The cognitive-affective schemas in their unity are analogous to heads and tails of the coin.

The cognition-affect balance varies along two dimensions—*conscious control* or awareness and *cognitive structural level*. It seems likely that, during the neonatal period, the infant, being at a sensorimotor level, would be more reflexive than reflective. However, during the reflexive period, the infant is involved in three forms of assimilation—reproduction, recognition and generalization. It is probable that during this period affect actions and reactions are reactive primarily to inner stress or the sudden unexpected environmental change. It may well be that, as the cognitive capability of the child unfolds, the interaction with feelings, emotional expressiveness, will alter. In this schematic, let it suffice to present the argument that cognitive structures evolve, and in their evolution generate differential responsivity to contextual demands. A young child, for example, may deal with death of an older person with minimum display of affect because the child does not understand the finality of death. However, the same event can create a profound sense of grief and loss, because at a later cognitive level the child understands the finality of death.

The child's shifting level of understanding of events involves feelings differentially. Understanding may intensify feelings, as in the death example, or reduce the intensity of feelings. Interaction between feelings and thoughts will, as indicated in the model, oscillate in the course of experiencing events, self, or others.

Two other factors interact with the thought-feeling schema: One is control and the other is awareness. Control refers to the conscious and unconscious inhibiting feelings (see Santostefano's discussion of cognitive control). Awareness refers to the developing understanding that individuals have feelings (referred to as empathy) and that one's own feelings are related to both internal and external states. In psychoanalytic terms, awareness and control can be construed as ego functions.

The equilibration model of cognitive-affective development that I propose should be viewed in the broader context of ego development, because the ego construct incorporates memory of the notions described earlier.

Working toward an integration, the equilibrated model incorporating some of Santostefano's ideas, especially of context, control, and metaphor, will in time provide a model that takes into account the integrative, holistic nature of the human organism as it engages in its milieu. The construction of such a model is an ongoing process that in my view must move away from the fragmented view of the human to an integrated one.

CONCLUSION

My purpose in this chapter is to reflect on a fundamental psychological riddle—the relationship between thought and emotions. We must continue to search for answers. But how can this be done when there is little effort at integration, little attempt to dialogue in a constructive, problem-solving way? Perhaps I may be accused of doing just what I am bemoaning. In my defense, I believe this chapter is a beginning search for an answer. I believe that Santostefano has provided a model with considerable potential for achieving that. For example, it would be interesting to investigate the relationship between the development and use of cognitive controls and the cognitive stages of Piaget. Seeking specific interests among the various conceptual models and evolving a developmental model may provide answers to the riddles.

Let me close with the following quote from Gergen (1982):

> The search for certainty is a child's romance, and like most, one holds fast to even the most fragile shard attesting to continued life. The question that must now be confronted is how to pass successfully into the maturity of a second century. A new romance is required to extinguish the old, and it appears that the overtures are at hand. (p. 209)

REFERENCES

Boesch, E. E. (1983 July/August). *The development of Affective Schemata*. Saarbruecken, West Germany: Social-Psychological Research Center on Developmental Planning, University of Saar.

Décarie, T. G. (1978). Affect development and cognition in a Piagetian context. In M. Lewis & L. A. Rosenblum (Eds.), *The development of affect* (pp. 183–204). New York: Plenum.

Erikson, E. (1950). *Childhood and society*. New York: Norton.

Erikson, E. (1959). Identity and the life cycle. *Psychological Issues, 1*(1). New York: International Universities Press.

Freud, A. (1946). *The ego and the mechanisms of defense*. New York: International Universities Press. (Originally published 1937)

Gardner, R., Holzman, P. S., Klein, G. S., Linton, H., & Spence, D. P. (1959). Cognitive control: A study of individual consistencies in cognitive behavior. [Monograph]. *Psychological Issues, 1*(4).

Gardner, R. W., & Moriarty, A. (1968). *Personality development of preadolescence: Explorations of structure formation*. Seattle: University of Washington Press.

Gergen, K. J. (1982). *Toward transformation in social knowledge*. New York: Springer-Verlag.

Izard, C. E. (1977). *Human emotions*. New York: Plenum.

Kagan, J.(1978). On emotion and its development: A working paper. In M. Lewis & L. A. Rosenblum (Eds.), *The development of affect* (pp. 11–41), New York: Plenum.

Kelly, G. A. (1955). *The psychology of personal constructs* (2 Vols.). New York: Norton.

Klein, G. S. (1958). Cognitive control and motivation. In G. Lindzey (Ed.), *Assessment of human motives* (pp. 87–118). New York: Rinehart.

Lakoff, G., & Johnson, M. (1980). *Metaphors we live by*. Chicago: University of Chicago Press.

Lazarus, R. S. (1982). Thoughts on the relations between emotion and cognition. *American Psychologist, 37*, 1019–1024.

Lazarus, R. S. (1984). On the primacy of cognition. *American Psychologist, 39*, 124–129.

Levenson, R. W., & Gottman, J. M. (1983). Marital interaction: Physiological linkage and affective exchange. *Journal of Personality and Social Psychology, 45*, 587–597.

Lewis, M., & Michalson, L. (1983). *Children's emotions and moods: Developmental theory and measurement*. New York: Plenum.

Lidz, T. (1968). *The person: His development throughout the life cycle*. New York: Basic Books.

Petrie, H. G. (1979). Metaphor and learning. In A. Ortony (Ed.), *Metaphor and thought* (pp. 438–461). New York: Cambridge University Press.

Piaget, J. (1951). *Play, dreams and imitation in childhood*. New York: Norton.

Piaget, J. (1981). *Intelligence and affectivity: Their relationship during child development* (T. A. Brown & C. E. Kaegi, Eds. & Trans.) Palo Alto, CA: Annual Reviews.

Polanyi, M. (1966). *Personal knowledge*. Chicago: University of Chicago Press.

Polanyi, M. (1967). *The tacit dimension*. Garden City, NJ: Anchor.

Santostefano, S. (1984). Cognitive control therapy with children: Rationale and technique. *Psychotherapy, 21*, 76–91.

Schank, R., & Abelson, R. (1977). *Scripts, plans, goals and understanding*. Hillsdale, NJ: Lawrence Erlbaum Associates.

Schön, D. A. (1979). Generative metaphor: A perspective on problem-setting in social policy. In A. Ortony (Ed.), *Metaphor and thought* (pp. 254–283). New York: Cambridge University Press.

Sigel, I. E. (1981). Child development research in learning and cognition in the 1980s: Continuities and discontinuities from the 1970s. *Merrill-Palmer Quarterly, 27*, 347–371.

Sigel, I. E. (1985). A conceptual analysis of beliefs. In I. E. Sigel (Ed.), *Parental belief systems: The psychological consequences for children*. Hillsdale, NJ: Lawrence Erlbaum Associates.

Witkin, H., & Goodenough, D. (1981). Cognitive styles: Essence and origins. *Psychological Issues, Monograph 51*. New York: International Universities Press.

Zajonc, R. B. (1980). Feeling and thinking: Preferences need no inferences. *American Psychologist, 35*, 151–175.

Zajonc, R B. (1984). On the primary of affect. *American Psychologist, 39*, 117–123.

Zimiles, H. (1981). Cognitive-affective interaction: A concept that exceeds the researcher's grasp. In E. K. Shapiro & E. Weber (Eds.), *Cognitive and affective growth* (pp. 47–63). Hillsdale, NJ: Lawrence Erlbaum Associates.

Author Index

Subject Index